Wagner and the Novel

Wagner's Operas and the European Realist Novel:
An exploration of genre

156 Internationale Forschungen zur
Allgemeinen und
Vergleichenden Literaturwissenschaft

Begründet von Alberto Martino und in Verbindung mit

Francis Claudon (Université Paris-Est Créteil Val de Marne) – Rüdiger Görner
(Queen Mary, University of London) – Achim Hölter (Universität Wien) –
Klaus Ley (Johannes Gutenberg-Universität Mainz) – John A. McCarthy
(Vanderbilt University) – Alfred Noe (Universität Wien) – Manfred Pfister
(Freie Universität Berlin) – Sven H. Rossel (Universität Wien)

herausgegeben von

Norbert Bachleitner
(Universität Wien)

Redaktion: Paul Ferstl und Rudolf Pölzer

Anschrift der Redaktion:
Institut für Vergleichende Literaturwissenschaft, Sensengasse 3A , A-1090 Wien

Wagner and the Novel

Wagner's Operas and the European Realist Novel:
An exploration of genre

Hugh Ridley

Rodopi

Amsterdam - New York, NY 2012

Cover Image: *Kompositionsskizze* for *Siegfried*, reproduced by kind permission of the Richard-Wagner-Museum Bayreuth, and of Alan Laing

Le papier sur lequel le présent ouvrage est imprimé remplit les prescriptions de "ISO 9706:1994, Information et documentation - Papier pour documents - Prescriptions pour la permanence".

The paper on which this book is printed meets the requirements of " ISO 9706:1994, Information and documentation - Paper for documents - Requirements for permanence".

Die Reihe "Internationale Forschungen zur Allgemeinen und Vergleichenden Literaturwissenschaft" wird ab dem Jahr 2005 gemeinsam von Editions Rodopi, Amsterdam – New York und dem Weidler Buchverlag, Berlin herausgegeben. Die Veröffentlichungen in deutscher Sprache erscheinen im Weidler Buchverlag, alle anderen bei Editions Rodopi.

From 2005 onward, the series "Internationale Forschungen zur Allgemeinen und Vergleichenden Literaturwissenschaft" will appear as a joint publication by Editions Rodopi, Amsterdam – New York and Weidler Buchverlag, Berlin. The German editions will be published by Weidler Buchverlag, all other publications by Editions Rodopi.

ISBN: 978-90-420-3521-8
E-Book ISBN: 978-94-012-0796-6
© Editions Rodopi B.V., Amsterdam - New York, NY 2012
Printed in The Netherlands

Table of Contents

1. Introduction

'The Germans do not only want to feel music, they want to think it.'
Richard Wagner, 1840

As Chesterton's detective Father Brown looked across the titles of books on the wall of a library in which a murdered body has been found, he deduces the presence of a false door, a wall painted like shelving. For the books standing on those shelves have titles behind which there could, he pointed out, be no reality and therefore no real book. From the 'Religion of Frederick the Great' to the 'Snakes of Ireland' – perhaps we should pass over the other title on the humor of the Swiss – these books could only be empty.

I fear that my own title qualifies this book for a place on those shelves. Wagner neither wrote novels, nor appears to have planned any; his lengthy aesthetic works contained few positive reference to the novel as genre – in that sense he partook of the same understanding which had informed classical aesthetics as it ignored the claims of the novel to be art – and even when Wagner used the word 'epic' it would often be incorrect to apply his opinions to the novel. Quite apart from the disposition of his own talents, which certainly pushed him towards the musical stage, it is inconceivable that the reading of Schopenhauer in 1854, which is claimed to have had such a marked effect on his operatic work, could have taken place without a further diminution in Wagner's view of the novel. In general, Schopenhauer succeeded in persuading Wagner of the complete superiority of music over all the other arts, an insight which caused Wagner to shelve that synthesis of the arts which had been his professed aim since 1848. In particular, Schopenhauer's scorn for that direct representation of 'the World as Will' which he saw in the novel is too evident to have been overlooked by Wagner.

My last but one negative (I promise that these prevarications will abruptly cease): I am not intending another book on the numerous novels in which Wagner and/or his works play a role. These novels are numerous and often readable, but stringing them together for study does not seem worthwhile. Those novels which have something to say should be read – they cluster around *Buddenbrooks*, D.H.Lawrence, and Heinrich Mann's *Man of Straw* – but those which might have something to say but do so in a context profoundly out of sympathy with today will not be resuscitated here: aficionados of flaxen-haired suburban heroines called Isolde, or of re-enactments of Norse myths in Wisconsin will find no rich pickings here. All too often music enters the novel as one ingredient too many. It is unreasonable to expect readers to follow lay descriptions of lay descriptions of unheard music – in the style of 'first of all the goblins, and then a trio of elephants dancing'. Often the authors of such novels have spent so much energy on evoking the music that they feel it must be transposed into a special metaphysical realm in which – as E.M. Forster, from whose *Howard's End* the above example comes, went on to remark – the 'braveness' of the music 'is why one can trust Beethoven when he says other things'. If I am skeptical about this type of writing, then readers may be reassured that I have no attention of 'trusting' Wagner when he says anything, let alone outside the language of music.

My question has three sources. I wish – with a general focus on Wagner – in the first instance to ask about the relationship between the opera as genre and other genres, in particular the novel. This involves questions about how differently the genres do similar things and how different are the things they do. This discussion starts in the third chapter with a consideration of two re-workings of other genres into opera: the longish path which the young Wagner took with *Rienzi*, and the much shorter trajectory which Victor Hugo's play *Le Roi S'Amuse* followed to become *Rigoletto*. It concludes with an examination of the sometimes conflicting formal ideas of Richard Strauss and Hugo von Hofmannsthal as they worked on *Der Rosenkavalier*. Here I am less interested in the brilliance of these two artists than in their perceptions of the other man's world, and in their search for a language in which they could communicate with each other from their different creative backgrounds.

Secondly: I am going to look at features of Wagner's operas in which his closeness to the contemporary novel can be seen, focusing on their 'Realism' in portraying social and interpersonal relations and on what, for all the looseness of the terminology, I wish to call the psychology of Wagner's operas. I want to argue that it is a different psychology than what the operas of his predecessors and contemporaries contained. On the basis that Wagner's use of psychology has its closest parallels in the contemporary novel, I shall consider the shifts in opera practice which took place to make this possible. My focus will be on dialogue and interaction, on the body, and on the range of psychological issues which Wagner examines in his work.

In the final section – which, knowing that my own passionate interest in national literary history is not necessarily widely shared, is kept to a minimal length – I shall explore the place of opera in the 'long' nineteenth century (i.e. from 1815 to 1914). Here we shall consider the media competition between the two great mass art-forms of that period, the novel and the opera, and speculate on those processes by which in at least two cultures (German and Italian) opera came to be dominant, both in the sense of reaching significant artistic expression and in the narrower sense of taking over the representative function for these two newly emergent nations. I am interested in understanding how Wagner happened in Germany, why his genius expressed itself through the medium of the opera and what function his work had in the overall cultural production in Germany at the end of the nineteenth century.

As if these questions are not enough, I wish to follow through an idea (is it a question?) which seems to underlie the above issues, and which – although it is posed here in the context of Wagner's work and biography – raises much broader issues about the nature of music and of art in general. It is the idea that great works of art represent, at levels which are not always understood, both a maturity in handling matters of the artist's personal development and interrelations, and also an appreciation of the world outside the artist, an appreciation which is beyond ideology and behind which we must diagnose a cognitive as well as emotional advance. When Virginia Woolf referred to Eliot's *Middlemarch* as one of very few novels written for adults, she was identifying elements of Eliot's work which come into this category. W.H. Auden, writing in 1935, offers a more precise account of the process which will interest us in Wagner: 'It is, in fact, largely the medium,' he remarks, 'and through familiarity with the medium, with its unexpected results, that enables the artist to develop from elementary uncontrolled fantasy, to deliberate fantasy directed towards understanding.'[1] We can see such a moment in the evolution of Thomas Mann's first novel, *Buddenbrooks* (1901). Expressed in theatrical terms (such as masks), it may have still greater affinity with Wagner's situation. Mann notes in a letter to his young friend Otto Grautoff that he has discovered in creating his fictional world both the road to self-understanding and a key to understanding society.[2] In the moment of achieving artistic greatness, Mann describes not only his coming into his own authentic voice but also managing to get the world itself into focus. All these remarks suggest that the inventions of great artists are more than self-realizations: they are adequate to the reality outside the artist. They operate therefore within a general project of the Enlightenment – something not always self-evident in interpretations of Wagner's work. Yet it is there to be found. In hearing Wagner's music a common experience is not

---

[1] In: *Psychology and Art Today*, quoted by Meisel (2007:166).
[2] Mann writes: 'I have suddenly become able to find the discreet forms and masks in which I can go into society with my experiences. Whereas previously, even if I wanted to communicate only with myself, I needed a secret diary' (Letter of 06.04.1897).

that of swirling, murky unclarity which the unfamiliar ear may register, but of its opposite: clarity and focus. Martin Gregor-Dellin's major biography of Wagner outlines this experience in a way which not only summarizes many of my own experiences, but, I suggest, is common to many readers and listeners, not only of Wagner:

> There is stupid and intelligent music. The level of its stupidity or intelligence does not depend on its complexity or the originality of its melodic invention, the freshness or novelty of its expression, execution or technical preparation. It does not depend on its particular style or method, nor on its sparse or dense orchestration, and it has nothing at all to do with the cleverness or academic expertise of the composer. There are clever musicians of genius who at times have written very stupid music. Specifically musical 'intelligence' reveals itself in what we may call the physiognomy of the melody (*melos*).
> Just as there are intelligent and stupid forms of facial beauty to be found in all classes of human society, so intelligent and stupid music can be found at every level, from light music up to opera, from the smallest piece of chamber music to the symphony. This cannot be more fully explained on paper or in words, you have to hear it. But it can be defined negatively, as something which is fundamentally missing from the beautiful or sophisticated effect of musical sound in time: it is an absence of triviality. (1983:162)

I quote this passage at length not because I regard its arguments as unassailable (indeed, I find suspicious its absence of historical consciousness and its readiness to ignore the place of desire in the appreciation of beauty), but because it touches centrally – in one musical composition[3] – on the illumination of the world which literature and music can achieve, and in which I would like to find a central affinity between Wagner's work and the rational, intelligent novels which were its contemporaries.

I am clear that opera and the Enlightenment are not natural partners. Not only does the artificiality which is so inbuilt into the genre potentially clash with Enlightenment virtues such as the victory of reason over illusion and myth: the whole paraphernalia of opera puts the genre into an economic dimension which is all but unthinkable without wealthy and aristocratic patronage. Historically a brief period existed when opera was recognizably part of the Enlightenment – Mozart's *Magic Flute* is often regarded as the high point of that period – but it is still more natural to think of those operas as enlightened which *parodied* grand opera (Gay's *Beggar's Opera*, picked up in the 1920s by Brecht and Weill, is the obvious example) rather than stayed within the genre. Again from a historical perspective, German opera

---

[3]   In fact it is one stage in development which is being characterized here. Gregor-Dellin – in common with many other critics – identifies this sudden achievement of maturity with *Der fliegende Holländer*. His broader point is that on which I focus here: that artistic maturity is emotionally and cognitively *intelligent*.

showed – most notably with Weber's *Der Freischütz* (1821) – a strong move towards national sentiment, and it is hard to understand that nationalism as what it was: a genuine part of the Enlightenment heritage. Even Mozart had looked forward fervently to the day 'when we Germans [*Teutsche*] could seriously begin thinking German, acting German, speaking German and singing German' (letter of 21 March 1785), and these were of course – in the age of feudal, absolute monarchs – sentiments of the Enlightenment. Although it is inappropriate in this book to work with an over-historical concept of the Enlightenment, I still wish to discuss Wagner's work against the background of a particular age, and of the particular legacy which went into the Realist novel.

Nearly two hundred years after his birth Wagner remains a controversial figure, and responses to his works are deeply polarized. It would be naïve for me to want to keep this book out of the argument. By putting Wagner next to the Realist novel I have already begun to take sides, but I hope not too polemically. For in looking at Wagner's relationship to enlightenment values through his relationship to the Realist novel, I am departing from the possibility of simply labeling Wagner 'progressive' or 'reactionary'. Self-evidently the Realists included elements of both camps in their ranks, and the central question of this book concerns a way of looking at and representing the world, rather than a 'position'. Perhaps methods can be debated less polemically than undiluted ideology: that would be my hope in these pages. There are obvious objections to placing Wagner within the Enlightenment, notably Adorno and Horkheimer's celebrated view of Enlightenment as 'the disenchantment of the world; the dissolution of myths and the substitution of knowledge for fancy' (1944:3) – it seems more usual to think with Starobinski of opera in the opposite way, as 'enchantress' (1984:19f). My approach will relativize these objections by placing Wagner in the context of Realism, just as the critique of Wagner's Enlightenment qualifications is modified by what Adorno and Horkheimer call the 'dialectic of enlightenment' – that is, the openness of enlightenment rationality to unfeeling bureaucracy, mechanical logic and ultimately to inhumanity. In picking the word Enlightenment I want to keep my text free of unreflected notions about what constitutes progressive and reactionary ideas, and yet shielded from any suspicion of sympathy with Wagner's anti-Semitism.

The final purpose of this approach is, I must admit, more partisan. I hope to offer an understanding of Wagner's work which opens out possibilities of greater enjoyment and appreciation. While there are few more annoying approaches than one which instructs readers how to enjoy themselves – sometimes under the mantle of telling them what to admire – I would rather run this risk than leave Wagner in a limbo where he can rest, stranded on philosophical obscurity by Schopenhauer, beached on sandbanks of German culture proud of their unapproachability to the normal European canon, and lined up with the cultural nationalism which the twentieth century had little reason to appreciate. Richard Wagner belongs with many aspects of the Enlightenment (many, but not all: that's the norm in his generation) and I want to explore these aspects by focusing on his work within the context of one of the literary forms of Enlightenment most favored by English-language culture, the novel. I hope people will like him more and feel more at ease with him, and those who already like him will find new avenues to reflect on their liking. It is seldom effective to interpret works into likeability, but in the case of Wagner the approach is inevitable. More than the novel, opera is dependent on an interpretation which precedes reception. Unlike Adorno's 'perfect listener'[4], most of us require conductor and orchestra, singers, stage and producer in order to appreciate opera: it does not leap off the page simultaneously into a reader's ears and eyes. None of the agencies of production can show the work without also interpreting it. For that reason it seems sensible to rehearse different interpretative possibilities which the work itself may contain.

Acknowledgements

This book has had the chance to benefit from discussions with many generous friends. I mention in particular Andrew Barker, Bill and Sheila Bell, Roger Clayton, Mary Cosgrove, Siobhán Donovan, Edmund Jephcott, Brian Jones, Caítriona Leahy, Guy and Simon Ridley, Lewis Ryder, Lothar Schneider, and Alf Smyth. In particular the project benefited from discussion with my friend and former colleague at the University of Kent, the gifted translator of libretti and librettist in his own right, Michael Irwin – and from the help of my friend, Gilbert Carr of Trinity College Dublin, with his infinite knowledge of *fin de siècle* Vienna. My debt to and admiration of the musicologists quoted in the text is huge, though of course – even surrounded by such excellent sources – I am capable of my own errors, and the text is my own, warts and all.

---

[4]   Adorno means a person so completely trained and gifted in music that all of music's techniques are revealed from the score without the need for performance, or – hardly a less utopian option – in the moment of first hearing. See below, p.19.

I wish also to thank my editor in Rodopi, Esther Roth, for all her help and encouragement, and the technical editor, MMag. Rudolf Poelzer, for his skill and, above all, his patience with my technical shortcomings.

The book is dedicated in gratitude to two people for the inspiration that they have given. First, to my wife, Jenny, who has lived with the project and thought along with it, and done everything to encourage me. Secondly to Alan Laing – pupil of Kenneth Leighton, subsequently Director of Music at the University of Kent at Canterbury and then Lecturer in Music at the University of Hull –, who first awoke my interest in Wagner over forty years ago, and, both as a lecturer and with baton in hand, caused that interest to develop. Alan's major stroke thirty years ago robbed musical life in Britain of real talent, and deprived Wagner studies of unpretentious enthusiasm and deep expertise. Alan's unpublished thesis – *Tonality in Wagner's 'Der Ring des Nibelungen'* (Ph.D., Edinburgh 1973) – at various times underpins my arguments, but, as a work of musicology, it makes many other and better arguments than those which surface here, at a high level of professional expertise. Without Alan's great enthusiasm this book would not have come to be written: it would be good to think that his own thesis might one day resurface in the specialist literature, for it constantly approaches major issues of Wagner scholarship with fresh and original eyes. It is poor thanks to Alan to have no more to offer than these pages as thanks, but they come in gratitude and sincere admiration and to his wife Jennie.

Canterbury/Lichtenberg

2. Establishing the Key-signature

'The more primitive one's first approaches to Wagner, the more
instructive they can be for the present.'
Ernst Bloch, 1911

Three general issues belong in this chapter. I hope to show that they are immediately relevant to any process of thinking about Wagner, and particularly central to the topic on which we are embarked. The first concerns the different levels of accessibility of music and the novel. We must discuss it here – even if the issues cannot finally be resolved – since what we have identified as the 'intelligence' of music cannot claim that description if it is merely an esoteric, inward dimension of the music. Its intelligence should be as communicable to Wagner's listeners as if it had been displayed in the form of the novel. Wagner's choice of medium cannot legitimate an avoidance of comprehensibility. The second problem directly concerns Wagner's choice of medium and illustrates the role of the market in one aspect of his artistic production. The third question in this chapter is more problematic, since in part it concerns the difficulties of approaching an artist who carries so much ideological baggage – some morally unacceptable, some merely heavy. This chapter has no intention of acting as an apologia for any of Wagner's ideas, nor does it try to offer any justification for embarking on this topic despite the unpleasantness of those ideas. But it does examine a possible separation of man and ideas, music and ideology. In the whole book, not just in the opening chapter, it is with Wagner's work and its relationship to the novel that we are concerned, not with Wagner's life and personality.

Monsieur Jourdain with a book and a CD-player

'If only they had invented electrical telegraphs to
make musical ubiquity possible' (Liszt)

Molière's satirical comedy *Le Bourgeois Gentilhomme* tells the story of the bourgeois Monsieur Jourdain, son of a draper who had made good. Monsieur Jourdain is trying to give himself the airs and snob-appeal of an aristocrat and to move out of the class into which he was born. In order to improve himself he needs to inform himself about the arts and to become proficient in them, that is in music, dancing and rhetoric. We can imagine his delight when he discovers that, without ever having had lessons in rhetoric, he is already able to speak prose. Indeed, all his life he has been speaking prose: he just has not known that that was what it was. Two hundred years later, in the heyday of the nineteenth century, Monsieur Jourdain would have been still more delighted to discover that a whole branch of literature and the arts had been evolved in order to cater for his unsuspected talent, and that the great geniuses of the century appeared to have little else in mind than to feed his appetite with novels, written in a prose often not dissimilar to what he discovers that he has already mastered.

As if that were not enough, another surprise would have been in store for M. Jourdain. The literature which his socialization and background had given him the talent to read insisted that it was written for him. The nineteenth century novelists gave up their interest in lofty aesthetic tales played out in aristocratic circles and tuned to the upper-class sensitive souls, the *schöne Seelen* of the eighteenth century. Instead the everyday lives of ordinary people like M. Jourdain became suddenly important to writers and to publishers. The Realist novel[1] seemed to be written in a language M. Jourdain could understand: it was written about him, about the world he inhabited and understood, and it was without reference to dancing or music.

And there's the rub, for our topic in this book brings together M. Jourdain's literary skills in the novel with the different and very differently specialized area of music, a problem at the levels of both primary reception (listening and reading) and criticism. Admittedly, the problem may have been still more basic than M. Jourdain suspected, for of course he did not really 'understand prose' any more than music or dancing, and the genre of the novel hung down like the grapes over Tantalus' head, apparently for him but always out of reach. Just in case he imagined that he did understand, ambitious novelists and critics soon took the novel itself and theorizing about it outside the orbit of his understanding. But even their efforts could not alter the situation of the unequal levels of approachability of the novel and music. Even if music is shown to be doing something similar to prose – for instance in descriptive or program music – the question remains as to whether

---

[1]   I discuss this category in more detail in Chapter Five. I use it here, loosely, to refer to the novels of Dickens, Thackeray and Eliot, Balzac, Stendhal, Sue, Flaubert and Zola (if we do need to differentiate between Realism and Naturalism, this is not the place), heaps of Scandinavians, Verga, Raabe, Freytag, Fontane, Heinrich and Thomas Mann, Tolstoy, Galdós and Eça de Queirós. Anticipating, I refer to Becker (1963) and Hemmings (1974).

listeners notice it as successfully as readers see what happens in novels. This dilemma will often lie behind our project in this book. It exists for critics, who – like me – have to admit an imbalance of skills between text and score, but in truth the biggest problem is to find equivalent levels of communicability across the two media, as well as to determine to what extent a feature of the music discerned by the critic can, or could, actually be appreciated by the listener. Did M. Jourdain in the nineteenth century have a chance to hear as well as he read?

Adorno's *Sociology of Music* contains an interesting section analyzing types of listener. At the top – for all his democratic credentials, Adorno operates a strict hierarchy of attitudes in aesthetics – just under the 'expert listener' is the 'good listener', who 'understands music more or less like understanding one's own language, even if one does not understand much of its grammar and syntax' (xiv,183). Adorno seems to assume an unrealistically high level of non-'expert' listening. More seriously, in his comparison with a native speaker's understanding of grammar and syntax, Adorno (normally suspicious of equations between music and language) invalidates his argument by ignoring what linguists call the 'reciprocity of discourse', which consists in the fact that native-speakers *produce* as well as understand their language, an activity which calls on a much greater level of understanding of grammar and syntax than is required for comprehension alone. Nevertheless, the question seems appropriate as to whether such a high level of expertise exists in respect of classical music in the way it might have done fifty years ago. Even if one presumes such a decline, it makes Adorno's comments still more applicable to the nineteenth century listener and leaves M. Jourdain's access to music still further out in the cold.

The disparity of music and prose is most obvious at the level of primary reception, While prose offers itself continuously and entirely to the scrutiny of the recipient – a scrutiny which can take the form of rereading a sentence or fast-forwarding to the end to check something out (we should not imagine that this accessibility means that texts have surrendered all their secrets: the text is simply the place in which some secrets can be most effectively hoarded) –, music is heard on the basis of immediacy, with effects, which cannot be checked out during the performance, although, admittedly, it is often enhanced by memory. Ironically, in contrast to the prose text, the musical score – although it is written in a specialist script, which M. Jourdain cannot read – contains all the details which may be analyzed subsequent to performance, ranging from key-signature and tempi to minute detail within the orchestration. It is like a marked-up text on a word-processor. Quite extraordinarily, the score preserves an extensive emotional notation too, indicating expressive gestures which are to be added in performance and therefore determine the reception of the piece – *ausdrucksvoll, herzhaft, scherzo*. It is well known that Beethoven added to the score of his *Pastoral Symphony* the instruction that feeling, not picture painting was the purpose of his score.[2] Paradoxically, for a medium written in code, music contains an elaborated set of conventionalities, audible and familiar to non-professional listeners, even if on a more basic level to that of performer and composer – I refer to rules of harmony and tonality, which lack obvious equivalence in prose, even though the function of metaphor or trope also come with conventionalized meaning and emotional coloring, as happens with major or minor keys.[3]

Perhaps the real difference lies in the anteriority of theory to musical practice. Tonality as a system predates both listening and critical reception, but it has a continuous presence at all stages of the evolution of the piece of music. Because the conventions are so sweeping, music does not need to emphasize them, or draw attention to them. They are taken as read. In contrast, the consciousness of author and reader in respect of the (perhaps no less) conventionalized systems of fiction is much smaller, or at least less formalized. Certainly, when we recall the bitter disputes about theories of the 'unities' in drama, the conventions of other media, such as the novel, seem to have been much less explicitly formed – a lack of openness greatly encouraged by Hegel's strictures against reflection and self-consciousness in narrative writing. The individual novel will avoid drawing attention to such aspects of the system in its own text. A novel may return to a particular location, it is much less likely to return to a particular style, as music returns to a key-signature. For that reason, it is unlikely that we find a structuring device as obvious as the *Leitmotiv* as commonly in prose as in music.

---

2   'Mehr Ausdruck der Empfindung als Mahlerei' (More expression of feeling than painting). How hard it is for novelists to give this sort of instruction: they must paint a scene in such a way as to show that it does not matter for itself, but matters instead on account of the action and the 'deeper' themes which lie behind it. It is so difficult for writers to paint such a scene convincingly, which is to say *substantially*, with detail, while getting the reader to understand that it does not matter, that the scene is really about something else. Kafka comes close to it when he dreams of describing a hammering noise which is both utterly real and 'a nothing' – but that is modernism. The problem existed no less for the Realists.

3   As music got out of the hands of musicologists and text theoreticians got involved, even apparent certainties of this kind were challenged. Hayden White, doyen of much of this writing, questions this unproblematic assumption of a link – even at the level of ascription, i.e. convention – between major key and positive attitude and minor (negative) (White 1992:301,308).

Without the presence of a clear system of conventions, the gap between the reading experience and the subsequent specialist criticism will tend to be larger than is the case in music. M. Jourdain might therefore understand the novel, but not criticism of the novel: if he understood the music, he would understand the analysis of the music. Such relationships lie behind a matter of great significance to all works of art: the *size* of an element required to achieve a particular effect. It is possible to argue that the more a genre is governed by convention, the greater the effect of small devices: from the minute clues which alter detective stories, to the slightest piece of chromaticism – the single accidental which is crucial. In contrast the scene of Emma Bovary's death (written when the conventionalities of the Realist novel are far from stable) shows the massive devices needed to achieve the effect. Not just in the codes of a work of art, therefore, but in the historically evolving reception of works of art, the situation of M. Jourdain raises difficulties in determining the degree of specialization required of the public.

Since my overall purpose in this book is to examine 'prosaic', rational, analytic qualities in Wagner's music, such as would have been identified without difficulty had he written novels in the style of his century, speculative questions of this kind cannot always be ducked. The Enlightenment was not a conspiracy, to be hidden from ordinary people: its devices had to be as comprehensible as its aims: M. Jourdain must be able to access them. There is another, still more fundamental issue in music criticism which stands in the way of our project. How can music be analytical, and therefore show Wagner's participation in the *intellectual* labors of the contemporary novel? Gregor-Dellin's comments on 'intelligent music' which we encountered in the Introduction make that question urgent, but still harder to answer. We confront not only the question of argument in music: its relationship to story-telling is highly problematic. How can music narrate, and thus place itself in the familiar environment of its listeners? Although drama itself might seem to suffer a similar obscuring as opera – in that the moment of attention constantly moves forward; unlike the written word, drama does not offer itself for immediate re-reading and checking – there is a focus on the spoken word, which only bad acting makes incomprehensible and which makes reflection and analysis more possible. Opera does not achieve that often, despite the modern tendency to put sur-titles over the stage, so that the audience can follow the text. But these projected texts too – unlike the written word – cannot be slowed or reversed. It could seem as if, by choosing opera, Wagner had deliberately selected the genre which had no features in common with the analytical novel of his day. Suddenly the book on Father Brown's shelves, *The Religion of Frederick the Great,* seems an easy book to write.

The difficulties are made worse by the familiar claim, made from many angles, namely that music is by its very nature primitive, non-intellectual and non-analytical. The argument is familiar in the banal form of equating music's constituting parameters (pitch and tempo) with primitive excitement, as expressed in the scream and in rapid speech or movement, by which reckoning the pizzicato of a string section is immediately identified as representing the human heart-beat. The one-time use of military bands to incite armies to attack seems to relate to these properties – it also involves some association of music with fervent national identity, to which we shall return in Chapter Eight –, and dance too offers continuous reinforcement of elements of such an argument. Similar assumptions are also behind the frequent dismissal of 'modern' music as cerebral and over-intellectual.

A different, but common use of this topos can be seen in critical response to unfamiliar new music (including pre-eminently, in his age, Wagner's). It was usual to complain that his music had descended into cacophony and chaos, which was then called 'barbaric', as if, as sound, all music were perched on the edge of barbarism and needed to be redeemed from the primitive by the Enlightenment. Similar assumptions lay behind the argument which was put forward, in a more sophisticated context, by the early sociologists of the city. Georg Simmel's ground-breaking essay on *The City and Intellectual Life* (1904), for instance, argued that the modern city favored the visual sense: only the eye was capable of the rapid movements and adjustments required to survive in the ever-changing city scene. In contrast, he asserted, the human ear was 'archaic', less adaptable, less capable of learning new ways. Simmel's remarks echoed those of the early film theorists, whose enthusiasm for the silent film based in part on their appreciation of the progressive nature of the 'analytical' eye as against the 'unconcentrated' and therefore passive ear – this view partly explained their hostility to the inclusion of sound in the film.

Such arguments narrow the area in which music can operate and be reckoned progressive, rational or analytic. They suggest that only a limited number of post-Wagnerian musical developments – Schönberg's systematic atonalism, Kurt Weill's and Hanns Eisler's ideologically aggressive music, or, less radically, Hindemith's *Gebrauchsmusik* – will ever be found to meet the criteria of the Enlightenment. The arguments possess too much authority to be brushed aside, yet they do not argue against the purpose of this book, which looks to a mapping of progressive, rational and analytic elements in Wagner not onto modern music, but onto the novels of his contemporaries. In fact I wish, in talking of Wagner, completely to abandon the discussion of the primitive in this sense. It is a very questionable category, and not least in music. That old conservative, Thomas Mann, was probably closest to the truth when the narrator of his great novel *Doktor Faustus* (a novel based to a large extent on the claim of its hero that music needs periodically to 'bathe in the elemental') remarked that naïveté – a synonym for the primitive – is a problematic concept, "for naïveté is at the very heart of all life, including the most conscious and complicated. Even the insoluble conflict between inhibition and the productive drive of genius [...] that too is naïveté' (Chapter 18). While the comment is a welcome reminder that form, morality, self-control – *inhibition,* as Mann's narrator calls it – are no less basic to humanity (and hence no less 'primitive') than their opposites, it does not help us in our search for musical equivalents of those features which make the nineteenth century novel distinct. But it does warn against absolutizing music as the primitive, inaccessible to reason and calculation.

While these problems seem deeply rooted in the nature of the two media of prose and music themselves, one element has changed significantly since the nineteenth century: the ability of the listener to reproduce *ad infinitum* the musical and visual experience of opera. When Walter Benjamin wrote his celebrated essay on *The Work of Art in the Age of Mechanical Reproduction* (1934), his central focus was on image and film, for which – following on the work of theorists such as Béla Balázs and the achievements of silent film, in both the USA and the Soviet Union – Benjamin claims limpid transparency.[4] Because of the technical nature of film, which Benjamin contrasts to the individual, 'inspirational' *aura* of traditional art; because every viewer of a film could use a camera and was therefore an expert, like M. Jourdain in prose; because of the collective nature of film production (no artistic geniuses needed there, and no special aura in the work: each film is only a copy); and finally because film dealt with a luminously communicative surface, Benjamin argued that viewers were able as equals to follow the *how* as well as the *what* in the film. It was therefore a democratic, indeed a socialist art form. If Benjamin had extended his theory to popular music – in which so many of his criteria are also met: the possibility of infinite reproduction of the music, the continuity of practice between amateur and professional, the collective nature of music production, the increasingly technical nature of the production apparatus – it would have remained persuasive, although here too,

---

[4]   Readers whose conspiratorial employer/government/financial advisor hide their exploitative intentions under the patina – worse still – under the *mission-statement* of transparency (and few do not) may need reminding of an age when belief in transparency was genuine. Unfortunately, it was also invariably misplaced.

no less than in film, the emergence of stardom and manipulative directing would have needed explanation. But it is strange to note that all music and in particular opera has been even more strongly influenced by technical changes than in the shift from Old Masters to film. Liszt's wishful dream, which we cited at the head of this section, has long since become true. Not only the hugely increased visibility of opera[5] which television and film have made possible, but also the easy access to recordings, including DVDs, which has led – if one believes the evidence of recorded-music periodicals – to an increasingly technical approach to the music, shown on the performance side in the virtual elimination of error and a corresponding standardization of performance, balance, sound, and, on the reception side, most significantly of all in the externalization of memory, represented by that button which enables the listener to play again and to graze[6] and which also, incidentally, all but changes every opera into a 'number opera'. M. Jourdain with a CD-player is a complex new appearance on the music stage, perhaps it offers a new road of Enlightenment into Wagner's work. Opera has become more like a book than in Wagner's day. If Monsieur Jourdain is not actually writing this book, I hope he is reading it.

How Many Nibelungen can there be?

There is more than one perspective on the question of the choice of genre. It is rare to find writers exclusively committed to the one genre with which we subsequently associate them, and often posterity oversimplifies and underrates artists' talents when it remembers them for only that one genre, walling in a talent which may have been broader. In an age richer in genres Shakespeare might well have added story-teller to dramatist and lyricist. Stifter painted in words and in oil. Nietzsche wrote (and, more surprisingly,

---

[5]   Schönberg claimed to have heard each Wagner opera 'twenty or thirty times' before he was twenty-five (Stuckenschmidt 1977:33). Quite apart from the time spent in the opera house, it is worth considering how long he had to wait before the works came round in repertory, this even in the heyday of Wagner's popularity. But not even Schönberg could wind a performance back and hear, anywhere other than in his inner ear, a particular piece of the opera again – he had to wait to the next performance. In this context we should remember that it was only on the last day of 1913 that Bayreuth's control over the performance of Wagner's work lapsed, and the general accessibility of his works increased. The first Wagner film – a twenty-minute silent version of *Parsifal* (1903) – was therefore issued outside Germany, in the USA. For more details cf. Carnegy's wonderful study (2006).

[6]   The political-aesthetic effects of that button are the subject of Adams/Goodman's opera *Nixon in China*, discussed in Peggy Kamuf's essay 'The Replay's the Thing' (1994).

was enormously proud of) poetry, In his creative writing Thomas Mann tried his hand at both lyric and drama (fortunately, his ability in self-criticism was much keener than Nietzsche's, and he pretty quickly stopped writing anything but fiction); every biography and fictionalized account of Henry James' life stresses the importance of a genre with which his present-day readers would otherwise completely fail to associate him, drama. It is not clear that writers need a visa to move into the territory of an adjacent genre, but one thing can tempt them over into neighboring genre: jealousy and the lure of success. While Wagner presents himself always as a double talent – as composer and as author of his own libretti – we should not underestimate the place which the desire for success played in his original choices.

In our day the novel is the favored genre. Partly it is the spread of travel which has made the airport book-purchase a significant element in the package holiday, just as the spread of the railways was responsible for the birth of a particular genre of prose fiction in the mid-nineteenth century. In part too the ability of the mass-media to make novels newsworthy, through the chat show or the sensationalizing of literary prizes, has come to mean that the novel enjoys special status. Not only do the so-called celebrities turn immediately to themselves writing in that genre when their need for further exposure becomes pressing (presumably they are, like M. Jourdain, gratified to realize that, without knowing it, they have been writing prose all their lives): but for the rank amateur the novel has apparently replaced the lyric as the genre of choice, even though it may have no other fate than to be consigned to the adolescent drawer. How seldom one hears anyone confessing at a cocktail party that they have sheaves of poetry in their drawer, yet there are circles in which the failure to have written (but not necessarily published) a couple of novels would be equated with a serious lack of imagination. In case we should think that this prioritizing of the novel has always taken place, a brief look back is in place.

Gustav Freytag – author of two best-selling novels, of popular histories of Germany, and the occasional successful drama (productions never subsequently repeated, such is the more durable quality of the novel) – made clear the different motivations of the various genres around the time at which Wagner was reaching artistic maturity. It shows a striking dissimilarity to the present situation. Drama is appealing to the young author, Freytag argued (1863), on the basis of its excitement, the smell of grease-paint, the deafening applause when the curtain comes down, those exquisite moments when the dramatist is dragged on stage to receive the plaudits of an enthusiastic public. In comparison, Freytag argues that the novel is for those shrinking violets who appreciate long hours of toil in solitude and, as outcome, at best the restrained admiration of the connoisseur. Whatever we might feel about Wagner's natural talent and inclination, artistic talent not only includes a predisposition to types of story, themes and topics, as well as to genre, but it also involves a recognition of the market situation. The ambition to succeed is – especially for the nineteenth century giants – part of what makes up artistic genius. It is hardly surprising that the plots of Wagner's operas include *two* singing competitions: they stylized an uncomfortable feature of his daily experience.

Repeatedly on these pages we will be concerned with questions of genre. We shall be concerned to establish what characteristics can be observed in the opera in contrast to the different features of the novel and drama and to understand what happens when themes and stories are moved from one medium to the other. At the same time, it should not be seen as a cheapening of aesthetic analysis to recognize the extent to which the choice between genres and media did not follow aesthetic theory, but was influenced by all-too human questions of status and prestige, such as those to which Freytag refers. In other words: the market-situation should never be forgotten. That is one advantage of putting Wagner's texts alongside the blockbusting market-leaders in the fiction of his day. To illustrate this – and to show that artists do not always work according to the laws of aesthetics: the laws of the jungle have a part to play too – we ask the question of the title of this section: How many Nibelungen could there be?

To some viewpoints this is a silly question. How could there be more than one *Anna Karenina*, one *Hamlet*, one Ninth Symphony? We should not forget that the singular here is a product of selection, of the number of works getting embedded in the academic or popular canon: it has little to do with the production side. A banal, but significant, truth would be that there were many Ninth Symphonies, but only one which occupies the space of that prestigious title. When we speak of *La Bohème* everyone thinks of Puccini, and very few remember Leoncavallo's *La Bohème*, first performed just fourteen months after Puccini's. Such patterns are easily demonstrable within classic prose fiction. Every topic which found success with the public of the day (and subsequently among the literary historians and readers of today) had many opposite numbers in the now forgotten fiction of its time. This is true of generic topics – in the previous century these might have been: east-west spy stories, adolescent diaries; in the nineteenth, the evil city, the sentimentalized miseries of the working-class, adultery (we should not forget how even a masterpiece such as *Madame Bovary* started as a restatement of what were *already* the greatest banalities of provincial life, including adultery[7]). It is also true of much more personalized stories. Writers needed to understand the market, and above all to recognize the fact that at a particular time certain stories worked (would work); they needed to know that there had been a partial success at one level of the market, or in one genre, and that it could successfully be shifted into another. How else could one explain the veritable passion of novelists in the mid-nineteenth century for transposing one type of story onto a different level. The story of Dorothea Brooke is not just a story of marriage, disillusionment and re-marriage in provincial England: it is the transference of the life of St Teresa into the genre of the realist novel. Keller's *A Village Romeo and Juliet* transfers the historical and aristocratic tragedy of Verona into a Swiss village in Keller's own day, where its feuding, blinkered peasants play out the roles of the Montagues and Capulets, and the transfer is so strikingly successful that Delius repeats and compounds it. Stendhal resituates the Napoleonic ambitions of France into a provincial saw-mill. A story's shelf-life is increased by combining it with something else, fitting it in to established frames of perception, whether an evergreen story or an identifiable trend of the present, and when something major happens which affects the national consciousness then the writers are in competition to find its parameters and to exploit it for sales. They follow the laws of the market.[8]

So the question of how many Nibelungen there can be is anything but trivial. At any one time the market will have a limited tolerance for Nibelungen, as for anything else. The fact that from the 1840s Germany was aspiring for a culturally sanctioned unification might make the country more tolerant of presentations of its ancient history and myth. Even then, however, market laws prevailed and popular nationalism was unable to increase the market's tolerance significantly. Wagner's Nibelungen are the victors, but they certainly did not have the field to themselves. By the mid-century at least four other authors had launched their Nibelungen on the market (Motte-

---

[7] Readers will observe that my argument here gratefully follows that of Hans Robert Jauss (1967) and his theory of reception history (Jauss gives detailed examples of the processes I summarize here). Another example is given by Theodor Fontane's novel of adultery, *Effi Briest* (1895), for which a number of unsuccessful, thematically almost identical contemporary novels can be discovered. Fontane may or may not be the best novelist of the time: he was – retrospectively at least – simply more successful than others.

[8] Only in poetry does the competition over topics seem less keen. The continued use of older forms, the ability in all ages to write on established themes within the poetic canon (autumn, morgues, unhappy love etc) suggest this view. But even then the challenge was to write about them *differently*.

Fouqué, Raupach, Jordan and Geibel[9]). Much more threatening to Wagner's project was the fact that one of Germany's major playwrights – Friedrich Hebbel, forerunner of Ibsen and master of the 'bourgeois tragedy' – was known to be working on the theme. Relations between the two men were hardly simplified by the fact that, before her marriage to Richard, Cosima had been an admirer of Hebbel (who in turn had good links with the circle around Cosima's father, Franz Liszt), indeed she had translated Hebbel's *Maria Magdalene* into French, with an enthusiastic preface of her own. This was hardly a recipe for her domestic happiness with Richard. In commercial terms Wagner had the disadvantage that, although he started his Nibelungen much earlier (*Siegfried's Death* dates from the revolutionary year 1848), the project took thirty years to finish – not necessarily a successful marketing strategy: customers do not care to wait so long for an unknown product and while waiting may decide on a rival model. In fact during these years Wagner had to watch Hebbel pick up the theme, write his drama text,[10] and then enjoy a great success with it, not only on the Viennese stage but also closer to home. The question of how many Nibelungen there could be was anything but academic to the writers – it was a question of life and death.

It is important to realize the considerable common ground our two artists had in their interest for this theme. Wagner would have agreed with Hebbel that the story was 'the great national epic [...] the great song of the German nation', but this common purpose was exactly the reason for the writers' increasing rivalry. It was in the importance of the theme that the deep, yet often amusing enmity had its origin. Their personal meetings were fraught with misunderstanding and hostility, their personal vanity, their inability to avoid personal invective and colorful exaggeration, and their massive potential inferiority complexes ensured that they would always rub each other up the wrong way, whatever happened with their works. The most bitterly

---

9   English-speaking readers' ignorance of these figures is hardly greater than that of present-day German literary historians. But Geibel (particularly since the King of Bavaria gave him a pension for life) was anything but obscure in nineteenth century literary life: he was certainly a celebrity, and what he did and wrote appealed to the media. Motte-Fouqué was a Romantic groupie, Jordan a local hero, without much national profile. If they had won the publicity contest, however, their Nibelungen might be household names.

10   Hebbel's play (itself a trilogy) concentrates on events subsequent to those described by Wagner. It will hardly be familiar to present day theatre-goers, since no theatre would dream of performing it today, but Fritz Lang *cognoscenti* will be familiar with its broad outlines, especially from Lang's classic silent film *Kriemhild's Revenge* (1924). (Kriemhild is the alternative name for Brünnhilde.) Hebbel's relationship to Wagner is well outlined in Mueller (1991): for their different approaches to the Nibelungen legend see Cicora (1999:55-89).

personal aspects of the controversy started in the early 1860s in Vienna, and were hardly interrupted either by Wagner's precipitous departure from the city with his debtors in pursuit or, more tragically, by Hebbel's death in 1863. There was no level on which they could find common ground. Hebbel's laughable visiting-card, which suggested that he had more honors than there was space for on the card, was a characteristically trivial point of friction. More telling was the fact that both felt threatened by the success of the other inside the Nibelung reservation. Wagner deliberately published the text of the *Ring* long before the music was ready as a desperate strategy to keep himself in the public eye at a time when Hebbel was milking his success (Hebbel's play was awarded the prestigious Schiller Prize in 1861), while Hebbel did not pass up the chance of writing a review of a concert in which the *Ride of the Valkyres* was played, praising the piece in the most offensive terms he could find for a serious composer: 'an excellent opening to the Vienna carnival'. About the only thing they agreed on was their joint (but separate) ridiculing of the previous efforts on the theme. Cosima (by now devoted to the Wagner side of the argument, a real turn-coat) recalls the Master reading out loud to her from Geibel's *Brunhild* 'with considerable hilarity', while Hebbel dismissed Raupach's work as 'a colossal misunderstanding of the theme': Raupach's Brünnhilde was 'a whale among flowers and butterflies' (a description not unfamiliar to many performances in nineteenth century opera houses), while the whole work was so turgid, Hebbel said, that it stopped the blood circulating in the audience's veins. Even jeering at their joint rivals, however, could not bring them together. It was not possible that they would accept the other's Nibelungen. Hebbel had already written, as if it were an accepted view, that Wagner was 'no poet' and Wagner had retaliated by calling Hebbel's work 'a disgrace [*eine Lumperei*]'.

   In perhaps the most revealing comment, Wagner called Hebbel's play a 'parody of the *Nibelungenlied*'. That was a particularly interesting comment from Wagner, because it emphasized his anxiety that the process of reception of his own work might have been jeopardized by Hebbel's getting there first: a sequel is one thing, but someone else's attempt at the same looks like plagiarism. More threatening still was the fear that audiences might start to see serious works as parodies of a theme – sometimes the borderline between seriousness and parody is uncomfortably narrow.[11] So despite the fact that,

---

[11]   These were very real fears, in fact for both writers. With the popular Viennese dramatist Johann Nestroy always on the look-out for plays to parody, no 'serious' dramatist could feel safe. Hebbel's *Judith* (retelling the Old Testament story of how Judith sacrificed her virginity to the pagan warrior Holofernes before killing him in order to rescue her people from his army) had been mercilessly sent up by Nestroy (who offered Holofernes' smelly

with hardly any significant thematic overlap – Kriemhild's revenge has no place whatsoever in Wagner's text, indeed Hebbel's play starts only at the end of the action of the *Ring*, and no other Valkyres ride – literary history suggests that there could only be one Nibelung, and Wagner showed by the continuous attacks on Hebbel way into the 1870s and 1880s that a rival could not be dead enough not to provide a threat,[12] In thinking of Wagner's work we should not merely recall the physical stages on which it was performed – from the austerity of Bayreuth and the opulence of the Paris Opéra to the provincial stages of small court theatres. No less significant in his enterprise was the wider and still more exposed stage of the market-place.

Listen to what I do, not what I say

I want here to introduce an approach to artistic production and to understanding texts which may help us in some discussions in later chapters in this book. It offers a profitable way of thinking about all artists, but has a particular relevance to Wagner, whose extensive works consisted of such consciously planned outlines and theoretical justifications.[13] We might say that the focus which he devoted to the *Ring* over nearly thirty years, interrupting its composition with *Tristan* and the *Meistersinger*, is unique in cultural history and testifies to the massive planning energies which he devoted to his material. With hardly less persistence he put forward outspoken opinions on everything musical and most things unmusical, changing them dogmatically and ignoring them at will. It would be hard to think of an artist more driven by plans for creative work and more convinced

---

feet as the reason for Judith's action), and the same fate had been visited by Nestroy on *Tannhäuser*. Parodies were no laughing matter for 'serious' writers. Beckmesser is certainly an indirect expression of Wagner's fears for what might happen to his own works, as well as an example of Wagner's own overriding self-confidence and scorn for his critics. The question of *what* literary parody reveals about the original, and thereby makes its serious reception impossible, is of great interest in many periods of literary history, and in all genres and was a major concern of the Russian Formalists.

[12]   On the menace which dead artists present to the living, see Harold Bloom's brilliant study *The Anxiety of Influence* (1973). It was Wagner who remarked of his predecessors: 'Plagiarism isn't enough, you have to kill.'

[13]   While the idea I am introducing can profitably be applied to long poems, the text of short lyric poetry – probably uniquely – does not involve different levels of attention being applied to different parts of it: a lot of such poetry's power depends on its being in continuous sharp focus. But of course there is a level under that detailed focus, and at that level many elements – for instance, elements of the poet's ideology or an unwished for confession – can slip out by 'default'.

by his own ostensible opinions. Parts of the approach I wish to introduce, as we shall see, have been glorified with a perhaps more imposing name within other literary theories,[14] but here I wish it to pass under a very everyday title, that of a writer's *default-setting*.

The metaphor is straightforward. When I fail to give my computer a particular instruction – for instance, relating to paragraphing or type-face – it does not do nothing and thus fail to carry out the general task which it assumes I am engaged on. The computer behaves without explicit instruction and gives me paragraphing and a type-face; it seems to carry out its job without being told how. This appearance is, of course, misleading. Some agency does tell it, or has told it, what to do; these instructions simply lie on a different level of consciousness than the instructions which I as operator normally give.

In the context of artistic production, the openness of the idea of a default-setting is useful: in German, for instance, the idea can be expressed only by referring specifically to another agency, one speaks of a computer's *Werkeinstellung* – the 'factory setting'. It is undeniably an accurate description, but does not necessarily correspond to the experience of the user. Default-setting remains a short-hand way to refer to processes which go on under the level of explicit and conscious commands – processes which go on inside artists still more than inside computers – and its openness accesses questions with which this book will continually be concerned.

We often express aspects of this idea impersonally, in a way which excludes the question of agency, when we say that certain elements of texts (I use the word 'text' to include pieces of music and many kinds of literary work) 'write themselves', and the phrase suggests a contrast between these elements and others that require effort and particular attention. There is often a value-judgment attached to the idea. What the author of the text focuses on is felt to correspond to what s/he may regard as their distinctive talent, and therefore these bits can be assumed to be better than what 'writes itself'. So a novel's plot will be constructed around episodes or generic situations to which the author is particularly attached, but the plot will also have to contain other scenes, of a different type, whose important, but (in the author's opinion) clearly subordinate function is to enable the preferred type of scene to take place. Perhaps the author 'specializes' in ironic misunderstandings and emotional mismatches: the plot will have to involve lots of other elements for the author's celebrated mis-understandings to take place at all.

---

[14] Dahlhaus shares this view of a gap between theory and practice: for him Wagner's theories *grew out of* the works (1996:146). That cannot, however, be true of Wagner's anti-Semitism.

For instance, the characters will have to be introduced, to be given character and background, they have to meet and establish 'normal' relations, to travel, have meals and – if they are unlucky – go to work. Only when all that has been provided for can the author devote time to those aspects s/he regards as meaningful, and around which the whole text has been planned. The author may be rather contemptuous of other aspects of the plot than those which s/he regards as meaningful, thinking, in our example: 'anyone can describe sex, anyone can portray working in an office, only I can do misunderstandings'. Sometimes, unusually, the author admits that another writer is better at what does not interest her/him.[15] One way or the other, however, in pride or in humility, the author will think of what s/he feels they can do best as being a trademark, that's how they want to be recognized and – eventually – remembered. In the mind's eye the author envisages reviews which draw attention to this particular skill, articles built round the author as a 'master' of this particular aspect of writing. This uniqueness is important to the author: to be remembered for anything else might seem like being praised for being able to spell. Two remarks of Wagner's most clearly reveal the importance of these attitudes. From the amazing tangle of erotic and artistic inspiration of the Tribchen years comes Wagner's description to Mathilde Wesendonk of 'my most subtle and profound art' (letter of 26.01.1859 – he is referring to the 'art of transition'). Recorded in Cosima's diary for April 4 1879 is the other absolute claim to interpret his own music: 'The way into my music is the A♭ major in *Tristan*. Beethoven, Bach, Mozart, they're fine, but *that* is my music.' Whether or not we agree with Wagner's self-assessment, the way he wishes to control his listeners' perception of himself is unmistakable.

Vanity has so many aspects. It blinds (not just) writers not only to their faults, but – more interestingly, as Nietzsche remarked (vi,3:415) – it blinds them also to what they do well. Blindness is contagious, easily spreading to critics, so that writers' default-settings get neglected, critics end up ignoring elements which they themselves might otherwise find particularly positive in a work, for the sole reason that these are not necessarily those features to which writers devote themselves obsessively, and through which they work hard at their fame, Readers and listeners can easily be mislead, yet within reason they should take their own decisions in the reception process. When Nietzsche claimed of Wagner that he was 'our greatest musical miniaturist' (vi,3:22), he was not simply trying to be offensive, but in the process he was

---

[15]   This involves often an uncomfortable degree of intimacy. Heinrich and Thomas Mann had a pretty realistic idea of where the other's strengths lay as novelists, but this recognition hardly brought them closer together, personally or as writers.

supporting the default-setting hypothesis. In fact, as Manfred Hermann Schmid pointed out, there need be no conflict between the over-lifesize qualities of Wagner's work and their exquisite sense of detail, for it is the slow progression and carefully modulated quality of the music – avoiding all suddenness and violence in transitions (the feature of his music of which Wagner, as we have just seen, boasted to Mathilde Wesendonck) – which stands in marked contrast to the monumentality of so much of the action and so many of the figures. For this creative aspect of Wagner's dual nature Nietzsche had no understanding.

Another area in which Nietzsche missed the point was how to understand his observation on the consciousness with which Wagner worked at his themes. Nietzsche commented that 'as a musician Wagner remained an orator, on principle he simply had to foreground "this is what that means"'. By this Nietzsche alleges that Wagner's music was concerned with making itself significant, with artificial rhetoric, rather than simply allowing music to 'speak for itself'.[16] In other words: Wagner spent a life-time with other explicit goals and themes through which he wished to convince people – he simply did not notice that, when he was not trying so hard at his big ideas, he was very good, not to say much more convincing, at something else. For of course music does not 'write itself' any more than novels do; someone writes them, and that person has to be the composer[17] – only s/he is 'not trying', not following big vanities, big ideas, 'specialties', s/he is just filling in until the next big moment comes along. And because everything which is not that big

---

[16] This is the theme of the tenth section of *The Wagner Case* (vi,3:22f). Manfred Hermann Schmid's work on Wagner has shown the musical dangers of attitudes such as Nietzsche critiqued here, but there is an important *caveat* to make when approaching Wagner through Nietzsche's remark. What Nietzsche describes is very close to the techniques of Brecht's epic theatre, the putting of actors' roles 'into quotation marks', one of the techniques by which Brecht hopes to create critical distance between spectator and character and offers opportunities for interpretation much wider than simple identification with the character. It suggests why Wagner and Brecht are particularly open to the possibility of 'default-setting', in part because critics do not necessarily like the significance which is being pointed out. What Schmid's argument does not include is the strong possibility that it was due to Nietzsche's *limitations* in musical understanding that he constantly criticized the nature of Wagner's musical talent. Martin Vogel's account of Nietzsche's embarrassing incompetence in music – set out with brutal clarity by Hans von Bülow, who referred to Nietzsche's 'regrettable piano-contortions' (*bedauerliche Klavierkrämpfe*) – reminds us of the danger of listening for too long to Nietzsche on these matters (1965).

[17] This is to leave aside questions which arise when composers leave someone else to do their orchestration – something which does not have much of an equivalent for the novel, except perhaps ghost writing. Is the writing better or worse when the celebrity picks up her pen? Certainly the ghost is the default-setting.

moment does not therefore really 'count', the author does not notice what s/he is capable of, and nor – all too often – does the critic.

Similar observations can be made concerning many composers. For illustration we will mention just Richard Strauss, who features prominently in the fourth chapter. The 'Dance of the Seven Veils' in *Salome* – whatever criticisms there may be of what Norman del Mar calls its 'offensive lapses of taste'[18] – illustrates our point exactly What Strauss really wanted was to be the best orientalist in Western music, so to speak out-Aïdaing *Aïda*. What happened when that ambition was overtaken by the practical problems of integrating the new music into the piece, when Strauss' ambition locked his mind and something else had to take over? The answer: a waltz, hardly the high-point of orientalism. Of course this is not to say that Strauss' default-setting *was* the waltz. As the correspondence shows, his most famous waltz (in *Der Rosenkavalier*) was the result of Hofmannsthal's suggestion, and to argue (as has happened elsewhere) that waltzes were 'in Strauss' blood' is neither acceptable, nor does it do justice to the facts. Our point is the disparity between ambition and execution – a distinction still more important to the ideologue Wagner than to the much more pragmatic Strauss.

We should note that this approach is very different from arguing that the artist is not *good at* certain things. There is no shortage of critical judgments in this spirit, such as: that George Eliot cannot do sensuality, or Henry James cannot manage action. There is nothing wrong in principle with these judgments, regardless of whether they originate from the writers themselves or from their critics, except that they can be wrong, and, worse still, by being accepted, they may prevent the real work of art being noticed. While many judgments of artists are based on an awareness of their low points – how much greater a poet Wordsworth would have been if he had learnt to throw away more of his work –, thinking of their default-setting does not systematize or even encourage this practice. In any case, if we did judge authors only by failure, who would escape a whipping? I am simply suggesting that an artist should not always be allowed to define his/her own high-points. We should question the expectation that the artist should not be good at those features in the work which s/he does not bother with, or is too

---

[18]   (1978:269). More problematic is the unreflected distinction which del Mar makes in Strauss' opera between inspiration (a state in which del Mar postulates most of the opera to have been written) and 'technique' – on to which Strauss had to 'fall back' when (the rest of the work completed) he was obliged to sit down and write the music for the dance. It does not seem helpful to think of 'inspiration' as something different to that process which produces the Dance. Again we refer to the *Doktor Faustus* argument on spontaneity which we outlined earlier in this chapter.

vain to notice. In this openness lies the implication of Nietzsche's ironic laudatory remark on Wagner the miniaturist. In fact, to think in terms of default-setting creates a context in which – unaffected by annoying critical or authorial opinion – listeners and readers might start to discover an artist's work for themselves. At a human level of artistic production, it is more likely even that the artist works better when relaxed, when s/he is not trying to live up their ambitions and straining every sinew to be marvelous, desperate to prove how good their 'specialties' are. It has been remarked that Wagner's composition of *Rienzi* involved a considerable amount of tidying up his own messes, patching up the uncomfortable spaces between his great ideas, hiding the evidence that certain of these ideas were not working out.[19] Again we note: there is a different, but by no means inferior type of creativity going on behind the big ideas, and this we can call Wagner's default-setting. He mentioned this in 1878 to Cosima. 'I'm not much of a musician', he said: only when he wrote without reflection could he achieve anything, once he started thinking how to transpose a theme into another key, he got muddled (cit. Laing 1973:89).

To point out the contrast between his theories and his actual composition, as Laing does, is not special pleading by or for Wagner, indeed it is worth remarking how widespread this phenomenon is. Some critics have argued persuasively, for instance, that Brecht was a better dramatist when he was not anxiously trying to prove Marxist theory, and there seems to be a general consensus that Zola was much better at describing exciting events than at ascribing every action of his characters to their genes.[20] Did Kipling really know that he was better at aesthetic description than action? If he knew, it would have been hard for him to admit it. Discussions of this kind are common in the analysis of sports performance. Finding a happy medium

---

[19] John Deathridge (1977:140-42) gives an excellent account of these processes, and shows very persuasively how Hanslick's critique of Wagner as a musical 'dilettante' not only based on Hanslick's acute recognition of the existence of these hand-to-mouth procedures, but was, more significantly, determined by Hanslick's failure to understand how real art comes into being, his inability to take a step outside the frame and to recognize the original genius of Wagner, shown precisely at his response to these theoretically uncertain moments, when his big ideas let him down.

[20] Martin Esslin's classic study of Brecht (1959) is essentially based on this premise. It may (or more likely may not) be true, but it is good example of the default-setting hypothesis. Theodor Fontane's view of Zola amounted to just what I have summarized. Forget the Naturalist theory, enjoy the stunning skill with which Zola simply describes and narrates – that was the essence of Fontane's opinion – making Fontane another follower of default-setting and an opponent of big-mouthed ambition in writers (but behind it all, a fierce campaigner for his own success).

between consciously trying to apply known principles (the so-called 'declarative knowledge') and relaxing with one's internalized skills ('procedural knowledge') has long been recognized as essential to good performances, bearing in mind that sporting performance is measured numerically, and by winning. Success in art – for some of the reasons Hebbel and Wagner illustrate – is harder to identify and it depends on external situations.

So we have suggested a number of parameters for a composer's default-setting: they have included the psychological, in as much as the idea depends on composers' ability to get out of the dominance of their Superego; but they affect the critical and receptive as well as the productive abilities. The philosopher Ernst Bloch pointed out many years ago critics' dependence on a series of false paradoxes about Wagner's work. Wagner studies are not the only field in which such false paradoxes abound, encouraged to large measure by the artists themselves: what is refreshing is Bloch's conviction that it is more than possible to discover 'a counter-Wagner within the genuine Wagner'. The key to this discovery is listening (1985:153). Similarly the metaphor of default-setting challenges listeners to train their ear to hear things other than what they are expecting to hear (whether or not they expected something pleasant or unpleasant), to pay attention at times other than when they are being nudged by artist and critic: in other words to be autonomous as a listener.

Here, and in all of our discussion so far, we have been focusing what goes on inside the producer's head. But the production side is only one dimension of our model: default-setting has to do also – indeed, primarily – with external, made objects, typefaces or paragraphing, and harmonic sequences. The further dimension concerns the medium itself, rather than with the creator. We can introduce this idea with a cheap anecdote. Cellists used to regale one another with stories of their recurring nightmare: they dreamt that they were playing in Handel's *Messiah* and woke up to find that they were. Nothing against somnambulistic art, but the implications of the dream for the music itself are clear. It implies that Handel's cello part is routine, that it took as little thought to write as to play, that both are automatic, unthinking processes. It was the Formalists who first used the concept of 'automation' to designate the moment when a particular style becomes mere routine: when what may have begun as a revolutionary and avant-garde technique ends as a cliché and thus reaches the end of its useful life. Some of the Formalists' argument might be used as a criticism of the music (in the spirit of: Handel should have 'taken more trouble' with the cello part, etc), and some of it merely a comment on the changing tastes of listeners (and performers) across the centuries. But it is simply one product of default-setting, and not all default-settings – at least from the point of view of composers and writers – have to end in bad, automated routine. Sometimes the most revolutionary elements of music happen when the composer is not 'really' trying and – as Deathridge shows – that happened in *Rienzi*. Historically, however, while we need to sharpen our attention for those moments when music seems derivative rather than original, routine rather than creative, we cannot immediately identify those moments with the composers' default-settings. Here we need to consider a relationship which we look at more fully in Chapter Eight: the relationship between the work of art and history, even national history.

Default-settings and high-points in musical history

In one shape or another all the relationships we have been considering are historical. Within the artist not only is there a development of the person across time, but there is also the development of the art-work within the person: these are the two processes which for Wagner culminated in the success of the *Der fliegende Holländer*. Secondly, art-works appear against the background of the ticking of a different clock, one whose note is heard almost exclusively within the specialist art-world. The clock marks the relentless development of genres, media and methods. It marks also the advance of new types of convention and expectation in the reception of works of art. It is to that clock that artists must pay attention when planning the quality and the success of their work. What is good one year will fail the next; what is impossible now may sweep the board and get taken into the Pantheon in five years' time. Neither type of historical development often finds its way into the history books,[21] but both follow the history that does. That history too has its default-settings. If one borrows from Hegel the idea of great art as a product of significant historical moments and significant historical forces, the idea must strike: how can great art be produced if the World Spirit is busy elsewhere, if one's life has been led out of the wind of History. A historian of the nineteenth century – especially when looking at

---

[21]   Those histories that come closest to following the second of the two clocks are either the (all too few) histories of the literary market (Martens, 1975, or Helmstetter on Fontane, 1997, come to mind) or the history of literature from the point of view of the reader of which Jauss speaks and which remains largely a dream.

countries or provinces some way off the beaten track [22] – has little choice than to conclude that there were times when history (including musical history) was not paying much attention, a kind of developmental lull had set in, impulses did not seem to be coming from the outside, and in art quiet polishing rather than innovation was the order of the day. The German writers called 'Epigones' in the fourth decade of the nineteenth century often felt like this: Goethe was dead, no-one could ever be so original as Goethe, so it was nearly pointless to write at all. [23] A celebrated writer of the restoration period, Ludwig Börne, more directly blamed political-historical factors for this choking of creativity. In such a situation, he despairs, 'where can we get novels from?' (1825:396). [24] By the end of his life Wagner's music had come to represent the moment of the nation's recovery from that feeling – whatever we may think of the intrinsic value of the historical movement which provided those new impulses, [25] the emergence of the German Empire, just as that of the united Italian state ten years previously, changed the rhythms inside the time-zones of personal and artistic history. But something needed to happen, and it lies rather outside the scope of this book to decide whether history is more to be feared at a moment of major innovation and change or in the quieter moments when it is running on its default-setting.

So it is not just at moments of stasis – in a quiet valley surrounded by the high and glowering peaks of theory –, or in accounting for the fact that the cello part of the *Messiah* seems to have been written on autopilot, that the highly pragmatic idea of a default-setting in artistic production shows its usefulness. One of its appeals is that the model helps us duck out of authoritarian accounts of absolute values such as 'quality' or meaning within individual works of art. In concluding this chapter I will take just one

---

[22] Heine remarked of the inhabitants of the French provinces that their faces were marked by their distance from Paris 'like milestones'. How much further from the World Spirit were many of the stations of Wagner's pilgrimage.

[23] Something similar affected composers after Wagner's death: they worried about where their music could go now, the *ne plus ultra* of Wagner's music frightened lesser successors into unproductive self-doubt. This is part of Harold Bloom's topic, cf. note 12.

[24] See Chapter Eight for a further discussion of Börne's position.

[25] We return to the artistic situation in 1871 (German unification) in the final chapter. Nevertheless, in Wagner's situation it would be absurd to see his productivity as an 'effect' of the *events* of 1871, if for no other reason than that most of his work was completed by that date. In any case, the mediation processes between History and the work of art are anything but direct. We might reflect on the fact that, for all the state's efforts and in marked contrast to situation in the Soviet Union in the 1920s, Hitler's Germany produced no culture whatsoever. Whether it is the paucity of the fascist ideology, the conditions under which artists worked, or simply luck, that caused such a patch of artistic unproductivity, is not an easy question to resolve.

example of a type of argument I am determined to avoid in this book. My quarrel is not with the individual essay, but with any argument that appears to legitimate ideologues' claim of 'meaningfulness' for bits of Wagner's work in support their views. I want to focus on how Wagner's operas work, not on what they 'mean'. It was not only the critics who put the focus in the wrong place, but the composer himself too. I abhor Wagner's views on Jewry in music, not only for the reasons that make all anti-Semitism unacceptable, but because his remarks very foolishly ascribe fixed quality and meaning to particular music, as he does to 'Jewishness'. I think we should object nearly as much if Wagner had said that he *liked* 'Jewish music'.[26]

In an article on 'understanding music' (1973) – in which Wagner is not mentioned – the eminent Polish musicologist Zofia Lissa argues that the distribution of 'meaning' in music is not even; that is, that some bits of music are 'meaningful' and that others are not. That is an argument in absolutes, which I do not accept. I argued above that out of vanity artists ascribe more meaning to one aspect of their work than to others, but that does not mean that such a meaning was or became *intrinsic* in the music. Meaning is ascribed to music, but we are not therefore obliged to share the ascription and thus accept a fixed meaning.[27] Using the analogy of non-musical language, Lissa distinguishes within an individual sentence language parts which *mean* something from parts of the sentence which lack meaning.[28] Rather than

---

[26] Chopin offers an interesting parallel here. As Charles Rosen wrote recently, Chopin showed 'little regard for the authentic reproduction of the folk elements' of Polish music, but was influenced 'by chromatic Jewish folk music heard in Poland, which did not prevent him from being offhandedly as conventionally anti-Semitic as many other Poles' (2010:5). Music, ideology and their subsequent perception can clearly diverge – to an improbably wide extent.

[27] I echo here the attack Carolyn Abbate (1989) launches on the referentiality of Wagner's motifs. Any referentiality which is ascribed exists only within the context of the work, outside that context a harmonic sequence or a short melody will not necessarily preserve the ascription – except as a quotation (e.g. Sachs' quoting of *Tristan* in Act 2 of *Meistersinger*). I am suggesting that, since music has no intrinsic referentiality but *acquires* it, Wagner's ascriptions are to be taken seriously only within the evaluation and reception of the work as a whole. (Cf. also Darcy 1993:50).

[28] Even if one accepts the analogy, one should point out that those parts of the sentence which are denied explicit meaning – the fillers such as 'well' or 'um', the *Partikel*, the redundancies and repetitions (the things that are invariably so hard to translate) – often have a clear pragmatic function in communication and the sustaining of dialogue: i.e. that meaning exists only within the context of the whole sentence. The whole topic of music and language is of great moment to aesthetic philosophers and philosophical musicologists, and has to do with the issue of whether one can 'read' and 'understand' music as one does text. Adorno's side-stepping comment that to understand a language means that we can explain it:

insisting that some bits of Wagner are meaningful (and therefore *must* be taken to be more important than others – this a comment on ideology *and* on artistic form) I want to limit the sense of meaning which this book accepts, and within which I hope individual listeners have their own free space, undirected by composer or critic.

Lissa's remarks on the greater or lesser presence of 'meaning' in music can be re-expressed less absolutely, without insisting on meaning as a black and white quality, in three ways:

1. It can strike the ear that one note stands out, that it more urgently requires the ascription of meaning than others. In the majority of cases this situation will simply refer to matters of conventional tonality, the resolution of a diminished seventh back into the dominant, the completion of a chord. Perhaps the idea of an accident/accidental is helpful here – just as a Freudian slip may be more 'meaningful' than the banal, everyday remark in which it is embedded, so perhaps accidentals (i.e. breaks in the accepted tonality of a piece of music, exceptions to a tonal pattern) have a similar effect in glowing with 'meaning'. But whatever that meaning may be, it is not absolute. It acquires meaning only within the work as a whole.

2. As a particular example of this: Meaning can appear to be created when one element in the music is repeated more than other material. This is obviously important in listening to Wagner's music, as it is in prose and poetry. When something is repeated, the reader and listener will assume it to be important, they will start thinking, speculating, investing this material with their search for meaning. Nevertheless, that element acquires 'meaning' only within the coherence of the work, that is 'narrationally'[29] – which is likely to

---

to understand music means that we *perform* it elegantly points up the difficulty of the topic, but does nothing to resolve it (cf. Dahlhaus 1973:37ff; Adorno xvi,253).

[29] Peter Rabinowitz (1992) gives a strong account of the pliability of the listening experience, stressing what is called the 'attributive' level, and by this approach he tries to counter the claims made in support of over-technical musical analysis as the only valid interpretative tool. It is, he argues, only the 'theories' and 'preconceived notions' about what music ought to be that allow a listener to turn the raw material of sound into a musical experience at all, whether or not they are based on musicologically defensible propositions. While, as we argued above, some of those conventionalities are all but inescapable (e.g. the tonal system), others are much more heuristic (Rabinowitz lists rules of 'notice', 'signification' – for instance, in interpreting actions hinted at within a sexual context – 'configuration' and 'coherence' without making, as reception theory was obliged to, sufficient safeguards against lapsing into 'psychologism', i.e. merely subjective opinion). The idea of default-

be equivalent to the meaning intended by the author, but that still does not have to amount to any absolute meaning which can be re-expressed outside the terms of the story. (It is possible, after all, that certain repeated elements – as it might be, Colonel Vronsky's white teeth in *Anna Karenina* – are no more than a mannerism on the author's part, rather than an image carrying particular meaning outside the work.)

3. Meaning also appears to be created when reviewers, critics, the author – anyone of these agencies start talking about a particular aspect of the work as being 'meaningful'. This book is liable to be dismissive of much of this. This occurs not through perversity on my part, but because I want to reposition elements of Wagner's work, and to shuffle the pack.

None of these arguments prevent us from finding meaning in some parts of Wagner's music rather than in others, but they leave this choice to the listener. In fact, I think they amount to a compelling argument for listeners to adopt just the approach which is implicit in the default-setting syndrome. We need to look behind the shop-window opened by the composer and assiduously maintained by critics and to see what it is that connects the high-points and ear-catchers of the music. We may admire Wagner when he really tries (of course some listeners do not care for him in that mood), but we know him only when we get to know how he behaves at less exalted moments. In particular with regard to the *Ring*: the *Leitmotiv* dominates so much discussion (in fairness to Wagner we need to remember that he himself *never* used the word) that we should find the listening energy to insist on the structure of the whole, which distributes meaning through the relations of the parts to the whole. That ambition is something of what Stravinsky meant when he critically described the *Leitmotiv* as a cloak-room ticket: it seems predetermined what the listener gets when the ticket is given in; it would be good to hand in the ticket and be surprised at what is handed back over the counter.[30] To the extent – let's put it at about ninety-nine per cent – that the reception of music, like that of all the arts, is historically conditioned, received by specific societies against the background of a series of functions

---

setting offers a modest possibility to reflect on and free up the listening experience and is meant only to make our ears suspicious, and does not offer a method of analysis.

[30] Cf. Bloch (1985:169). The reference comes in a passage setting up both Debussy's comparison of *Leitmotiv* and address-book and Bloch's own comparison of (i.e. a warning against) *Leitmotiv* and trademark, in the spirit of 'Persil washes whiter'. All the examples argue against the institutionalization of the reception process and the need to ask other questions in other to discover levels in the music other than the label.

and completing claims to meaning, canonized, or ignored by specific societies: – to that extent it seems reasonable to praise the artist, apart from their particular technical skills, for creating polysemantic structures, in which almost every element stands in possible relationships with almost every other element, and in which meaning – or a sense that the thing matters – overflows contagiously and promiscuously rather than being identifiable specifically, as it might be as the hardened residue on the test-tube glass. We don't assume that we can distinguish what is meaningful from what is not, and the argument of this book is certainly not that the 'Realist' elements of Wagner are more important than others. Our greatest wish would be to have them properly included in an overall sense of the elements which make up Wagner's works. We suggest contexts in which listeners develop their own sense of meaning. The book itself will be evasive when it comes to establishing one meaning.

So we do not need to be philosophers of music to work with the idea of the default-setting and to use it to encourage ourselves to be open to appreciating aspects of Wagner's works which are so often taken for granted. We should notice skills which the composer would never have been [dis]credited with, and allow ourselves the freedom to see behind the big to what we may subsequently experience as the meaningful. Wagner may well impress us most when he is not trying to do so. Perhaps he was a secret novelist and did not wish to admit it. It is in this spirit that we have embarked on a book with a theme that seems to qualify it for a place on Chesterton's false shelves. Our hope is that the door will lead to insights, and that for some the corpse on the floor of the library may even come to life.

3. Wagner and the Novel: the existing view

'Music is something quite different than the art of hearing'
Ernst Kurth, 1923

Our approach to the question of Wagner and the novel in the following chapters of this book may seem unorthodox, but the topic itself is not new, simply underdeveloped. Since the beginning of the last century it has been a cliché to compare Wagner's operas to novels, if only *en passant*. Often critics and fellow artists have meant nothing more serious than that Wagner's operas are long and have complex, sometimes multiple, plots and would therefore sustain more extended treatment. An explicit, but rather more considered position to this effect was reached by Thomas Mann, whose acutely sensitive account of Wagner and his works (in various essays, culminating in 1933[1]) identified in Wagner the epic breadth of Zola's novels. Much earlier Mann had stressed general features of the novel to be found in Wagner's work: their 'Homeric origin' and vivid characterization made Wagner's works into 'secret novels' (Mann 1908). Mann's response was certainly unusual among novelists in his generation. Quite apart from the fact that Wagner was frequently the butt of satirical treatment in novels, since the performance of his operas offered the opportunity to study the cultural pretensions of the European elite, even his admirers hesitated to think of him in the context of the novel. It was more usual for novelists to use Wagner as a way of making their own works *less* novel-like, more 'musical', and they seldom had their eyes open to Wagner's novel skills, whether real or potential. In the earlier period, Wagner's contemporaries were either locked in rivalry or their reception of his works too strongly overlapped with ideological and social aspects of Wagnerianism for the idea that these were novels to catch on. Bayreuth and the big social events in Berlin and Vienna represented by productions of Wagner did not suggest subtlety or detailed social observation on anyone's part, not even that of the composer. In recent years only two

---

[1] With the Nazification of Bayreuth during the Weimar Republic Mann moved away from Wagner as a topic: his last major essay was a deliberate affront to nationalist readings of Wagner and caused uproar in the Germany from which Mann was about to depart into exile. Best known of his 'Wagnerian' works – apart from *Buddenbrooks* – are the stories *Blood of the Walsungs* and *Tristan*, dating from the first decade of the last century. All these works are poised between critique and admiration of Wagner's work.

critics have briefly looked at the issue: Ingenhoff (1987) and Borchmeyer (1989).

Serious critics – and above all the advocates the Wagner's work – had a further strong reason not to draw the comparison: namely the poor standing of the novel as a genre in the aesthetic canon of nineteenth century Germany. The idealist view of art gave little prominence to forms which set out to reproduce social reality: the novel was neither among the art forms sanctioned by antiquity nor did it meet post-Kantian criteria of ideality. Significantly – for Wagner too – Hegel identified the novel with modernity, but only at the cost of seeing it as part of a general and irreversible decline in art. As a result perhaps, although there were hundreds of novels being published in Germany (as everywhere else), they never achieved critical prestige. There may or may not be a connection between the aesthetic prestige of a genre and the readiness of artists to work in it – as the previous chapter suggested, money and success are more important motivations –, but there certainly is a connection between that prestige and critics' readiness to give recognition to new works. Only Wagner's enemies would have thought of disparaging him by comparing his works to novels. As late as 1908 Mann was well aware of the hostility which his opinions on Wagner and the novel would meet from 'the conceptual apparatus of an aesthetic which even today refuses the novel a place within the kingdom of poetry' (1908:32) – the greater hostility of the nineteenth century can well be imagined.

Mann wrote these words at an early stage of his career as a novelist. He was to say of those years that his novels were European, rather than German in inspiration. Zola, the Goncourt brothers, Tolstoy, together with some lesser known Scandinavians had been his guiding spirits. This was not just a personal account, but involved a diagnosis of the absence of the novel from the German tradition: from 1850s on a German writer who wanted to write novels had to learn the art either from England (where Scott and Dickens' reputation was huge) or from France. The novel was not 'really German'. In the climate of fervent nationalism which dominated all European countries at the end of the nineteenth century it was most unlikely that German critics would dream of associating Wagner with a foreign genre such as the novel. Cosima determined Wagner's reception as a German, riding the wave of patriotism following the establishment of the German Empire in 1871. In this readiness to distort elements of the legacy, she strongly resembled the other strong-headed woman responsible for passing on a major corpus of work to the next generation, Elisabeth Förster-Nietzsche, who ran her brother's affairs during the decade of his mental illness and after his death. Cosima knew how Richard was to be packaged successfully, and that package certainly did not include the European novel. Her hints were dutifully followed both in literary criticism and in specialized study.

These attitudes prevailed not simply in general literary criticism, but in musicological circles. This is well illustrated in a major study of Wagner's harmony by Ernst Kurth, first published in 1923 and still part of the musicological debate fifty years later. We shall return to some of its claims when we turn to the topic of Wagner and psychology in Chapter Seven, but here we should emphasize two elements, first: the dominance of Schopenhauerian aesthetics, shown both in the understanding of music as the supreme art because of music's closeness to the Will, rather than to the surface appearances of the world; and also in the rejection of any mimetic element in music. Even the depiction of nature – one of the particular skills of Romantic music, and of Wagner in particular – is no imitation (*Spiegelung*) of nature. Even a Beethoven sonata (Nr. 31) does not give 'a portrayal of the storm, but the experience of its forces'. By this Kurth means that the forces of nature are transferred by analogy outside the area of immediate experience, that is, abstracted from the everyday experience. Secondly: Kurth insists – consequentially enough – on the primitive, elemental, non-conscious nature of music.

Other Schopenhauerian readings of Wagner's music draw the same conclusion, repeating Wagner's view 'that the vocal line, as a linguistic expression of the individual is part of *the world of appearances*, whereas instrumental music in essence belongs as a *secondary world* to the pre-conceptual and elemental world' (Schmidt 1981:142, italics in original). Hence, so the argument goes, the increasing importance of the orchestra across all nineteenth century opera, as the voice is increasingly submerged in ever richer instrumental music. Such arguments suggest that opera moved further and further away from the expression of individual feeling and experience which characterizes the novel. Music was related either to the ideal-abstract 'secondary world' or (as illustrated in the previous chapter) to the elemental: never to reality. Those who worked within that tradition would never think of describing Wagner himself as a novelist; indeed – as Grey comments – no music critics in the nineteenth century were interested in ascribing any 'narrative or metaphorical significance [to] long-term tonal relations' (1992:109). Music was related to the ideal and the abstract, or the elemental, but never to reality.

My argument in this book is not simply a protest at this type of traditionalism. It cannot be denied that these critics were true to many of Wagner's words, as well as to Schopenhauer's ideas. The question is rather whether they are true to Wagner's practices. There are many reasons to be suspicious of these opinions. Two short examples will suffice here. First we need to discuss Wagner's increasing move away from ensemble writing in the course of the years, up to the famous compositional break in the middle of Act 2 of *Siegfried*. It is clear that he was using individual voice for a *positive* statement of personality, one which was not to be buried in ensemble or whose melody needed to be strengthened by ensemble. Instead, individual voice is for 'personalities who need for the musical assertion of their individuality a multi-voiced symphonic support (that is: clarification of their melody)'.[2] While this is an appropriate description of the use of voice in *Die Walküre*, which is all about the attempts to individuals to achieve freedom and autonomy, the shift towards ensemble which is observed in Act 3 of *Siegfried* and *Götterdämmerung* cannot by any stretch of the imagination be equated with the submerging of individuality in the elemental. Not only the final duet of *Siegfried* – a triumphant statement of individual commitment and love – but the strongly social nature of the world of Gunther and Gutrune make it hard to diagnose a principled shift away from individuality in the opera. Ackermann points out that the restoration of duet and ensemble in *Götterdämmerung* has a different structure, based on a 'longer, more open, dialogic structure': i.e. he does not accept that voice is invariably associated with the ephemeral aspects of individuality in the world as appearance (1981:124). Indeed, in places *Götterdämmerung* is more like a novel than anything which has gone before. Secondly, it would surely ignore the clearly rational, analytical aspect of the *Leitmotiv* if we accepted the view that the orchestra is there merely to represent a chthonic and unstructured unconscious. A great deal of Wagner's intellectual commentary on the action is left to the orchestra. Whatever large-scale theories may say, the practice is different. The orchestra is not abstract, but a shrewd commentator on the reality of the action played out on stage. As the opening pages of this book suggested, it is preferable to listen to what Wagner does rather than simply to what he says.

Whatever critical opinions got set in concrete around him and his work, and however dogmatic his own pronouncements might be on occasion, Wagner himself was nothing if not an unorthodox and unconventional thinker, it is unlikely that we shall find him holding to traditional opinions. This was true not only for the brief period of his explicitly political ideas, the years when Bakunin and other, less well-known revolutionaries were his friends, but of his aesthetics. His opera plots, especially the *Ring* and

---

[2]   Quoted from *The Art-Work of the Future* by Ackermann (1981:123). By 'support' Wagner refers to orchestral backing, rather than integration in an ensemble.

Parsifal, showed – often maddening his supporters in the process – an absolutely uncontrolled contagiousness in his thinking: stories, disparate myths, conflicting sources and ideologies, all got mixed up, leaving more straight-laced critics struggling to tie his operas down to just one meaning. An artist of that kind was incapable of *not* thinking of himself from time to time in the same way as a novelist, just as at various times in his life he thought of himself as politician, philosopher and historian. Wagner would slip repeatedly into mixed ways of thinking, use the most unlikely analogies, and then argue the contrary with equal conviction. Above all, despite the focus on the national culture which can be seen in Wagner's later life, he was anything but averse to European influences and reception.[3] Above all he was not constrained by any clear aesthetic credo. As we shall see in the next chapter, Hofmannsthal and Strauss did him no injustice in finding him a wonderful practitioner and above all *pragmatic* thinker in the art of opera – something which, alas, few aestheticians in Germany managed to do. Wagner was not one to throw away creative ideas for the sake of aesthetic theory.

There is no need to emphasize that Wagner *read* novels. He read virtually everything, adored Scott and above all Balzac. He respected other types of novel – of course he loved the prose of the Romantics such as E.T.A. Hoffmann and the mixed forms practiced by Heine, indeed his own prose-writings in Paris in the 1840s showed both influences clearly. He read and respected the *Bildungsroman*, the novel of education initiated by Goethe[4] - *Parsifal* and *Siegfried* contain clear elements of the *Bildungsroman* tradition. Yet at the same time he could not fail to hear and respond to Goethe's words: 'The modern artist cannot do without even the barbaric advantages of the novel, if he wants to reflect the complexity of contemporary life in his own work' (cit. Borchmeyer 1989:133. By 'barbaric' Goethe meant exactly the kind of vulgar imitation of social reality and the moving into the intimate lives of ordinary people which characterized the Realist novel.) So it's not surprising that Wagner's focus on the novel picked out the European style of the genre, the realistic historical and social novel – starting with Bulwer

---

[3] When Nietzsche triumphantly consigns Wagner to the Paris Opéra (vi,3:425f) we should recognize that he has shown himself – rather than Wagner – to be provincial, a prisoner of petty nationalism. Where else, in the Germany of the nineteenth century, should a composer wish to shine, where else can he learn serious and modern attitudes to art except in Paris?

[4] Not surprisingly he also loved Goethe's *Wahlverwandtschaften*, (translated as *Elective Affinities*) with its extraordinary mixture of wife-swapping and (very appealing in the context of Wagner's own personal history) children resembling their non-biological father. Making a classicist of Wagner is one thing: ignoring the potential chaos and moral ambiguity of German classicism is another.

Lytton's novel as the basis for his first operatic success, *Rienzi*. His maturity involved growing out of the narrow provincialism of so much German writing. In any case, as Eva Roden (2006) points out, novels such as Balzac's *Lost Illusions* must have read to him like an account of his own experiences in Paris. The novel was the only artistic form which could recognize the characteristic nature of his own biography. Small wonder that the genre remained always on his mind.

Yet in his theoretical writings Wagner's attitude was anything but consistent. *Opera and Drama* (1852) stresses the importance of knowledge in art and celebrates the novel as having carried out the move from the understanding of nature (in which he sees the achievement of previous periods of literature, notably the lyric and the drama) to what Wagner calls 'the bed-rock of history [...] the social nature of man' (iv,50). Not surprisingly he lauds the novel as expressing 'the sum total of human intelligence in the present' and sees in the novel 'the real core of our poetry' (iv,6). The dilemma facing critics, however, is that Wagner directly contradicts these opinions – what's more, in the same publication. He launches a traditional, and therefore from his pen surprising, attack on the very genre he has just been praising. He accuses it of an absence of aesthetic force, 'lacking beauty and form' and claims that the cost of describing public life and 'the individual and social nature of man' has been too high. 'The novel became journalism, its content fragmented into political articles, its art became platform rhetoric and its discourse was infused by appeals to the people' (iv,53). This might be a defensible reaction to some of the less successful Young German novels – to Ernst Willkomm possibly, perhaps Karl Gutzkow too (though his principal work did not appear until 1851 the year before the publication of *Opera and Drama*[5]) – but what about Balzac? It hardly makes sense.

At the worst therefore we have Wagner betraying the novel. Such a betrayal is sometimes seen in the context of his move away from politics after 1848 – which involved worse forms of betrayal than simply pulling up the aesthetic drawbridge on the failed world of politics. But it is questionable that the betrayal actually took place. To argue that it did ignores the obvious novelistic features in the works after 1848 – these are *innovations* in comparison to the pre-revolutionary works. It seems more likely that we are dealing with a deep uncertainty about the novel on Wagner's part, a refusal to

---

[5]   Repeatedly in his autobiographical writings Wagner returns to his dislike of Gutzkow (with whom he had to work in the Dresden years). Perhaps – despite his one-time enthusiasm for Gutzkow's *Wally* (cf. Wagner *SB* II,18) – his public attacks on the novel had a strong element of personal motivation.

give up on the Enlightenment heritage of the pursuit of knowledge and the exploration of man's social nature which the novel supported, combined with a determination to push his own music dramas into the space which the novel threatened to take over. Certainly there is no attempt to reconcile that heritage with the Schopenhauerian aesthetic which it is customary to see Wagner adopting in the years after that famous letter to Röckel.[6] Just a situation with those ambiguities and mixed motivations suggests that Wagner and the novel is an intriguing topic.

Another clue is how little evidence there is in Wagner's subsequent writing of the importance to him of the traditional aesthetics which his radical – and very modern – praise of the novel had caused him to abandon, albeit briefly. It was amongst his opponents, notably Eduard Hanslick, that these traditional ideas were most strong. Indeed Wagner's opponents were right to use that aesthetic against his works, for these works bore very little relation to traditional ideas of form and offended both against the classical idea of tragedy (with their choruses, unities etc) and against the much more focused structure which Realist drama such as Hebbel, or later Ibsen, introduced and which – in the guise of the 'well-made play' – came to take on near classical status. Wagner is drawn to the open and untidy form of theatre, pulled along by its epic breadth, rushed by catastrophes. It was unusual to find these features in an artist, Hanslick (2007:64)) commented, who was supposed to be a master of 'retarding' the action – in short, Wagner was felt incapable of aesthetic focus and form.

Those comments related to the plots of the operas, but very similar arguments persist in evaluating the music. Even modern musicologists have found it hard to establish formal patterns covering the entire length of the operas. Those who tried – notably Alfred Lorenz,[7] with his influential elaboration of Wagner's theory of the 'poetic-musical period' – to discover overall formal shapes (thus reflecting classical harmony and unity) have been increasingly cut down to size, the formal patterns appearing recognizable

---

[6]   This letter (dated 23 August 1854) appears to tell the story of the most complete conversion to Schopenhauer's philosophy, to which Georg Herwegh had introduced him. There are many suggestions in the literature that that conversion was less complete than the letter suggested.

[7]   Not only a typical representative of nationalist, Schopenhauerian aesthetics (increasingly replaced by a popularized form of Nietzscheanism), Lorenz was an active member of the National Socialist Party. Post-war Wagner studies make clear that one can distinguish between his meticulous musical analysis and his unacceptable ideology (cf. McClatchie 1998). In his musical analyses Carl Dahlhaus – to whom this book will often refer in gratitude – emerged as one of Lorenz' most persuasive critics (cf. Abbate and Parker 1989:1-24, also Darcy 1993:52f and Schmid 1981:149f).

only within much smaller units than the whole work. The over-ideologized understanding of the structural function of *Leitmotiv* and *unendliche Melodie* is no longer felt to be a proper base for formal analysis. It is no coincidence that this critical process leaves Wagner's works very much in the position of the novel: the formal structures (never a *forte* of the novel) are now sought much more in small units and scenes, and the unity of the work is fundamentally challenged, as Adorno remarked of Mahler's novel-like music (see below). Instead its openness is praised (cf. Brown 1989:187f), and formal arrangement is felt to lie in smaller-scale rhetorical devices. In any consideration of his own operas and in comparison to the dramas of his century, the accusation of formlessness against Wagner has much justification. It is no coincidence that one of Wagner's most famous remarks on the place of *reason* in the work of art (and therefore, its supremacy over form – it had been Hegel who famously critiqued reflection in art) was addressed to Hanslick: 'Don't underestimate the power of reflection,' he tells the critic in 1847, 'the work of art produced unconsciously is a product of ages far removed from our own: the work of art of the higher period of culture cannot be anything other than a product of the consciousness' (cit. Gregor-Dellin 1985:99).

One particular development in criticism makes my topic less inappropriate than it would have seemed a century ago. We touched on an aspect of this development in the first chapter – the emergence of musicologists, philosophers and literary critics prepared to embark on the analysis of music at a point of maximum distance from Kurth. These critics explore the relationship of text and music not through hierarchy (as it might be, using the music to 'set' the text – in which activity traditional critics understood a master-slave relationship), but on the basis of equality, understanding both as conventionally operating semiotic systems, whose use of the technical devices inherent to their medium can be mapped on to tropes and rhetorical structures anterior to both media. They relativize both language and music and with them the genres which proceed from them. In doing this they seem to learn from the creative practitioners of these arts. Working across the media, Hofmannsthal and Strauss, and Verdi-Piave clearly perceived structures which antedated specific medium-based scenarios and sketches. Within his own head, Wagner obviously did the same. For these artists neither medium nor genre was primary and any effective practices they discovered fitted both arts.

This critical background – associated with Anthony Newcomb, Lawrence Kramer and Steven Peter Scher – not only encourages us to think flexibly between genres: it offers a possibility of understanding that conventional ways of speaking about Wagner's music – for instance those implying that a passage of music *narrates*, that the orchestra *comments*, that an individual harmony is materializing a particular *thought* – are more than shallow metaphors. We shall not use these arguments often in the pages that follow, although their complexity means that M. Jourdain's situation, as outlined in Chapter Two, remains relevant. Nevertheless, they offer reassurance that in the terrain we are exploring there *are* paths and other routes which lead to the type of conclusion we seek. The established critical methods do not rule our central question out of order any more than recent critical re-positionings automatically validate it.[8] In any case, as I made clear at the very start of this book, my aim is less to manufacture an answer to the question of Wagner and the novel than to see what insights drop into our hands as we address it.

Before the work of these critics, this interdisciplinary writing about music had been largely the province of two celebrated philosopher-critics, both writing from an unorthodox Marxist position: Theodor W. Adorno and Ernst Bloch. We will encounter their arguments fragmentarily at various points of this book, but in concluding this chapter, and without implying that either Adorno or Bloch represent any kind of orthodoxy, it is appropriate to outline their approach to our question.

Bloch locates himself at the middle of the issue with his essay of 1929 comparing Wagner and Karl May. This was serious iconoclasm: to compare Balzac to Wagner might offend the purists, but to compare him to Karl May offends everyone, for Karl May – pulp-fiction creator of the Wild West, with Winnetou and Old Shatterhand – represented about the lowest form of novel-writing of which middle-class men, remembering their childhood reading, would admit knowledge. Bloch is interested in the function of Wagner and May in the culture of high capitalism, and much of his effort goes into showing similar functions for their works in that society, from escapism to *Ersatz* metaphysics and 'meaning'. He speaks of the 'birth of metaphysics

---

[8] Apart from my lack of expertise in these new critical methods I confess to a historical sense that wishes to make more absolute the genres which these methods dissolve, and to a simultaneous failure to define with the necessary historical rigour the genres which support my argument. In a similar way, my approach leaves out of consideration the massive contribution of structural anthropology to discussions of Wagner. Claude Lévi-Strauss' many pronouncements on Wagner absorb Wagner's work within a dazzling intellectual system and constantly illuminate his texts. While this approach even more radically – and for my argument: usefully – dissolves any essentialist concept of both classical beauty and traditional genre, I reluctantly must avoid it here because it contains no place for the historical form of the Realist novel nor does it help to relate music to Enlightenment ideas. My arguments in this book clearly depend on both elements. (cf. Wiseman 2007:1ff,106f,167ff).

from the spirit of pulp fiction' (1929:5). At the same time, his distinctive
approach is seen, not only to Wagner, but to all the nineteenth century
culture. Bloch was determined to find a progressive perspective which after
1933 could prevent the Nazis from taking over still more of bourgeois culture
for their own purposes. (It might be remembered that Karl May enjoyed
much unthinking support from the ideological right-wing, which gave Bloch
this impulse. In Wagner's case it was a bit late for that – the Nazification of
Bayreuth had taken place long before the end of the Weimar Republic.[9])
That's why the concept of the utopian plays such an important part in Bloch's
work: he knew he was working against the grain of history.

Adorno's writing on Wagner came later than Bloch's. His views, as we
suggested, were marked by observing the massive exploitation of Wagner in
the day to day practice of Hitler's state and wars. In consequence of this,
however, much of Adorno's positive thinking on the relationship between
music and the novel deliberately stops short of Wagner, and to find his view
on this relationship we need to look instead at Adorno's book on Mahler
(1960). From that study I want to suggest five elements which may
accompany our thoughts on Wagner and the novel. There's no evidence that
these ideas have been taken up by modern criticism, but Adorno remains an
established voice in aesthetic debates in the twentieth century and we should
consider his views briefly here.

The first reason to regard much of Mahler's music as 'Novel' (the title of
an entire essay in the volume – xiii,209-229) is the contrast between
'pedestrian', i.e. commonplace material, and musical artistry. In Mahler's
case the 'pedestrian' material to which Adorno refers includes the folksy
Ländler and marches which he uses (the equivalent, Adorno argues, of the
adventure novels and pulp fiction of the nineteenth century). These represent
a commitment on Mahler's part to ordinary reality, to the ephemeral things in
life: something which the novel, rather than music, is good at. These are
features, Adorno remarks, of Flaubert's *Madame Bovary*, that 'novel of
novels' (xiii,209).

Adorno turns from the material of these genres to the form of their
presentation. He speaks at length of the gesture of narrating which he finds in
Mahler. He summarizes Mahler's basic attitude as 'Just listen, I want to play
you something', and calls this gesture the epitome of the novelist, indeed it's
Balzacian in its basic narrativity. Adorno does not stray into the issues of the
ability of music to tell stories – that was where later critics were to begin. His
interest is to show a composer 'who wants to make music in the way that

---

[9]   Carnegy (2006:235).

other people tell stories' (xiii,209). What he calls the *Habitus* of the narrator can be seen not only in the music, but in the type of text which Mahler's works contain. In support of Adorno's argument we might suggest that the *Kindertotenlieder* (whose subject is perhaps the most personal of griefs) are structured not round immediate identification with feeling, but round telling stories.

In terms of form, Adorno points to the openness which is typical of Mahler's compositions. Rather than adopting the closed forms of traditional classical music, Mahler is open always to new themes, like a novelist always ready to introduce new characters, which may – Adorno quotes Proust on this point (xiii,220) – come from nowhere to dominate the work. Rather than have fixed meanings or set equivalents for the parts of movements, within formal structures, Mahler operates flexibly, and shows himself the brother of the novelist.

Time is a fourth element in the approach of the artist. The classical symphony aimed to make time shorter, to help it to pass faster. In contrast, the 'epic symphony' regards time as part of its material (this clearly a product of the historicizing of experience), just as the nineteenth century novel showed 'lack of consideration' towards the readers, who were forced to plough through hundreds, not to say thousands of pages (xiii,221). When Thomas Mann (subsequently while writing *Doktor Faustus*, a keen, if rather selective reader of Adorno) spoke in *The Magic Mountain* of 'narrating time' (in the first sentence of Chapter Seven), he was conscious of taking over a musical habit which was itself a take-over from the novel.

Lastly – we touched on this issue in Chapter Two – Adorno detects in Mahler a discontent with the social position of the musician, and a longing for the higher status of the novelist. Mahler (b. 1860) saw differently the shifting fortunes of novel and music, and perhaps he approached the choice of media with different feelings than Wagner two generations before. What is refreshing for us on our exploration of Wagner and the novel is that Adorno regards as a natural instrument of analysis an approach which for many critics would not be thought likely to bring rewards. Undaunted therefore by past criticism, indeed rather cheered by it, we may move on to the substantial work of seeing Wagner's operas as novels. We do so neither to denigrate Wagner's music, nor to mitigate any of its weaknesses, but – as Adorno's approach to Mahler makes clear – in response to the historical situation in which this music and the art form of the novel came to full flowering.

In the next chapter we start our enquiry by looking at the form of opera in contrast to the forms from which, in two of our examples, it was derived: novel and the drama. Here, as in Chapter Five, I hope to show both the distinctive differences between these genres and the way in which opera can feed on the insights and techniques of other genres. At the end I am unlikely to discover any new Wagner operas hiding as 'secret novels' in his work: my aim is to show how many elements of the operas we do know derive from the novel and how close – despite the judgments of aestheticians – the two genres really are. We shall go on from that discussion to place Wagner's work more squarely within the thematic concerns of the Realist novel.

4. Forms of Collaboration across the Genres

Wagner's *Rienzi* : from novel to opera via drama

'Artists often do not know what they do best: they are too vain'
Nietzsche: *The Wagner Case*

From a composer often thought of as archetypically German, *Rienzi* is a
strongly cosmopolitan work. Without Gibbon's *Decline and Fall of the
Roman Empire*, continental Europeans would hardly have been aware of the
name, Rienzi, and without Bulwer Lytton this charismatic populist leader
would hardly have come to the attention of an age looking to the past for
expressions of anti-authoritarian and populist aspiration. It is worth
remembering that Wagner's opera remained his greatest popular success for
much of the nineteenth century. Other matters apart, present-day reception of
the work has suffered from the fact that *Rienzi* was also Hitler's favorite
among Wagner's operas, and therefore the most frequently performed in the
Third Reich – although never in Bayreuth. It is assumed that the original full
score was lost in the final chaos of Hitler's bunker (having been presented to
the Führer by the family) – not a matter for prolonged reflection. But it does
explain modern readers' surprise when Adorno's celebrated study of Wagner
(first written in 1938/39) begins with the opera they do not know, *Rienzi*, and
Adorno is more harsh on Wagner as a result of starting with this work.[1] The
work of musicologists has been hindered not only by the textual uncertainties
caused by the loss of the original score, but by the political implications of
the circumstances of that loss, and they have often hesitated to discuss the
work because of its fateful provenance. Concert-goers will be familiar with
the compelling overture, but few will have experienced the whole work.[2] We
focus on it here in no spirit of rehabilitation, but because of the circumstances
in which it was written: it is only one of two instances in Wagner's work of

---

[1] Another feature of the time may be identified in the often rather naïve acceptance by Adorno
of Nietzsche's critiques of Wagner, a strategy seen as subversive during the years when
Nietzsche too might have been in the Nazi Pantheon. In this book – perhaps this is also
general among musicologists, who have little reason to respect Nietzsche (cf. Vogel 1965) –
a much more critical view is taken of Nietzsche's remarks. To echo the words of the
Introduction: I'm certainly not suggesting that we trust Nietzsche *either*.

[2] The Deutsche Oper in Berlin revived it in January 2010.

an opera being based on a modern prose-work, which – via a successful adaptation into drama – became opera.[3] It thus raises elements of our general theme in an exemplary fashion.

Lytton's novel enjoyed moderate popular success. Its relationship to the English novel of the century accurately reflects its publication date (1835). It owes more to Scott's broad historical canvases than to the intimate social observations of Jane Austen. When later English novelists resolved to understand themselves as 'historians of the present' – a tendency unmistakable in Thackeray's *Vanity Fair* (1848) and the works of George Eliot – Lytton's work (with Scott's) would have been a point of reference, but not of imitation. Lytton belongs within that great drive towards the reinvigoration of history, seeking 'to disentomb the spirit of the Past', for which so many writers – Carlyle, Emerson and Nietzsche come immediately to mind – argued. While Lytton declared his readiness to desert 'the art of fiction [...] for the fidelity of history' (p.257), he is at pains throughout the novel to show the positive relevance of his story to the changing times in which he was living. He deliberately critiques in Gibbon 'the cold and sneering skepticism which so often deforms the gigantic work of that great writer' and commits his portrait of the past to capturing the 'sincere and urgent enthusiasm' of its actors (p.186). That is the very essence of Emerson – and via Emerson (as well as via Wagner!) of Nietzsche.

A strong narrative voice is present throughout the novel. Lytton was not one of those writers who, like Flaubert, believed in the 'impassibility' and 'impersonality' of a novel's style. Nevertheless, the voice is constantly stressing objective elements in the story it is telling – and often when it departs from impersonal narration it does so in the interests of objectivity. Lytton is concerned with verifiable, source-based content for the story of Rienzi and his time, and eschews the romantic mode, for instance directly criticizing Petrarch for giving too 'rosy' a picture of the Colonna (p.19). He insists that, properly understood, Rienzi's story has great relevance to the present and should therefore be approached as part of a broad historical context. Early in the novel readers are warned that only 'those who dislike to understand what they read' (p.17) are exempt from confronting that historical background. His preference for history is therefore, in Nietzsche's famous terms, neither monumental, nor antiquarian: it is passionately *critical*.

Lytton was especially popular among German intellectuals from about 1830. It is a clear sign of Wagner's revolutionary stance that he chose

---

[3]   The other - *Die hohe Braut* – is based on Heinrich König's novel of 1833 (cf. Rüland 1986:75f). Other operas before *Rienzi* were based on Romantic texts, but not novels.

Lytton's theme for his work. In fact Friedrich Engels too had planned a drama on that subject. Lytton represented not merely the type of writer who, the Germans hoped, would rescue their literature from the *salon* and (a still greater danger) from the study and re-connect literature with serious public issues. His particular interest lay in his use of the political character sketch, in which the exploration of individual character did not follow the quirky and the eccentric (as so many Romantic writers had done), but understood character as the distillation of social, political and historical forces within an individual person. Similar literature was arising in France, as German intellectuals – among them Heine and Börne, acknowledged masters of journalistic writing – were well aware, but the first German writer explicitly to follow this example as a novelist was Karl Gutzkow, a writer whose work only belatedly has begun to receive the critical and scholarly attention it deserves. He gave the name Bulwer Lytton currency in Germany, publishing his own *Moderne Charaktere* in 1835 under that pseudonym – less an example of laxity in matters of intellectual property than as a device to outmaneuver the censors. So it is hardly surprising that Bulwer Lytton's work was familiar to Wagner and that Wagner's interest combined a broadened understanding of the function of literature, a sense of the historical basis of art, and an overriding interest in the social psychology of his characters. In his *Mitteilung an die Freunde* Wagner makes clear that it was reading Lytton which determined him to break with the limitations of the German stage of his day (iv,256f). During a visit to England he visited the House of Lords in the hope of catching sight of the man he had so admired.

The plot of Bulwer Lytton's novel *Rienzi; the last of the Roman Tribunes* is rich and far-reaching. It starts with the casual killing of Rienzi's younger brother in a skirmish between the warring families of Orsini and Colonna, and shows how Rienzi commits himself to breaking the power of these families, who have reduced Rome to anarchy and lawlessness. In its first phase, the story shows in detail this growing anarchy from 1347 onwards. It relates Rienzi's successful coup against the greed and irresponsibility of the Roman nobility and its culmination, which sees Rienzi installed as the Tribune of Rome. It shows how the first success had to be followed up with a costly military action against the noble families, the *nobili*. In the course of this story the novel establishes – and offers a broad historical explanation for – the intense passion of the two love-stories which run through the novel. Lytton shows within his material the archetypal and timeless power of the great stories of human history – in this case, of *Romeo and Juliet* – but he goes further in offering an objective explanation for the power of love in Italian culture (p.50f). In doing so he followed a common conceit of later

Realists, who (as the example of Victor Hugo will show in the next section) delighted in discovering the patterns of great tragedy and the outlines of heroic myth being repeated in the lives of their everyday characters: in just this way George Eliot constructed the character of Dorothea Brooke as a re-enactment of the sacrificial life of Theresa of Avila. The two love-stories concern Adrian di Castello (a member of the Colonna family) and Rienzi's sister Irene (here the Romeo and Juliet overtones are strongest) and Rienzi himself and Nina di Raselli, whom Bulwer characterizes as an archetype ('breathing image', p.65) of five centuries of Italian history.

The second phase of the novel traces the involvement of the (Avignon) papacy in the barons' fight-back against Rienzi, as it withdraws the support which it originally gave him and pronounces the ban. It gives a short account of Rienzi's time in exile, separated from Nina. It narrates the successful intrigues by which Nina gains the Pope's limited support for Rienzi, as a result of which Rienzi is restored to power in Rome with the apparent blessing of the Church. It tells of Rienzi's death at the hands of the Roman populace, who refuse to support him against the barons – who have risen up against Rienzi for the third time –, and finishes on the restoration of anarchy and lawlessness to the Eternal City.

Within this story-line there are two compelling side-plots. Modern readers may even find them more to their taste than the principal action, with its heavy emphasis on political issues. The first (p.125f) concerns the Provençal mercenary knight, Walter de Montreal. From his brutally cynical involvement with the various factions of the barons, Walter emerges as a complex character, happiest in idyllic retreat from the world in an almost fairy-story castle, with his mistress Adeline – whom his knightly order had forbidden him to marry. He hides the personal tragedy of his life – a son whom he has lost – behind romantic scenes of chivalry, jousting and singing. The second theme comes out in Lytton's description of the plague years (p.228f): the time in which Rienzi has escaped from Rome following the first reinstatement of the barons. These years are traced through Adrian, who searches for Irene, knowing that her life is threatened by her brother's fall, only to discover in the plague a still greater threat. In a nightmare sequence of scenes Adrian combs the convents and charnel-houses of Florence in search of his mistress. The writing is of great power, exceeding that with which Lytton evokes the cataclysm in his more popular *Last Days of Pompeii*.

Reading Lytton's novel one can hardly fail to think of its transposition into another medium. A film, perhaps, certainly from a costume-drama obsessed Hollywood which had its success with Spartacus. It's less than likely that, without our extra-textual knowledge about the opera score,

Lytton's text would have suggested a fanatic's downfall in the bunker - in any case, when Adrian, Irene and Nina leave Rome on the last pages of the text the echoes are of Aeneas' leaving Rome, rather than fast-forwarding to Hitler (although it is clear which elements of the story would have appealed to him). Adorno's critique of Rienzi's self-glorification and pomp – he describes these as 'characteristics of Wagner's whole output and the essence of fascism' (xiii,13)) – picks on elements of the character certainly prominent in Lytton's text. Transposing the story would require pre-eminently perhaps a musical setting, a tone-poem, offering within the structure of Rienzi's rise and fall the two contrasting elements of escapist dream and a descent into the inferno. We wonder what Berlioz would have made of it, for these strong contrasts are the stuff of program music. But not, apparently, of opera.

In fact Wagner – though it is established that he was extremely familiar with Lytton's work (it's a striking feature of Wagner's autobiographical writings that he has little tendency to secrecy when it comes to his sources) – turned to a forerunner of Lytton's novel which had adapted the story of Rienzi for the stage. It is significant to observe that Wagner's ambition – which he subsequently admitted to have been that of *outdoing* grand opera: an ambition in conflict both with Wagner's evolving views on *Opera and Drama* and with the actual models whom Wagner admired – did not require the dizzy heights of Lytton's narrative, but the more restrained world of Mary Mitford's drama *Rienzi*. Mitford mentions Gibbon and Sadé [4] as her sources, but she was concerned to cut the story down to size, to pare off elements which she felt excessive or irrelevant to drama and which she felt might be unhelpful in observing the unity of action and place. Her later preface to the play (1855) stressed the formal innovation of her work, but that innovation consisted merely in doing without a prologue, rather in than anything more imaginative. The overall effect of Mitford's play is conventional. She abbreviates the political history drastically, Rienzi's story becomes one movement of rise and fall, and the scene does not venture outside Rome. Nina does not appear, but Claudia (Rienzi's daughter) takes a central role – "For the female characters I am wholly responsible", Mitford claimed in her Preface – although that is not obviously a matter for pride. Claudia's

---

[4]   It's not clear whom Mitford refers to here. Most likely is the ancient family (from which Petrach's Laura came) which had published in the eighteenth century on aspects to the background of Petrach and of Rienzi. It is less clear where the accent on the 'e' came from. Mitford clearly had much less trouble with Gibbon's cutting comments on Roman characters and with Petrach's rosy views than a politically committed novelist such as Lytton. Lytton is highly critical in his Preface to the novel of Mitford's lack of interest in historical background and historical facts.

dilemma is to choose between her loyalty to her father and that to her lover, Angelo, himself torn between loyalty to Claudia and duty to his noble family, which is determined to destroy Rienzi. For all the power of these conflicts, and for all the Shakespearean cadences which the verse strikes, the work is extremely staid: it is more of a mould into which music can be poured than a work crying out for full realization. Certainly, as we shall see in the next section, *Le Roi S'Amuse* offered much more substantial fare, morally and emotionally exploring a wider range, but it was not for its drama, rather for its shape, that Wagner borrowed from Mitford. We should also remember that the German stage at the time had much in common with that narrow provinciality which marks Mitford's work: the great days of Schiller's theatrical revolution were past, Büchner's *Woyzeck* remained unknown and new greatness lay in the future. While of course Hugo's imagination soared above similar petty restrictions of his contemporary stage, at least such an imagination could catch fire on the French stage. Nevertheless it's hard to think that Mitford would have inspired Wagner as Lytton had: except that she showed him how to convert novels into stage works, that in crossing genres *structure* is more important than content.

In der Beschränkung zeigt sich erst der Meister, Goethe famously remarked. Only in limitation is the master revealed. Perhaps it is the case that all opera requires a formal focus and a restricted basis, even if only in order that its overpowering surplus of energy has something to overflow. All texts will be inadequate to their setting. In a charming (but not particularly thought out) remark Stendhal once commented on this contrast between opera music (Rossini's *Otello*) and its somewhat artificial basis, the text: 'the magnificent musical quality of the songs [and] the incomparable beauty of the [musical] theme' are so overwhelming, he wrote, 'that we invent our own libretto to match' (cit. Kimbell:1991:452). Mitford's text certainly does nothing to get in the way of such invention, and at all events, in contrast to the program music which the full novel would require, Wagner's *Rienzi* has a tight structure. As John Deathridge has shown, in rearranging Mitford's material Wagner restructured the acts to give full prominence to Rienzi (and in particular to his entries on stage) and arranged his characters in strikingly symmetrical constellations: a formal symmetry which Lytton's text neither aimed at nor achieved. But in fact the debts to Mitford are little more than structural. Her drama makes clear how the historical material can be tidied up and made manageable, and Wagner gratefully takes it up, even when doing so caused him difficulties of his own.

In consequence, Wagner is obliged to accept that strange coalescence of Lytton's Adrian di Castello and Angelo (Walter de Montreal's lost son) into the one composite figure, whom Mitford calls Angelo (and Wagner Adriano).[5] The price of this coalescence can be seen in the improbably quick shifts of loyalty which Adriano has to make, from devotion to Rienzi to sworn vengeance. Nina's loyalty to Rienzi transfers to Irene. Mitford had tried to involve the young female lead (Claudia) in the upper-class marriage intrigues of the Colonna family, creating in Lady Colonna a sort of Roman version of Wilde's Lady Bracknell, both reproaching the men-folk for their lamentable behavior in carrying through their 'private feuds' (as if the disorders of Rome were little more than a feud between rival private schools) and yet offering some kind of sanctuary to Claudia after the tragic dénouement. Rather than turn his story into a tale of upper-crust discord and misfortune, Wagner takes over an uncharted brother-sister relationship, to which we must return shortly.

Clearly Wagner's interest is far removed from polite society. In considering his qualifications as a Realist novelist, we must see his lack of interest in the domestic life and social intrigues of the *nobili* as quite a start. When we think of the obsessive interest which so many of his Young German contemporaries took in the aristocracy,[6] Wagner is a true revolutionary in his story-line, a Realist *avant la lettre*. Yet why? Was it simply that the grand opera he wished to write[7] demanded certain formal features, among these most notably a pantomime ballet (which takes up nearly forty minutes in the second act) and large prominent choruses (as he insisted to Dresden, where the first performance was to take place, nothing but the best should be put in here). But these formal features made possible a clear socio-political line in the final work. The multiple choruses required the staging of what are political elements: the separate choruses of clergy, of Roman citizens (foolishly alternating between wild enthusiasm and violent hatred for Rienzi), nobles, legates and ambassadors drive Wagner into political generalization and lead him to show Rienzi in constant confrontation

---

[5]   These names become maddeningly confusing as soon as comparisons take place. In Lytton: Rienzi, Nina (Rienzi's wife), Irene (his sister), Adrian di Castello (Irene's lover, member of Colonna family), Angelo; In Mitford: Rienzi, Claudia (Rienzi's daughter), Angelo (Claudia's lover, member of Colonna family); In Wagner: Rienzi, Irene (his sister), Adriano Colonna (Irene's lover).

[6]   It would be hard to find any Young German plot not dominated by the aristocracy, from Gutzkow's *Wally* (where the 'progressively' presented dilemmas take place in the highest echelons of society) to Ernst Willkomm's industrial novels, to which the *Almanach de Gotha* is a better guide than any trade register.

[7]   *Rienzi* was subsequently described as 'Meyerbeer's best opera': in fact, Wagner's admiration for Bellini was more instrumental in his ambition. Adorno's argument less flatteringly places *Rienzi* in the tradition of the still earlier *opera seria*. (xiii,55).

with these groups as *political* forces – something Mitford conspicuously did not attempt. Even the ballet has a political theme. In an age which prided itself on what in a famous phrase Gutzkow called 'the smuggling of ideas' (Hömberg 1975) even grand opera had its uses.

A similar overlap of aesthetic and political intention can be seen in the way in which Wagner follows Lytton closely in his fascination with Rienzi's political charisma – a feature which was a *sine qua non* for any self-respecting hero of grand opera. We see this in the repeated scenes in which Adrian(o) succumbs to the persuasiveness of Rienzi's vision for Rome, and in Rienzi's initial but repeated power over the people. Mitford was less than open to this element in Rienzi, in part, one suspects, because it broke the terms of those *moral* dilemmas on which her play focused. Instead she turns Rienzi into a Shakespearean tragic hero, showing in his life 'the common tale of low ambition' (her word 'common' certainly has intentional ambiguity), like Macbeth inappropriately wishing to be king. In keeping with this, Mitford offers Rienzi in the last lines of the play the positive epitaph: 'treat the corpse with reverence; for surely, / Though stained with much ambition, he was one / Of the earth's great spirits'. In the absence of political interests, Mitford's only explanation for Rienzi's ambition is given in the motive of vengeance on the *nobili* for the death of his brother.

Wagner gives dramatic and musical prominence to this motivation too, but the line 'Woe to the man who must avenge his family's blood' becomes a recurring motif for Adriano too, being quoted as Adriano looks up at Rienzi from his father's corpse towards the end of Act 3. Vengeance is therefore part of the driving energy of the whole opera and not just of Rienzi's character. Lytton's approach would have encouraged Wagner to think of it (like the love of Adrian and Irene) as a historical feature of the age, rather than as a merely personal quality in individuals. The central ambiguity within Rienzi between selfish love of power and altruistic love of Rome is a central issue in the entire story, and essentially political in its portrayal, for it throws into question the legitimation of populist régimes. Lytton leaves the ambiguity unresolved, seeing Rienzi as 'a patriot who knows himself sincere' (p.40) – although he does not hold back in his contempt for Church and *nobili*, and for the citizenry who value Rome only 'as a commercial speculation' (p.313) –, while Mitford has no time for explanations of Rienzi's high-mindedness: for her more significantly all revolutions end in fresh tyranny. Rienzi is a potentially noble character, but a social upstart and the world is best left in the hands of Lady Colonna and her ilk.

Wagner is not prepared to accept either account. He takes from Lytton an extended interest in the role of the Church in Rienzi's fate (Mitford amazingly leaves out the Church, clearly believing it not to be a suitable topic for the stage), and develops the metaphor of the Church as the Bride of Christ into a major element in Rienzi's motivation: Rienzi's bride is Rome, he loves her and will sacrifice himself to her. (Such secularizations of religious sentiment were a common feature of the works of the Young Germans, as their use of titles such as *Madonna* – a fashionable novel by Theodor Mundt – illustrates.) But Wagner goes one step further. Minutes before the final catastrophe, in which she, Rienzi and Adriano will perish when the burning Capitol engulfs them, Irene makes an extraordinary remark. She asks Rienzi to reflect on the sacrifice which she is making, as she renounces her lover Adriano in favor of Rienzi's vision of Rome. 'Do you know, she asks, what it means to renounce one's love?' And she is forced to reply to her own question: 'No, you have never loved.' She has not been impressed by his talk of Rome as his bride, but it is only thanks to Wagner reducing Rienzi's family connection still more radically than Mitford that Irene can make this remark at all. (As we pointed out above, the love-story of Rienzi and Nina is one of the most compelling and prominent elements of Lytton's novel.) A penetrating psychological interest involving the renunciation of love[8] has thus come into the drama, insufficiently motivated, no doubt, but very powerful. And it is followed up shortly after, even closer to the final moment, when Adriano, desperately trying to talk Irene out of the immolation on which she has by then set her heart (Irene: 'Here I stand, a Roman [...] I feel a giant's power, God helps me to resist you'), is forced to comment on the selfishness of that sacrifice. He has to tell her that her death will affect him – something which seems not to have occurred to her as she prepares for her great moment. So Wagner is deeply interested in political dimensions of Rienzi's fate, but is searching for ways to follow through what are in fact psychological questions of a more pathological kind, and for which grand opera may well not offer the best format. Perhaps we should note that this insight into Rienzi is – if we follow Martin Gregor-Dellin's suggestion that Irene owes much to Rosalie, Wagner's much loved sister, who died in 1837 (1983:130) – potentially very revealing about the young Wagner. So too is Wagner's comment that the mature works of a composer tell little about the mature artist, in contrast to a writer's early works, in which the seeds of the future works can always be found (cit. Graf 1911:1). If true, Gregor-Dellin's remark would make *Rienzi* still more fascinating.

We return to our word 'undermotivated', with a brief reflection on practice and theory. The idea of Rienzi's incapacity for love is without

---

[8] The importance of this theme in the *Ring* – and elsewhere – needs no emphasis.

precedent in the material: it represents Wagner's innovation, and not surprisingly the material he works through gives him no support. But it's worth reflecting on what support the work itself (either as novel or as opera/drama) would require for such an innovation to be effective. In prose, Irene's one-liner could never achieve the force it is meant to have. Her accusation needs preparation, not just in the previous action, but by the narrative voice pointing up the action, showing the reader what to expect, and making plausible this final judgment. A similar moment is reached, for instance, in Theodor Fontane's celebrated novel of adultery *Effi Briest* (1895), when, shortly before her death and for the first time *ever*, Effi passes judgment on her ex-husband. He was a good man, she remarks, considering that he was a man 'without love'. While Fontane deliberately leaves Effi's phrase ambiguous; the remark causes a whole series of events and responses to fall into place. The innovation and surprise effect of Effi's remark is not destroyed by preparation of this kind; the preparation is the only thing which makes it effective: its ambiguity rounds off the whole action, because it strikes the same chord as an entirety of narrative voice, which throughout the novel has been pointing up the small heartlessnesses and lack of warmth in the man. And if the musical metaphor of the chord is appropriate here, then we may continue it. Of all arts, music supremely can hold together a plurality of ambiguities, while yet reminding the listener, at a moment of revelation, of what s/he *already* knows.

Wagner realizes here that he needs two features of the novel: first the secret accord between narrator and story if he wishes to achieve his psychological effects, and secondly the presence of a memory marker, involving harmony and melodic shape to remind his listeners of what they already know. From here came what Wagner called the 'motif of remembrance' (*Erinnerungsmotiv*) to which criticism has given the more familiar name of *Leitmotiv*. Drama needs perhaps a much narrower focus on interpersonal relations than the major political canvas permitted which Wagner took over with Lytton's material, and Mitford had no sense of the psychological depths which drama might wish to reach. However empty the shell of her story, however, it was – until that last moment – more or less appropriate to Wagner's wishes – it was only in retrospect that the advantages of the novel became clear.

In summary, we may conclude that *Rienzi* showed Wagner some of the drawbacks of the novel and conventional drama if he wished to do justice to the themes which interested him. Although the music contained nothing by way of *Leitmotiv* it certainly revealed to him his need for such a device. His later works, as we shall see, reveal his use of the orchestra as the narrative voice of opera, with a function which moves far beyond merely accompanying individual characters' remarks and offers reminders (it would be hard not to think of them as psychological *comments*) on the action. Irene's remark – had it been highlighted by such devices and had the orchestra taken it up into the dialogue with the audience – could have focused the opera: without such support the insight is merely swallowed up in the turbulent and imperfectly organized maelstrom of Wagner's music. We should remember that Wagner was having too many significant problems with the cohesion and development of his music for more subtle relations to be established within his text. While the original prose version has but one music reference scrawled in the margin, the verse text is treated cavalierly, as Wagner struggles with the music (Deathridge 1977:123f,141f). His grand opera is, in its day, magnificent and compelling, but neither in form nor in content did it meet the real needs Wagner felt as an artist. He wanted to write a novel of political and psychological pathology, but his artistic techniques met only part of that program. He was too vain and ambitious for glory to understand what he really wanted. To meet his ambitions he needed the novel.

Drama to Opera: *Rigoletto*

In the final chapter we shall touch upon the place of Verdi within the Italian cultural situation in the second half of the nineteenth century, and hope to show that Verdi and Wagner shared much more than the year of their birth (1813). It is clear that Wagner and Verdi participated in a similar project as far as the development of opera was concerned. This is reflected in the present-day debates about the role of Wagner's music in Verdi's increasingly complex orchestration, and in Verdi's move towards a 'symphonic' opera form[9] – nevertheless, their individual operas are markedly distinct. In particular, in this preliminary chapter on opera and other forms, Verdi's *Rigoletto* – despite the opening scene which could have been copied from *Rienzi*'s first scene (in which Irene is being abducted by the *nobili*) – offers contrast rather than similarity with Wagner's work. We have chosen it for discussion because, as with *Rienzi* – a character incidentally on whom Verdi more than once planned to write an opera –, the relationship between the

---

[9] Verdi's pronouncements of the matter were characteristically direct. Speaking – tolerantly – of Puccini's use of 'symphonic element', Verdi remarked: 'Opera is opera; symphony is symphony, and I do not think it is good to do a symphonic section in an opera, just for the joy of making the orchestra dance' (cit. Phillips-Matz 1993:677).

finished opera and its original expresses significant aspects of the generic nature of opera, aspects which have relevance to Wagner's work.

Rigoletto is based on an adaptation of Victor Hugo's drama *Le Roi S'Amuse*, and Verdi's choice of model is distinctive for many features of his work.[10]

Le Roi S'Amuse drew the displeasure of the French censors in 1832 through the effrontery of its presentation of the libertine king, François I. But the play itself, so little changed in its adaptation by Verdi's librettist, Francesco Maria Piave, does not really depend on the character of the king. Indeed, the shift in the title of Verdi's opera corresponds closely to the actual balance of Hugo's original, in which the royal jester, Triboulet, is obviously the central character, and Rigoletto himself is constructed closely and entirely on Triboulet. Triboulet might well have given Hugo his title too,[11] were it not for a particular type of expectation of drama in its portrayal of society (an expectation on which the response of the censors was to a large extent based). It was Verdi who drew Piave's attention to Hugo's play, which he had called 'one of the greatest creations that the theatre can boast of', being particularly impressed by the character of Triboulet, 'deformed and ridiculous on the outside and passionate and full of love inside'. It is fair to say that Triboulet's case is the result of a search for heroic tragedy rather than of a carefully plotted psychological development.

Triboulet's story depends on the possibilities of corruption opened to him by his service of the king, as Triboulet exploits his position as court jester to initiate the crude rapine which fuels the king's 'love' affairs, but it is his tragedy on which the play depends, and it is this which Piave/Verdi take over unchanged. Like so many of Verdi's operas, the force of the play lies in the extraordinary power of the dénouement, although this dénouement does not involve the king at all, indeed his absence and non-involvement is crucial to the ending. Triboulet, attempting revenge on the king for corrupting his daughter Blanche, discovers not only that has he unwittingly aided the king in that corruption, but that he is responsible for the killing of his daughter. The body in the sack which he is to throw into the Seine contains Blanche's body, not that of the king, as his revenge had foreseen. Towards the recognition of that horrendous truth the whole play is constructed; not only the extraordinary figure of the professional assassin Saltabaldi, with his

---

[10]   I'm grateful to Dr Roger Clark for access to his program notes for the Covent Garden production of *Rigoletto*.

[11]   In fact the title came from a parody of Hugo's play: *Rigoletti, ou le dernier des fous* (cf. Phillips-Matz 1993: 273) – yet another example of the crucial importance of parody in literary history.

carefully adjusted range of services and charges ('you see that I am an honest man [...] I am paid half in advance and half afterwards'), but the complexity of Blanche's character. She is split between a sensualist – 'don't listen to him', she implores God, as Triboulet promises revenge on the king, 'for I love him still' – and that sacrificial nature which not only has made her compliant to her father's bizarre instructions, but in the final dénouement leads her to offer herself to Saltabaldi's weapon in place of his intended victim, the king. Both of these dramatic elements are more or less submerged in their function of engineering the final scene of recognition. Perhaps the drama shares with Verdi's opera a certain negligence about the plausibility of these elements, although, after all, they are no less plausible than that, after being stabbed to the heart, Blanche should carry off her final duet in fine voice. But the final scene is all, and to it everything else is subordinate.

It follows that Hugo and Piave/Verdi strongly share a sense of the weight to be given to psychology in their story. There are potential explanations for Blanche's behavior: lacking human contact, locked away by a jealous father, whose name she does not even know, and of whose love she is merely the object ('I needed you, needed a heart which loves me', Triboulet tells her), Blanche's actions can be explained, but her character lacks the necessary depth for explanation. Saltabaldi and his sister Maguelonne illustrate the same point. They show those extremes of sentimentality and depravity of which Eugène Sue was to make the principles of his world-famous novel *Les Mystères de Paris* (1842): Maguelonne 'a very beautiful girl who dances in the street and whom men find compliant', yet she admires François as 'baby Jesus' as he sleeps. Perhaps beyond economic necessity these two have their particular reasons for behaving as they do, but these reasons remain hidden. Hugo subordinates them to Triboulet's fate; the characters' function is to be instruments of the curse which M. de Saint-Vallier (another father whose daughter has been made a victim of François' fatal predilections) delivers to the king and Triboulet equally. While the curse is powerless over the king – Saint-Vallier remarks with bitter truth at the end of Act 3 'this king will prosper': as we have seen, Triboulet's attempt to take over vengeance on the king fails spectacularly – the curse rings repeatedly throughout the play within Triboulet's head, and this is the mainspring of the action, carried along without profound characterization of the supporting roles. Heroic or tragic greatness seems to depend more on contrast than on psychological depth.

When original and adaptation are so close, then it is reasonable to assume that the differences between Hugo's play and Verdi's opera have to do with genre. Doing the same thing, exploring the same topic through the same characters, opera and drama work differently and comparisons of the two works may shed light on the genre relationships between drama and opera.

In choosing Hugo's play Verdi embarked on something highly innovative in Italian opera, in particular in its structure. The *Gazetta Uffiziale* reported on its first performance in March 1851: 'Yesterday we were overwhelmed by the novelty, the novelty or unusualness of the subject, novelty in the music, in the style and even in the form of the pieces' (cit. Capra 2001:137). Hugo's play and its individual acts neither begin nor close on set-piece, large-scale scenes suitable for operatic chorus. The play ends with deliberate banality, with the surgeon confirming Blanche's death, and although Piave/Verdi shortened the play by a few pages – ending 'she is dead, ah: the curse!' – the scene remains private, if highly dramatic. The first act had ended on a similarly personal note, the curse of Saint-Vallier which, as the first line of Act 2 makes clear, only Triboulet has taken personally. The play had opened *in media res*, with the king planning another seduction (only at the start of Act 2 does the audience realize that Triboulet's Blanche is to be the king's next victim). These are informal, fluid scenes, with wit and humor, which Piave is careful to retain – such as Marot's comment that it is unusual to encounter a king who did not leave the job of amusing himself to others (a remark from the age of Büchner's Woyzeck, who was convinced that, even if they ever got to heaven, people from his background would have to do the hard work, like making the thunder). There clearly is the potential for an operatic chorus: most obviously in the large number of hardly differentiated courtiers, but Verdi makes almost no use of this potential. Triboulet's curse on them – its directness being one of the elements which offended the censors of 1832 – takes away any collective dignity which they might possess in the eyes of the audience. They represent nothing but the foolishness and sycophancy in which Triboulet fully participated. They lack that normalcy and positive lack of individuality which Nietzsche was to show as the distinctive feature of Greek tragedy, and which we see in Verdi's predecessors as well as in others of his own works.

We must go further than this and point out that at certain moments the musical element of *Rigoletto* is straightforwardly naturalistic. In Hugo's play the king happens to sing – particularly when on his predatory raids for women – and his catchy, cynical number becomes a kind of trademark. This song gives Triboulet the first inkling that Saltabaldi has not killed the king. Having spoken his last words to the corpse in the sack – 'À l'eau, François premier!' – Triboulet is appalled to hear the song ringing out from a nearby street: that is enough to tell him that the king is alive, the sack must contain something else. There is nothing symbolic about this moment, the song is no

Leitmotiv hidden in the orchestra and in Triboulet's memory: the king sings and Triboulet reacts to what he, and the audience, hears. Exactly the same happens in *Rigoletto*. 'La donna e mobile' owes its stunning effect to the same naturalistic freshness and its lack of musical integration into the rest of the opera. The absence of writing for chorus makes the same point, cutting out stylization and conventional formalism which is evident in the ensembles. Translated into opera this range in Hugo's play makes for a great deal of self-reflectiveness.

In literary-historical terms we are dealing in Hugo with an early example of stage realism, one which Piave/Verdi are more than happy to continue. Although less well known than *Hernani* and less discussed by the aestheticians than the preface to *Cromwell*, *Le Roi S'Amuse* is a shining example of the shift from classical to Realist drama, a shift which can be followed in all European countries from the 1830s on and in which Hugo was a pioneer. The new drama takes its heroes not from kings and gods, but from ordinary mortals, reflecting the awareness of the dramatist – in the words of Friedrich Hebbel, an important German follower of the trend (and virulent enemy of Wagner's, as we have observed) – that 'one did not need to be a princess to have a fate, and in certain circumstances a tragic fate' (i,326). It includes often sordid details of ordinary lives, it embeds the action in a surrounding everyday reality and is constructed on the idea that people act for material reasons, not for any ideals they may pretend to have. It eschews classical verse – few duels were more bitterly fought than Hugo's fight against the hexameter – and is happy to use money and sex as driving-springs of the action. Verdi/Piave make clear in their title that they subscribe to these innovative ideas, nowhere more obviously than in the fact that the noble hero strolls banally out of the action, while it is the lowly character who attains tragic greatness. And in most other ways too the similarity between Hugo's text and Verdi's libretto is strikingly close: we understand why Wagner regarded the 'inner laws of music' as being 'those inner laws by which drama is constructed' (cit. Stein 1960:159f). We need to remind ourselves that Hugo and Verdi were writing in different genres – it's small wonder that Eduard Hanslick called Hugo's plays 'libretti which have not yet been composed' (cit. Kimbell 1991:498), or that Hugo felt his name should have been on Verdi's posters.

Of the five elements distinctive to opera – chorus, with or without individual voice, recitative, instrumental interlude (including overture, perhaps even ballet), aria and ensemble – the first two can most naturally match the structure of drama. As we said, *Rigoletto* does have choral elements, but not only are these not used for large set-piece conclusions: they have the same element of farcical emasculation that Hugo's courtiers display. Kidnapping Gilda or breathlessly relating their exploits to the Duke, the courtiers are ridiculous, their music a parody of the collective – closer to Arthur Sullivan than to *Rienzi*. Recitative obviously is crucial to both opera and drama, it drives the plot on, creates spaces for interaction; but it was in the nature of the developments with which Verdi and Wagner were associated that composers were increasingly expected to show skill (and occasionally virtuosity) in handling recitative, integrating it with the other elements of the music. Strikingly, the most amazing examples of that skill and originality are located in identical moments within the separate work of Hugo and Verdi. Hugo's writing in the first scene when Triboulet is approached by Saltabaldi, the professional assassin, is breathtaking and innovative: understated, telegraphic, starkly materialistic, although – of course – the scene has the character of dream-fulfillment, since Saltabaldi has no way of knowing that Triboulet might be on the look-out for an assassin: indeed, when Saltabaldi accosts him on the street, Triboulet is hardly aware of that urge in himself. Verdi's technique in the parallel scene with Sparafucile – which Deirdre O'Grady calls 'a masterpiece of self-analysis' (2000:15) – is no less amazing. Verdi drives the scene along on a syncopated urban melody, orchestrated to echo like a hurdy-gurdy, brilliantly evoking the decay and threat of a city, of course much more nineteenth century than medieval.[12] The fate which waits on kings is found not in the heavens above nor among Poseidon's monsters of the deep, but in the everyday vice which passes in the big-city street: it lies in the unpredictability of the anonymous. The closeness of the two scenes and Verdi's transposition of Hugo into music shows Verdi's ability to grasp the essence of the original and to find for it (he called this 'the hardest work of all') the corresponding 'idea, the basic musical mood'.

Rigoletto uses the briefest of interludes or overtures and dispenses with ballet – as other serious composers of Verdi's time wished to – as a mere irrelevance. Modern critics comment on the way in which the arias break with the form traditional to Italian opera,[13] and it is worth also noting the subordinate place taken in them by conspicuous vocal virtuosity – it was part of the spirit of the age that, just as the tragic effect could be achieved out of the traditional classes, the whole range of emotion was available for a more naturalistic vocal output. (Virtuosity did not, of course, cease to be required

---

[12]   In this respect (among others) it would be impossible to claim any striving for historical accuracy in either text.
[13]   Kimbell's notes on *Rigoletto* accompanying the Deutsche Grammophon CD of the opera.

of the singer – it was a question of the form in which it was to be displayed: today no-one imagines that it is *easier* to play Hedda Gabler than Lady Macbeth.) In other words, while the obvious affinities between Hugo and Verdi/Piave are on a thematic level, the real closeness lies in the handling of the technical resources of the two genres. The texture of the orchestration and the use of tonalities in *Rigoletto* are closer to Hugo even than the characters Triboulet and Rigoletto.

In turning to duets we encounter a series of difficult problems. Once we accept as duet a type of operatic singing in which the two participants do not have to sing at the same time – it's very noticeable that not until Act 3 of *Siegfried* does the *Ring* contain any other form of duet – the closeness of opera and drama becomes still greater. For drama also regards the duet as a special form, whether it is the quick-fire exchanges of Benedick and Beatrice, or Jessica and Lorenzo's famous duet 'In such a night as this' (*Merchant of Venice* V,1). The formal, rhythmic and stanza-like construction and the progression through the exchanges make the scene obviously musical. In a different key would be the scene of intense rivalry between Mary Stuart and Elisabeth in Schiller's *Maria Stuart*, no less consciously structured with tempo, rhythm and pitch and leading to Elizabeth's passionate decision to put Maria to death. Such scenes are the set-pieces of classical drama, no less eagerly awaited than a favorite operatic number.

It is this institutionalizing of forms which creative artists – much as they may enjoy the applause it reaps for them – most fear. This fear, no less than their pursuit of the 'symphonic element', drove Verdi and Wagner's anxiety to overcome the 'number opera'. The artificiality of Mozartian duets,[14] reflected in their perfect formal symmetry, strongly resists integration into the rest of the opera, and what was true of opera applied no less to drama. Modern drama tried to move away from such high scenes, and Ibsen – still more strongly than Hugo – shows a clear tendency to achieve effects with smaller means and to ensure that the action and its motivation was not obscured behind rhetorical fog. We need only to remind ourselves of the

---

[14] Let no one imagine that Wagner was anything other than a whole-hearted admirer of Mozart, or that his championing of Beethoven diminished that regard. If today there is tendency to identify 'camps' of opera-goers, some of whom 'do' Mozart and 'don't do' Wagner, it had no basis in the attitude of Wagner himself (Mozart being spared that dilemma), who of course conducted Mozart operas on numerous occasions. Many of Wagner's innovations applied to the way in which he conducted the work of other composers; the malaise of the European opera-house had infected other composers' works than his own. What Mozart did was brilliant, but could not be repeated in the 1840s, the clock moves on.

anonymous way in which Hedda Gabler leaves the family home to see the contrast. It is not fanciful to see elements of this desire in *Rigoletto*. In this way he is reminiscent of Brecht, who – recognizing the spell cast by the set-pieces of his great predecessors and above all their institutionalization in the audience's anticipation – endeavored to take the steam out of them, to make the audience open to a response other than the cloying identification and empathy (*Einfühlung*) traditional to 'Aristotelian' theatre. He wrote exercises for actors who had to perform these big scenes, in which the objective frame of the scene is reasserted without the emotional idealizations. Elisabeth and Mary Stuart have to rehearse their scene in the role of two fish-wives, accusing each other of selling stale fish, and of not smelling any better themselves. When they have learnt to use the duets to make visible real events and processes, Brecht believed they would play the original scene differently.[15]

When Verdi took over Hugo's drama he achieved, within his chosen genre, a shift in practice which is hardly less radical. On one hand the formal structures of the duets are made dependent on the processes which are driving the action at the time: this we see most notably in Verdi's altering of the weighting of the two voices according to their ascendancy in the father-daughter relationship (Gilda is clearly more assertive in the second duet). At the same time Verdi is naturalizing what had become a merely conventional device. Music is being used to highlight elements of the processes taking place on the stage, rather than simply intensifying the emotional enchantment which the characters exercise over the audience. It would not be out of place to stress the *gestic* quality of such writing, no less than in the other ensembles in *Rigoletto*.

The exquisite quartet 'Bella figlia dell' amore' in Act 3 is given its motivation – no less than 'La donna e mobile' – naturalistically. Hugo's play has Triboulet and Blanche watching the king's advances to Maguelonne from outside Saltabaldi's house. The king and Maguelonne play out their own drama, full of wit on both sides and flirtatious threats ('you read that in a book', Maguelonne says of one of the king's gallantries: even when he is

---

[15]   Referring to his exercises for *Macbeth* II,2 and *Maria Stuart* III, Brecht wrote: 'For years our theaters have stopped playing these scenes for the processes which take place, and only for the temperamental outbursts which these processes make possible. These exercises restore spectators' interests in the processes and refresh the actors' interest in the stylization and poetic language of the original texts, as special, additional feature of the scene' (22,830). We see here unmistakably Brecht's interest in rescuing traditional aesthetic features of the classics, rather than – as is too easily assumed – merely debasing traditional aesthetic considerations in the service of politics.

quoting Solomon, she sees that he goes to the theater more often than to church). Triboulet and Blanche have a common stance. Blanche – unable to watch any more: 'he says to this woman the things he has already said to me!' (but the audience continue to watch) – lets her father pursue his plan for revenge. Her spirit is broken by what she watches the king do, and she agrees to his will: 'Do what you want', yet as she hears his instructions she trembles with fear at his plan. 'Great God,' – she says to Triboulet – 'you are terrifying'.

It would be hard to imagine an operatic quartet more naturalistically inaugurated, or a more natural occasion for a quartet. Music has a different language to drama, where speed, volume and pitch – let alone harmony – play, if any, a subordinate role. Yet both Hugo and Verdi seem to be reading from the same score in this number. If the dramatist or composer were to have kept a shorthand scenario of the scene they wished to create, then Hugo and Verdi could be seen to have worked from the same notes. Did Verdi see this structure beneath the skin when he first encountered Hugo's play, or was it 'just' the theme (sublimity behind a disfigured exterior), the visible aesthetics, which attracted him to Hugo's play? At times we could be forgiven for thinking that he could read Hugo's most secret notes. Working across the genres demands a level of aesthetic sensitivity which the practitioner of only one genre seldom requires. Only we should not fail to see the role played by genre convention, even at moments of such striking proximity. We notice at once that a quartet is fundamentally different from four characters being on stage and singing. The quartet starts some time after the scene starts, the situation is the frame for the quartet, rather than its structure. And Hugo's text has very uneven goods to offer Piave/Verdi in this scene. François, for instance, has only one line in the section of the play to be set. In general his witticisms and – a greater loss still – those of Maguelonne are cut out and the charm and grace which they bestow on his character in Hugo's play (it must be half ways plausible that Blanche is prepared to die for him: he has to be more than simply a serial lecherer) are left to his music, rather than his words, to convey. Gilda and Rigoletto lapse strikingly into a very conventional language for the duration of the quartet, and this is interrupted only when Rigoletto starts to give Gilda her instructions (which start only after the quartet as such is finished). We see here, therefore, in this set ensemble number more strongly than in the duets the characteristic of opera to suspend action, to express the relationships between characters within a suspended moment. It's a freezing which drama doesn't manage – perhaps the soliloquy managed that, perhaps the framed dramatic narratives can achieve it, but drama seems always to have to move on, because it needs words to sustain its length and cannot shift into image (as the film does) or into music. In a similar if rather more trivial process, the overarching music of an ensemble piece can embrace actions by other characters – actions for which the stage-play had required a separate scene – and makes unmistakable the focus of the work.[16] Wagner was not the only composer who wanted the spirit of music to be seen as the force from which all action sprang, starting from inside the relationships music moves out to embrace the action.

So the renewal of opera in Verdi – that 'overwhelming novelty' which its first audiences experienced – came from a closeness to Realism, in which drama and opera could participate equally, even if neither set out to achieve a directly political message. Innovations were largely technical, consisting of shifts from unreflected tradition practices. We suggested Brechtian terms to explain this shifts which music brought to Hugo's play, and as Verdi moved from a more conventional frame and allowed more reality to impinge on the action. At times it seemed as if elements of these arguments might apply to Wagner also; at others this possibility seemed more remote. While Hugo's text helped Piave and Verdi down the route of his development – although it would be hard to detect any strong political direction in the opera –, Wagner was forced to rely on his own writing alone, and as we shall see in later chapters the naturalism of his work got pushed into less discernible corners than in Verdi's case. Yet fundamentally the conventions of opera, especially in the direction of the reforms which Verdi and Wagner were achieving, set up possibilities for the Enlightenment heritage in which he had developed, and the space between story and music, between music development and stage action would prove capable of being filled by something other than pomp and convention.

Presenting the Rosenkavalier – the claims of word and music

On the assumption that a letter which I sent some ten days ago to your presumed address (Knesebeckstrasse 30) may perhaps not have reached you, due to some unknown circumstances, or other, for I should find it almost impossible to understand that you would not have replied to it, by a line of rejection at the very least, I permit myself to repeat its content.

This decidedly unpromising sentence opened the first letter Richard Strauss received from Hugo von Hofmannsthal in November 1900 (perhaps he *did*

---

[16] So for instance Rigoletto's cross-examination of Giovanna about her locking the house door and about strangers who might have followed Gilda is included in the duet 'Figlia' in Act 1.

get the first letter and had simply not bothered to reply, so that their whole relationship started from Strauss' guilty conscience). Thus began one of the most celebrated operatic collaborations of the twentieth century, producing first *Elektra* (1907), then *Der Rosenkavalier* (1911) – not to mention *Die Frau ohne Schatten* (1917), of which Hofmannsthal remarked that it could become 'the most beautiful of all existing operas'. This opening sentence was prickly and unfortunate, but it revealed in Hofmannsthal not merely an anxiety over social forms and a sensitivity to slight which might have boded ill for future collaboration, but a latent precocity about the poet's 'content', even when that content had been committed to a form as ephemeral as a letter.

If that sentence had been Strauss' only acquaintance with Hofmannsthal's writing, the opera repertoire would have been short of some of its masterpieces. But, although there is no evidence in the correspondence that Strauss was actually familiar with Hofmannsthal's previous work, he must have known his reputation. Perhaps Strauss was not the person to respond to the approach with flattering appreciation – sensitivities were not all on one side –, but he might without exaggeration have replied to Hofmannsthal: I am honored that the greatest lyrical prodigy since Goethe turns to me for collaboration. Strauss, who at the end of his life would convert Hermann Hesse's mediocre poems into the unsurpassed genius of his four last songs, could well have suspected that Hofmannsthal – the person behind the *nom de plume* 'Loris', who at sixteen years old had taken the literary world by storm – had something special to offer.

It was hardly likely that, on its own, the ballet which Hofmannsthal wished to negotiate – under the title, *Kythere*, his draft remained without a musical score – would have caught Strauss' imagination. By the same token, the project Strauss was working on at the time – the opera *Feuersnot*, with its iconoclastic, directly lavatorial humor: scatological, as the jargon goes –, would hardly have been the work to appeal to Hofmannsthal. Author of the *Chandos-Letter* (a sensitively written, lyrically conceived reflection, in the form of an historical letter, on the inadequacy of language to express any worthwhile truth), Hofmannsthal had shot to fame as the creator of subtlety, fleeting nuance and rich ambiguity. His search was for anything but the corporeal, and certainly not for the coarse provincialism which Hans von Wolzogen's satirical libretto had offered Strauss.

Not only their past works were radically different, there's no doubt that the two great artists were on separate trajectories when this letter was finally read: Strauss was trying to move beyond the tone-poems and, subsequently, to get *Salome* out of his system, and was hesitant about collaboration since he expected that 'the symphonist who has been dormant in me for the last 2 years will burst out violently' – and of course he would not have needed a collaborator for that. In view of the fact that Hofmannsthal was trying to achieve a footing elsewhere than in the esoteric and to establish himself in real society, outside literature, neither giving offence nor pushing back the boundaries of taste was his metier. He had, however, come to attach much importance to practical theatre as a way to embed his especially sensitive language in reality. The principal area which might have brought the two men together – their self-conscious embrace of family happiness, as a haven of reality amidst all the relativities and uncertainties of their age – was never identified in their correspondence as a further common ground. This may be nothing more than a reflection of the formality and professional focus of their relationship, yet one could argue that from the mid-1890s onwards Hofmannsthal was trying to write a lyrical version of what Strauss had achieved in his *Sinfonia Domestica* (1903): perhaps it's as well that – for all the importance he attached to domestic life as an anchorage in his life – Hofmannsthal never succeeded in writing an equivalent piece.[17]

Strauss' initially hesitant response to Hofmannsthal's letter eventually changed, largely as a result of Strauss' response to Max Reinhardt's staging of Hofmannsthal's *Elektra*, and the collaboration started. Rather than tell it as narrative (readers unfamiliar with its course can find excellent accounts of their collaboration in a number of secondary sources) I want to use the relationship to focus on those elements of our overall themes which have already been identified in this chapter. A reason for this approach lies in the obvious fact that this correspondence takes place in an explicitly post-Wagnerian context. The lessons of Wagner's practice have already been absorbed, not only by the composer but by the librettist, lessons which included both negative implications and an admiration which wishes to walk in the footsteps of genius. The orchestral richness of *Salome* and *Elektra* is obviously both Wagnerian and post-Wagnerian, and although *Der Rosenkavalier* is strongly broken up into 'numbers' (indeed, Hofmannsthal

---

[17] Originator of the phrase 'conservative revolution' Hofmannsthal's thinking (with its emphasis on such anchorage – not just in marriage, but in his language community and in its cultural traditions – would have been identified as worryingly right-wing, had its sensitivity and decency not been so patent. This tendency of his work makes his professional appreciation of Wagner in the correspondence impressive in its lack of ideological underpinning and in its focus on the *craftsmanship* of opera-writing. In any case, it's hard to think of any work of Hofmannsthal being reviewed under the rubric 'Papa and Momma and Baby Celebrated', as notoriously happened to Strauss after the US première of the *Domestic Symphony*.

was very pleased to have got the important elements of his plot and characterization into those numbers, rather than having excessive recourse to recitative) they are musically far less separate than – for instance – in the Mozartian model. Hofmannsthal, fascinated at the chance of creating something entirely original, saw 'all development in art as following a rhythmic course' – by which he meant that, in order to move forward, opera had to go *back* to styles which predated the *Meistersinger,* the great comic opera of the previous century. Hofmannsthal's opinion contradicts neither a shared admiration for Wagner's opera, nor even the two artists taking up important aspects from it. Surely Strauss and Hofmannsthal's joint amusement at Octavian ending up with Sophie – she is simply 'the first halfways suitable young woman to turn up' – echoes the question mark hanging over Eva and Walter von Stolzing,[18] while the plot which sees the Marschallin renouncing her younger lover and working for his union with Sophie was inconceivable without the model of Sachs passing Eva on to Walter.[19]

For his part Strauss admits, not without irony, to being 'always on the look-out for *Zukunftsmusik*', and when Hofmannsthal expresses his delight at the music Strauss has written for *Rosenkavalier* we notice that he expresses his admiration in terms originally coined in Wagner circles: the first half of his praise is conventionally phrased: 'a garland of pure flowers', the second half more revealing 'and so magically organic in its transitions'.[20] What's interesting about these lessons is how often they ignore those matters which concern today's critics of Wagner – semi-extraneous questions of ideology, or of the artist's personality – and focus instead on the prime relationships which constitute opera: those between word, music and stage. That focus becomes very sharp in Hofmannsthal's comments on Wagner's characterization of Beckmesser. As he worked on the character of Baron Ochs, Hofmannsthal sharply criticized the *fortissimo* Strauss has used for one of Ochs' remarks to the Marschallin.[21] It is revealing to see the justification he offers for his criticism: 'Here the music must literally force the singer into good and correct acting, as Wagner so beautifully succeeds in doing.' He (as

---

[18]   Cf. below, p.104.
[19]   For a general study of Wagnerian influences on Hofmannsthal's plots cf. Cicora (1992:91-129).
[20]   We recall Wagner's self-praise (amply justified and echoed unsycophantically by his analysts) for his 'genius at transitions' (*Übergänge*) (letter to Mathilde Wesendonk, 26.01.1859).
[21]   The line was 'muß halt eine Frau in der Nähe dabei sein' (Act I) (there must be a woman close by).

in part Strauss also) sees the gestic quality of Wagner's music, the interrelation of composer, librettist and stage-manager in the effort to *communicate*,[22] and he bases his own work on exploring those skills. *Der Rosenkavalier* may try to go back before Wagner, but it could not have been written without the skills Wagner so innovatively brought to opera.

Although Hofmannsthal constantly insists that, in musical terms, he is a layman, that was clearly an overstatement. He takes great interest in earlier opera and constantly reflects on music's relationship to words, constantly using the examples of Wagner and of da Ponte. He hates certain musical elements of what has become operatic convention – for instance the 'roaring' of Wagnerian love-duets. It was perhaps for that reason too that Strauss, from the very start of the project, scored the opera for alto and soprano, leaving out the *Heldentenor* completely. It's his collaboration with Strauss that teaches him the detail, but Hofmannsthal is no unwritten page, indeed he is anxious lest his 'lack of respect for what is *conventionally* operatic' may not have gone too far. Strauss' iconoclasm (which in the correspondence he insisted had represented an important feature of many of his previous works) was glad to hear that, but, on the other hand, he is quite adamant that his area of expertise is not only 'the music', but also the dramatic effect and the theatrical conventions. He patronizingly assures Hofmannsthal that it is much harder to write a good libretto than a good stage-play, and the clear implication is that he, Strauss, is the judge of both. Hofmannsthal is frustrated because Strauss would not accept his wish to make a stage play out of the *Rosenkavalier* and only then to turn it into a libretto. On one hand Strauss argued from the commercial reason of not throwing away a good *coup de theatre* before the opera itself was known, but the real dispute was over both men's claim to understand theater success better than the other: the vanities of authorship are not confined to pride in one's own text. Strauss goes further and argues, both on principle and in detail, for placing of moments of 'rest' in dramatic scenes. He complains to Hofmannsthal that his draft for Act 2 of *Rosenkavalier* is dramatically uninteresting – you can do better, he upbraids his collaborator, and Hofmannsthal agrees and does better. As we read the correspondence, Strauss' occasional bullying tone often jars, but it is about the craft of making an opera that he is most adamant, and the jarring effect is mitigated every time he is proved right. He had learned the difference between dramatic and operatic tension while working on Oscar

---

22   A praise of Wagner immediately offensive to all Brechtians and liberal opponents of Wagner. We shall come back to the idea in more detail, but leave it here with the reminder that 'progressive' attitudes can be found elsewhere than in the explicit ideology of a work and its composer.

Wilde's text of *Salomé*, for instance when he left out the scene with the young Syrian and his page. He had realized – to quote Norman del Mar – 'that the inexorable progress of the tragedy was better maintained by a symphonic passage that would develop and build to a climax' (1978:254). And this experience helped him with *Rosenkavalier*.

Yet there was a still more basic level of consensus between the two. As we saw in Wagner's struggle with Hebbel, the common language is artistic pride and a nose for commercial success. Strauss makes an interesting judgment on a contemporary production of *Aïda* – it has eclipsed all the Wagner productions for no better reason than that it has new scenery, by a famous 'designer' (a circumstance which sounds familiar enough today). The appeal to audiences has, according to Strauss, little to do with the music or the subtleties of plot: an exotic setting will always win the day. Hofmannsthal supports this as he outlines his view that the work must appeal to both the refined and the coarse elements of the public: 'the [refined elements] create that prestige without which we are as lost as if we had no popular success'. Echoes of this position are heard when, having finished the work, they discuss the classification of the *Rosenkavalier*, as comic, burlesque opera, or – in the agreed version – 'Komödie für Musik' (anything not to be confused with *The Mikado*). We can feel Strauss' excitement even more strongly therefore when he looks at Hofmannsthal's draft of Act 1 and knows not only that they will make big money out of the work (at that moment that seems more exciting than holding a work of genius in his hand), but that it is absolutely right for the stage: setting it to music will be as easy as 'Öl und Butterschmalz' (a high-calorie version of the English phrase 'easy peasy').

Strauss feels (rightly, we suspect) that Hofmannsthal does not understand three significant features of his trade as musician. Quite clearly Strauss insists on his own sense of the appropriateness of particular musical effects, and in particular a sense of those which no longer work in music. After all, it is he who is locked in the micro-historical situation of the composer, and only he who has the understanding to find a way out. Within his own chosen art, Hofmannsthal possesses exactly the equivalent insight – that was the background point of the celebrated *Chandos-Letter* – namely, an acute sense of the wear and tear on language and the need for renewal, so it is he who warns Strauss off the Renaissance themes which Strauss had wanted him to provide poetic texts for. In literature, Hofmannsthal explains, the Renaissance has become impossible and such a choice of theme amounts in the present to little else than a short-cut to bad writing.[23] Hofmannsthal exposes his musical ignorance more naively when he fails to understand the unlimited number of possibilities in musical setting. He shows typical linguistic flexibility when challenged by Strauss in trying to find a good formulation for the line in Ochs' refrain which became 'Nur ein Lerchenau hat a solches Glück' in the final text, and Hofmannsthal's original suggestion does not do the trick. The music has to show its own far greater rhythmic and sequencing flexibility. Hofmannsthal is amazed at the absolute virtuosity not just of Strauss' personal musical talent, but of music itself in being able to set different text versions. He has to concede to music the palm for fluid, amorphous richness of association, for which his own poetry had rightly been praised. Perhaps he slightly resents the fact that his carefully composed text can be trumped by that infinite variety of possibilities, tonal and rhythmic, over which his collaborator holds sway. But there is another sensitivity of Strauss' to which Hofmannsthal has no access: the openness of the work of high art to parody. It is Strauss who has a sense of the danger of writing something which can be parodied – this was hardly surprising in view of the embarrassing mistake he had made in *Aus Italien* (1886), where he mistook the commercial ditty 'Finiculi, Finiculà' for a genuine Neapolitan folk-song. After that experience he begins his objections to a line of Hofmannsthal by referring to a popular song which shares the same rhythms as the original – 'denn dort in Lindenau / da ist der Himmel blau'. Perhaps his music had always been closer to cliché than Hofmannsthal's – the route back from the avant-garde music of *Elektra* was bound to include the risk of that. Of course Strauss was used to dealing with extreme subjects (heads on plates, for a start) and this type of subject, as both Hebbel and Wagner had discovered, is an invitation to the parodists.

Finally, in their efforts to balance out the course of the third act of the *Rosenkavalier*, Hofmannsthal's role is reversed. Strauss' ultra-confidence in his music's theatricality comes out. Initially Hofmannsthal had found it hard to accept the power of music to carry all before it, wanting instead a more crafted drama. He worried that the end of *Rosenkavalier* lacked dramatic force: Strauss has to reassure him with the bad news (for the librettist) that his music can handle that kind of weakness, can make climaxes and dramatic conclusions even where the drama text lags behind. And as early as April 1909 Hofmannsthal is talked into conceding the point.[24] Yet it is he who

---

23   This was the precise argument put forward some three years previously in Thomas Mann's short-story *Tonio Kröger*, down to the choice of examples of impossible bad taste, namely Cesare Borgia: Mann had already had his failure with Strauss' other suggestion, Savaronola.

24   With some reluctance, however, for Hofmannsthal insisted on printing his original version of Act 3 in the libretto – even though it had not even been set.

instructs Strauss to write 'an old fashioned, sweet-cheeky Viennese waltz' to hold the Third Act together, and – with this suggestion – put the final seal on the opera's success. So Verdi must have looked at Hugo's play and seen potential even where probability, motivation and plot lagged behind – or, we wonder, was it perhaps Piave (as in the above case Hofmannsthal) who produced the musical idea? At all events it is clear that a common language existed between the two halves of the production.

We suggested earlier that Piave/Verdi and Hugo seemed to have been able to read a 'secret scenario', by which, in a language which was neither that of music nor a poetic language, the real inner structure of the work could be appreciated and developed into opera. The Strauss-Hofmannsthal correspondence seems to confirm this suggestion – partly because of the two artists' ability to have insights into the other discipline, partly too in the 'instinctive' sense which both of them had into the as yet unfinished work. Some of this was certainly a recognition of the external formal requirements for an opera text – this had been the case with *Elektra*, whose simplicity of formal structure immediately told Strauss of its suitability for setting to music. But we need to look also for a vision of form which goes even before external form in the composition process. Although it was only Hofmannsthal who articulated this awareness, it is hard to see how – in view of the collaborators' potential for misunderstanding and the relative incomprehension about the other medium – *Rosenkavalier* could have come into being without what Hofmannsthal describes being an experience common to both of them. He tells Strauss in March 1911 (by now, of course, their collaboration has moved on to a different opera: *Der Rosenkavalier* is already that stage success which Strauss had predicted) that he had recently been giving himself over to

> that hardest and most rewarding work, involving introducing the psychological motives of the piece. I mean: I've been establishing the links between the individual characters as well as between the individual parts of the work – sketching out the exact scheme of inner motives. It's that scheme which the poet needs in his head – just like you need a symphonic structure – if the work is to interest us, attract us and absorb our energies.

Seldom is the existence of form clearer, not as external rules of arrangement, but as mental shape, and with it the central parallels of music and text more plausibly established. Perhaps artistic form in this guise – a mental structure anterior to the *Praxis* of the two distinctive arts – has much greater closeness to everyday, non-artistic experience than its elusive abstraction might lead one to suspect. Lawrence Kramer's influential study of *Music and Poetry* finds the common ground in suggesting the structure of both music and

poetry to be 'a kinetic form of meaning', driven by what – using Freudian
terminology – he calls the *cathexis* of rhythm: namely, 'the process,
described by psychoanalysis, by which a subject invests a portion of its
psychic energy in an object and thereby makes the object meaningful for
itself' (1984:19).[25] Another – perhaps less close – analogy can be drawn from
applied linguistics. At one time the concept of 'interlanguage' (Selinker
1972) was influential, referring to an internal language, situated *between*
formally articulated languages, an *intermediate* mental structure on the basis
of which language learners develop their production of the finished product,
the so-called 'target language'. Both ideas touch on something akin to
Hofmannsthal's idea: a forming impulse and a personal identification with
the material which pre-dates expression within the fixed code of the finished
language – whether that language is music, poetry, or schoolboy French!

Alongside this insight, which links back to much that we have observed
between the separate medial forms of the individual works, Hofmannsthal
makes one further fascinating remark about his gifts as a librettist. He has had
to fight off Strauss' rather patronizing assurances to him that they were 'born
for each other', and that Hofmannsthal was a 'born librettist'. While these
remarks give the impression that Strauss has the head of his collaborator on a
plate, in fairness to Strauss we should note that he was aware that there were
other goals which a lyricist might set himself. All the same, Strauss was
hardly wrong in his judgment. Still, Hofmannsthal has his own pride and this
comes out when he reflects on what a librettist's verse should contribute to
the whole process of the creation of an opera. His reflections on his own
operatic writing are formulated in such a way as to apply equally to his lyric
writing: 'my verse is not dynamic or flowery, the quality which it has (and

---

[25]   Kramer's study is emphatically of 'non dramatic music only', and he implies that dramatic
music shares with dramatic poetry an essentially different kind of 'kinetic' drive, one which
lies outside the purely formal processes of both arts. In fact, however, the interface between
text and music with which we are concerned in opera suggests that in both media the artist's
search for form participates in the same processes as in non-dramatic branches of their art.
Hofmannsthal and Strauss show this throughout their collaboration, in which the energy for
composition does not exclusively derive from the need to produce dramatic effect or from a
simplistic view of the unproblematic meaning of language (language is therefore not
immediately instrumentalized when placed in the dramatic mode). It seems that Strauss
nowhere tended to read Hofmannsthal's text in this sense 'naturalistically'. In Wagner's
operas, where the separation of text and music is not reflected in a personal division of
labor, the existence of these structures may be harder to identify, but the questions raised re-
emphasize the usefulness of the concept of a default-setting, the recognition that conscious
ideas are by no means the only or the most interesting building-blocks of an artistic work,
and that both music and language enjoy their moments of autonomy, even in their eventual
merger.

which it's hard to deny it has) lies somewhere else: it has something to say, it's to the point, it's rhythmically flexible. Nowhere does it go slack, sentimental, or off the point'.[26] In another letter (June 1911) he explicitly speaks of his talent as something 'artistic in a quite general sense [*ganz allgemein Künstlerisches*]: my purpose is to create contrasts, yet through these contrasts achieve harmony'. Something similar could be said of Victor Hugo's contribution to *Rigoletto*. We need to bear in mind that the usability of Hugo's text identifies qualities which were present in his own lyrical output and which – had they not existed – would have made the writing of his plays impossible: his wonderful poem 'Tout conjuge le verbe aimer' is not devoid of intellectual placing and distanced structure – in other words, his Romantic poetry too, for all its dependence on feeling, participates in the kind of precision which the librettist needs. No wonder Hugo felt *used* by Piave/ Verdi, and wanted his name on the libretto. None of his work was, he must have felt, merely inert matter; it was instrumental, and did not need its realization in opera for it to be made practical. In just this spirit Hofmannsthal was very careful to insist that that no text of his would ever have that absolute lyrical flexibility or diffuseness which 'left the model of characterization to the composer' (June 1908). There is no poetic quality which does not aim to organize the world it creates. Again we see that the idea of gestic art – i.e. poetry and music that accomplishes the characterization – was a daily reality within this collaboration, and that Richard Wagner was in important respects its model.

The division of labor in opera and ideology

We have looked, all too briefly, at three moments of transition, three reports from the no-man's land between opera and the neighboring genres from which it came. We saw initially the transition of a story from novel to opera, passing through drama, a process which highlighted Wagner's difficulty in incorporating historical-political understanding and psychological insight – both of which featured happily in the contemporary novel – into the conventional forms of opera. The transformation of the *Rienzi* material led

---

[26]   Hofmannsthal's point here illustrates the reason I suggested above (p.30) that the idea of default-setting needs modification to be applicable to lyric poetry of quality. His remark from June 1911, which follows (and is quoted above), offers a perfect example of the Russian Formalists' understanding of poetry – as a system of contrasts in balance within which theme or 'content' is generally indifferent. It is balance not theme that holds poems together.

directly to other transformations inside the frontiers of opera itself. Despite its conventionalities and the border formalities on which opera insists, opera was in the process of radical change. We identified composers' desire to discover the type of opera most suited to the changing times in which they lived, thereby endeavoring both to modify the function of opera within the cultural system of their individual country and to respond to significant innovations which were taking place generally in the other arts. Such a situation is typical of the situation of all the arts, at any moment of their evolution, caught within a general historical moment and striving for specific originality within and beyond that moment.

In part some of these transitions were driven by 'the market' and involved an acute awareness of those factors which we may generalize as 'reception': changing audiences and public, the need for innovation if opera is not going to be confined to a museum, and the need for success, money. On the other hand we encountered a deeper drive of operatic composers to develop themselves as artists, that is: to find forms in which their own particular talents can find full expression, and to assert that individuality not only against the various dominant traditions into which the historical moment of their birth catapulted them, but also in competition with other talents which are finding favor with their own solutions to these same historical problems. Strauss and Hofmannsthal had the good fortune to find, for a brief period only, a common purpose in the shaping of their artistic lives – *Der Rosenkavalier* gave direction, as well as world-fame, to their later activities, even after the trajectories of their lives had separated again. Similar processes are at work in our other examples. For all Verdi's self-understanding as a national figure, *Rigoletto* bears particularly clearly the marks of general developments in contemporary art; it also shows Piave/Verdi's extraordinary sensitivity to the inner voice of other art-forms, while drawing attention to the subtle differences between the forms of expression in handling an 'identical' theme. As an early work of Wagner's, *Rienzi* is weakened by the all-too direct involvement of the artist's personality in character depiction. Perhaps, however, this was less a product of Wagner's immaturity: more a symptom of the difficulty experienced by opera (in contrast to the novel, where even a writer of limited talent, such as Bulwer Lytton, could handle such matters more comfortably) in reaching balanced, distanced views of its characters. One of the obvious roads to such balanced distance – a psychological understanding of human behavior – was, we noted, not available to the opera forms he inherited. While his youthful ambition made Wagner determined to *outdo* grand opera, his real need was to develop it in the direction of his deeper interests. These real concerns were emerging only gradually, and he had not quite understood their relevance to the theme with which he had landed himself. Eventually Wagner would realize the deficiency and realign his effort.[27]

One aspect of his work distinguished Wagner in these examples. Neither his vanity, his secret ambitions nor his desire for success are essentially different from those of Verdi or Strauss. What is different is the place of ideology in his early work. This is hardly surprising, for Wagner shared with his generation – not only Verdi, but Karl Marx and Georg Büchner share their birth-year with him – the fundamentally ideological enthusiasms of their time. They spread these enthusiasms to other European countries – not even (to quote Oscar Wilde) the splendid physiques of the English made them immune to such ideological pandemics – but perhaps they alone felt the urgency of the need to rethink the foundations of their world, as they set to work to digest the massive legacy of revolutionary thinking bequeathed by Kant, Hegel and the Young Hegelians and then, subsequently, to come to terms with the major historical upheavals of their own day. It would also be hard to overestimate the effect on that generation of their own social dislocation and (certainly in Wagner's case) downright poverty. Wagner's theoretical writings – from pamphleteering to aesthetics, from the thoughtful to the mindless and prejudiced – are the characteristic products of his time, but more characteristic still is the absolutism of his arguments. This is not just a reflection of personal aggression and the black and white thinking shown in his early hero Rienzi, but a generational affliction: the insistence on asking fundamental questions. 'Everything lives and continues because of the inner necessity of its being, the needs of its essential nature' (*Opera and Drama* iii,233) – in writing on opera Wagner feels compelled to start from this theological statement of opera's place within the scheme of things. What cannot justify its existence in the universe by means of theory, he is claiming, will not exist in practice.[28] In such attitudes Wagner revealed his generation's drive to take things back to their essence, to challenge and to create only on the bed-rock of the absolute. It makes his work at times hard going for modern generations which are suspicious of absolutes and prefer their social dislocation to be clothed in relativity; his background makes still more unacceptable Wagner's lazy take-over of cheap prejudice and stereotype. By inviting readers to become observant of all that is happening under the level

---

[27]   Wagner's arch-rival Hebbel used a felicitous image to describe this process (in his own work). The artist catches hold of an idea like a boy grabs a bird flying past him in the field. Only when he opens his hand to examine the bird, does he know what it is and can start to think what he is going to do with it.

[28]   A variant of Hegel's famous dictum 'What exists is reasonable'.

of Wagner's constant theorizing and attitudinizing, I have no wish to excuse any of his opinions. I wonder simply how central they were to his finished works.

Nevertheless, I hope that this chapter will serve to contextualize the more inherently artistic issues in Wagner's preoccupations, and to suggest how much of his real work was done at an unseen coalface of technical innovation and genre-based rethinking. What Strauss and Hofmannsthal observed and admired in him as they worked on *Rosenkavalier* suggests that *Opera and Drama* (the work most obviously situated on the fault-lines of social and artistic transition) is really a work concerned with the reform of the opera *as genre* rather than merely of the kind of ideological statement which critics can so easily abstract from it. The last chapter showed how acutely *Opera and Drama* analyzes the differences between the novel and opera – while Chapter Five will suggest the closeness of the *Meistersinger* to the core concerns of the contemporary European novel. Verdi's example in this chapter indicates how far Wagner had followed his age down the road to ordinariness (at the same time it indicates that operatic conventions could move some, but not all of the way towards Realism) and Wagner's operas of the following years underline the continuity of this transition. *Der fliegende Holländer* follows the democrat Rienzi in exploring the lives of the commoners – we need only to hear the chorus of Senta's friends to know that we have left grand opera behind and entered middle-class domestic life – at least in brief alternations with high seas drama. *Tannhäuser* is imbued with 'progressive' Feuerbachian materialism and contrasts the worlds of sensual and spiritual love in a way which many Realist novelists were to adopt. Moreover, at least in the Paris version, it makes huge concessions to expressing the form of love which thrived in the modern city – leaving modern productions torn between presenting the *Venusberg* as some version of a lap-dancing club and treating it as a sort of medieval boarding-school. Even *Lohengrin* – whose world combines the supernatural with a certain sham medievalism – bases on an explicitly modernist reading of religion, in which the philosophers Feuerbach and David Friedrich Strauss[29] were

---

[29]   The importance of both of these figures to George Eliot and hence to the English tradition of realism and secular thought has been frequently examined, seldom exaggerated. That's why it seems legitimate to describe this tradition and *Tannhäuser* as 'progressive' (a word not to be confused with prescriptive). In addition, the strongly anti-Catholic slant of the final scene (the Pope has repudiated Tannhäuser's repentance, and his pilgrimage to Rome has been no more than a waste of time) belonged within the anti-authoritarian traditions of the 1840s. It's worth noting too that – while *Parsifal* seems to portray the pure fool moving on to an ascetic, certainly a-sexual life in the Grail community – Lohengrin is proud to identify

Wagner's lode-stars, and Wagner was anxious that critics understood the opera as celebrating human virtues and qualities through the general metaphor of gods coming to earth. We should not merely read these elements as ideology, but as Wagner's engagement with the movements of which *Rigoletto* is another important expression. And *Opera and Drama* finally reveals itself – alongside Cosima's diaries and the disappointingly vacuous *Brown Book* (over which another Superego than Wagner's – namely Cosima's – held its unproductive sway and filtered out what might have been interesting, not after publication but before it had even been written) – as a dialogue between collaborators (who just happened to occupy the same body), puzzling over the relationship of genres which is central to opera, the relationship of word to music, of speech to song, stage action to music. That's why we start where we do.

Parsifal as his father. That particular fudge on sexuality was one of the causes of Nietzsche's vitriolic hatred for *Parsifal*. Watch what I do, not what I say remains a useful principle in dealing with Wagner's work.

5. Wagner and the Realist Novel – mostly about *Die Meistersinger* with some *Ring*

The six sections of this central chapter have a common purpose: that of establishing links between Wagner's operas and the Realist novel with which they were contemporary. This first section discusses similar symptoms of crisis in music and novel, from which the idea of 'musical prose' may take on new meaning. The established idea of musical prose is examined critically in the second section, encouraging us in the third section to ignore genre differences and to cast the *Meistersinger* in the form of a novel. The comparison is broadened in the fourth section at the level of Wagner's plots, and contextualized in an account of musicological discussions in the final sections. Arguing in this way bypasses any discussion of the *intrinsic*, historically distinct nature of the genres. We do not start, as Wagner and his century loved to do, from the early origins of the various arts and their rooting in the necessities of history or of the human personality. We are not trying, as it were, to identify ancient land-bridges which once joined genres now mapped as separate continents, as if there were once a time when objective truth and imaginative story, rational idea and impressionistic motif, argument and structure were inseparable in some pre-lapsarian, mystic unity. Our enquiry will keep to the immediate period of Wagner's work and consider the practical options which faced creative artists in prose and music at that time. For the producers and the consumers of art in Wagner's generation opera and novel were on the same menu.

Opera and novel in crisis

Before turning to the *Meistersinger*, a comment on *Tristan* and the novel is necessary, for that opera represents a blatant contradiction to most of what this chapter has to say. Paradoxically for a work of such historic importance, *Tristan* appears in Wagner's development almost as an episode, slipped in before the *Meistersinger* and the conclusion of the *Ring*. It represents a moment of maximum change in Wagner's development, as well as in that of opera in general, and in fact of music too. *Tristan* shows this radical change in three of its principal features. From the first phrase of the whole opera, the listener is confronted by the dissolution of traditional harmony and harmonic development, and must face the challenge of a musical sequence which is not given by the rules of harmonic convention, but seems to be reinvented in every situation. *Tristan* shows, secondly, the complete abandonment of the 'number opera', and, finally, the almost complete withering of action and recognizable place. It's not just that these elements have withered: their absence directly strikes the readers and challenges established ways of experiencing opera. We look in vain for the public actions, let alone court events or collective experiences of traditional opera: compared to the *Meistersinger* the action of *Tristan* is closer to Huysman's *Against Nature*, a withdrawal into inactivity and inwardness, than to any of its Realist contemporaries. And it is to the (rather better) successors of Huysman's text – in particular to Proust and Joyce – that critics have immediately turned to find equivalents of *Tristan* in the novel.

In fact, to find the work's plausible affinities in the novel we should really go back to *Tristram Shandy* (1760), even though it predates *Tristan* by a whole century. To justify that comparison we refer to two aspects of Formalist theory. The Formalists believed first that parody is serious: a symptom of crisis in the particular art-form, a sign that innovation and renewal are required, showing usefully the hollowness of outlived art-forms – and pointing to the shape of innovation to come. The second argument follows directly: they argue that the best art is that which goes beyond the conventions of its time. The more radically art goes beyond, the better it is. Furthermore, the progressiveness of any art is a product, not of its ideas but of its handling of the technical resources of the genre.[1] Works that achieve that transcendence from their age offer models for the future development of the medium – even if this potential is not always recognized at the time of their first appearance.

By defining progressiveness in a way that excludes all considerations of ideological content, the Formalists managed to integrate very diverse poetic material into the pantheon of the early art of the Soviet Union. Adorno's idea of the negative dialectic comes close to their opinion, and its consequences are hardly less radical. We should recognize, however, that their argument is not identical to that of Martin Gregor-Dellin quoted in the Introduction, which is less explicitly dependent on a linear view of art's development and is not without ideological overtones. For the same reason, their argument also strongly diverges from the account given by Walter Benjamin of the pleasures of listening even to archaic opera. Benjamin cherished this experience as a reminder that it was not the princes and bishops who had

---

[1]   See Šklovski and Éjxenbaum (quoted in this transliteration by Matejka and Pomorska 1971: 226,19f).

written these works, but that these works had been permanently marked by the artists who had carried through the commissions of these notables and who did not subscribe to the same ideas as their supposedly all-powerful lords and masters (cit. Hermand 2008:11). For the Formalists, artistic skill existed outside ideology, as something technical. For that reason in part they were fascinated by *Tristram Shandy* and (potentially) by *Tristan*.

Just as harmonic development, tonality and consequentiality of plot are the immediate casualties of *Tristan* – no less than the hero himself, these technical aspects of the opera lie expiring on Tristan's island – so in *Tristram Shandy* it is the technical devices of the novel whose demise (or crisis, or simple non-functioning) creates the effect, unheard of in its day. Three such structuring devices are obviously in crisis in Sterne's novel: the stability of the narrative position, the link between external and internal events, and the logical sequencing of the action. From the very first page we watch the narrator's futile attempts to gain control over his narrative; however he cannot do so until he has established his own identity, and this drives him to investigate his own origins (which turn out to be narrational, rather than purely biological). As a result the story loses all continuity and proves incapable of being told; the link between external events and internal states of mind – on which novels depend – is rendered absurd in the analogy between his father winding up the clock and begetting him. The novel fragments and, rather than resting comfortably on the conventional assumptions of the genre, the reader has to live with, and enjoy, those fragments and the uncertainty which they create.

My point here is a simple one and follows from the suggestion of basic structures which predate a work's assignment to one or other genre. Across genres, the structures of works of art can resemble one another so closely that differences of subject matter or externals fade into insignificance. They resemble one another because of their identical understanding of their respective technical resources. At turning-points within individual art-forms, the symptoms of crisis and change are all but identical, and they reveal themselves not merely to the expert's eye or only after long technical debates, but in the most simple reception process. Reading *Tristram Shandy*, listening to *Tristan*, one feels distinctly a sense not of progress in the narrative, not of progression through a musical structure, but rather of falling into deeper and deeper water,[2] losing certainties with every sentence and every fresh chord.

---

[2]   It was Nietzsche who compared listening to Wagner's music to the experience of swimming – more accurately, drowning (vi,3:420). Thomas Mann took up that image in *Death in Venice*, and Visconti's film version translates it into Mahler's Adagio, rather than *Tristan*.

Readers are left with little choice but to let go expectation and convention and throw themselves into the maelstrom.

When related to fiction, the experience I briefly describe is often denoted as a musical experience, where the word 'musical' is taken to imply less the structured forms of classical music, but rather a general diffuseness, a lack of direction and a loss of external reference. This sense of drowning in music, of falling deeper into inconsequentiality, is very obviously not a feature of *all* music, and no less obviously not even of all Wagner's music. Even when his music sets out to create another, an ethereal world – such as in the prelude to *Lohengrin* – it uses conventionalities of harmony, pitch and orchestral color which are highly consequential and task-orientated. Similarly, the *Meistersinger* represents a strongly narrative and milieu-specific music, in which only Beckmesser's muddled renderings of Walter's song are disorientating – the rest is as purposeful as the Prize Song itself on its way to victory. It is unlikely that listeners will drown in its harmonies.[3] The resulting apparent unevenness of Wagner's development across his operas (*Tristan* and the *Meistersinger* are composed within two years of each other) is, however, as the comparison with Sterne suggests, not unusual. In a similar way the run-of-the-mill fiction of the nineteenth century, which moved beyond the radical questioning of its bases by Sterne, shares none of the disorientation and inconsequentiality of *Tristram Shandy* – in part because it has taken up the technique of objective narration, and thus moved beyond the crisis to which Sterne responded. The world of the novel appears to stands firm by 1830 (until the crises represented by Huysmans and the symbolist novels of Gide), whereas opera seems far from settled, often unsure as to its form and rationale. The example of Sterne reminds us that crisis and uncertainty are built into all genres, and that music – like the novel – knows both order and crisis, its history is an alternation of confident direction and the search for new order. The more we recognize this, the less whimsical it becomes to seek to understand Wagner's operas as novels.

Musicality in Prose – all prose is musical

To explore this relationship, before our principal discussion of the *Meistersinger*, I shall glance at a couple of nineteenth century novels and

---

[3] We should remember, however, something which Nietzsche appears not to have realized: that the music of the *Meistersinger* is not a return to pre-*Tristan* harmonic systems – it is not an anachronistic piece of tonality, but a highly artificial construct, the archaic 'wrapped in modernity' (Dahlhaus 1996:106f).

suggest that even here there is a huge amount of 'musical' construction, and that the essence of the works belongs to a scenario written in a language beyond genre. The fact that these are not novels by Proust or Joyce makes the argument harder to conduct, but the similarities with musical discourse more persuasive. We start *in media res*, with the opening paragraph of a famous Balzac novel, under the chapter title 'A provincial printing office':

> At the time when this story begins, the Stanhope press and inking-rollers were not yet in use in small provincial printing-offices. Angoulême, although its paper-making industry kept it in contact with Parisian printing, was still using those wooden presses from which the more obsolete metaphor 'making the presses groan' originated. Printing there was so much behind the times that the pressmen still used leather balls spread with ink to dab on the characters. The bed of the press holding the letter-filled 'forme' to which the paper is applied was still made of stone and so justified its name 'marble'. The ravenous machines of our times have so completely superseded this mechanism – to which, despite its imperfections, we owe the fine books printed by the Elzevirs, the Plantins, the Aldi and the Didots – that it is necessary to mention this antiquated equipment which Jérome-Nicolas Séchard held in superstitious affection; it has its part to play in this great and trivial work. (Balzac: *Les Illusions Perdues*, translated by Herbert J. Hunt)

For all the historical furniture of this opening, the text neither is a historical chronicle nor can its apparent factuality conceal the overarching ambiguity of the passage. The smallness of the provincial environment is stressed, yet the end of the paragraph enigmatically claims for the whole work that it will be 'great and trivial'. The second sentence focuses on the contrast between the smallness of Angoulême and the dynamic changes which are sweeping through the world, and which are continuously portrayed as being poised at the moment before full implementation: the Stanhope press is 'not yet' in use, the provinces are 'still' behind the times. These are not arguments, but resemble musical statements, made meaningful by juxtaposition and development. What is being portrayed is not a particular historical moment, much rather a dynamic interrelation of past and future, whose evaluation is not formulated as an idea, consistently and carefully worked out, but rather as a combination of effects, of delayed fulfillments and reconciliation of contrasts. New machines have completely superseded the old machines, yet the books produced on the old machines were nevertheless 'fine'; an overstated loyalty to the past seems suggested in the 'superstitious affection' with which Séchard holds to the old, yet this must be balanced against the intrusive and 'ravenous' voice of the new.

The first sentence sets up a general proposition, without apparent reflective space (indicated by the absence of adjectives or modal verbs). The second sentence restates the proposition, but with variation, i.e. the localizing detail (the place Angoulême and the predecessors of the Stanhope press). The statement is contextualized within a related theme (paper making). The third sentence offers a further variation, specifying the predecessors of the inking-rollers; the fourth ('The bed of the press [...]') relates to a lithic, perhaps even a classic age, while the next one, as we saw, varies the first theme: the Stanhope press becomes 'the ravenous machines'. We are encouraged in this reading by the reflective nature of the language. The machines are de-substantiated, not merely by being shown tossed to and fro within larger historical movements, but an ironic discourse is established between the archaic terms in which the old machines were apostrophized – the next paragraph goes further, listing the old words for the machines with their 'groaning', their 'forme' and 'marble' and tells of the 'bears', 'monkeys' and 'gaffers' who worked them. The *theme* of old and new turns into a form of expression: it is not argued, it is simply arranged. It is all but meaningless to wish to differentiate argument from structure and expression in a passage of this kind, the material of the paragraph is subsumed in its arrangement. And even in this archetypically Realist text we find quite appropriate the language of music: statement, restatement with variation, juxtaposition, perhaps development (even within the first paragraph). The narrative voice is not just unmistakably Balzacian: it is both modern and traditional, the changes have a minor and a major key.

We contrast this text with the opening paragraph of a novel written towards the end of the Realist period. Despite its lack of the type of historical specificity which we identify in Balzac, the text begins not in the contrast of past and present, but with an explicit person, with his emphatic 'now' and his 'first question [...] when'.

Strether's first question, when he reached the hotel, was about his friend; yet on his learning that Waymarsh was apparently not to arrive till evening he was not wholly disconcerted. A telegram from him bespeaking a room 'only if not noisy', with the answer paid, was produced for the inquirer at the office, so that the understanding that they should meet at Chester rather than at Liverpool remained to that extent sound. The same secret principle, however, that had prompted Strether not absolutely to desire Waymarsh's presence at the dock, that had led him thus to postpone for a few hours his enjoyment of it, now operated to make him feel that he could still wait without disappointment. They would dine together at the worst, and, with all respect to dear old Waymarsh – if not even, for that matter, to himself – there was little fear that in the sequel they should not see enough of each other. The principle I have just mentioned as operating had been, with the most newly-disembarked of the two men, wholly instinctive – the fruit of a sharp sense that, delightful as it would be to find himself looking, after so much separation, into his comrade's face, his business would be a trifle bungled should he simply arrange that this countenance should present itself to the nearing steamer as the first 'note', for him, of Europe. Mixed with

everything was the apprehension, already, on Strether's part, that he would at best, throughout, prove the note of Europe in quite a sufficient degree.
This note had been meanwhile – since the previous afternoon, thanks to this happier device – such a consciousness of personal freedom as he had not known for years [...] (Henry James:*The Ambassadors*)

The plural in the novel's title suggest the importance of Strether's relationship with Waymarsh, perhaps this relationship (a 'friend' becomes 'comrade', then 'dear old', finally just a 'countenance') will constitute the event for which one searches in reading ('when he reached the hotel'), perhaps the question has become ambiguous, and by the end of the paragraph the event has been postponed, and in the process transformed. The efficiency of the initial action now presents itself as misleading, Strether did *not* want to meet Waymarsh. Postponing and 'without disappointment' reveal their emotional qualities within the presumed relationship, and are obviously not just a mannerism of James' narrative style. The individual sentences pick up the habit of mind of the central character, clarity is avoided and deferred: Strether is led 'not absolutely to desire' Waymarsh's presence, plans to a different end would have been a 'trifle bungled' – the very ponderousness of the phrases is designed to resist clarity. Not to mention readers' uncertainty about what may be behind 'at the worst' dining with 'dear old' Waymarsh; their arrangement to meet at Chester rather than at Liverpool remained 'to that extent sound'. The language suggests a stolid certainty which the development of the text consistently undermines. The paragraph culminates in a self-consciously synaesthetic metaphor. Waymarsh's face ought not to be the 'first "note", for him, of Europe', repeated in the final sentence of the paragraph in Strether's fear that he might 'prove' (a nice ambiguity between the two meanings: to establish something definitively and to experience at first hand) 'the note of Europe in quite a sufficient degree' (again the resistance here: a bureaucratic phrase, as if sufficiency can be carefully measured out, rather than fully enjoyed). This uncertainty is multiplied when we learn that the whole process of caution, tentative feelings, the emotional juice squeezed out of double negatives – that all this amounts to 'a consciousness of personal freedom which he had not known for years'.

So we could identify this as a prose which likes and cultivates ambiguity and dissolves certainties. Even where it sets out from the concreteness of a *now* and an event in the present, the drive of the writing is to move away from events, stories and explanations, and into a state of hovering ambiguity. It does so, in part at least, by consciously focusing on the form of expression, constantly implying the inadequacy of the phrase to grasp the true meaning of emotional states. It would be hard not to think of this writing – no less than

Balzac's – in terms which did not overlap with those we use to think of music, as dissonances mark borderlines between realms of harmonic certainty, constantly questioning that certainty, and as a prose constructed not round a progressive modulation – as it might be moving from one certainty to the next –, but much rather constructed on continuous, disorientating modulation, performed if not for its own sake then at least for the effect which it produces when repeated, that is: the suspension of progression and the stress on retrospective questioning. It is true that the purpose of this suspension is identified with Strether's freedom, but we note that it is neither a freedom *from* (the idea that all he wishes to be is free from is the autocratic Mrs Newsome is not fully sustained) nor a freedom *to*: there are no liberties to which Strether will wish to devote himself actively. Indeed, his first meeting with Mme de Vionnet shows his determination to 'stick with' the view he took of this lady as 'unassailably innocent' – that is to say, it is an act of will on Strether's part to contain her, the most disorientating of all his experiences in France, within the confines of the morality with which he arrived in Europe. The freedom of which Strether is conscious is a freedom without direction, either in escape or in aim: it is a freedom to *modulate*.

In short: there has been a tendency by critics to think of 'musical prose' too narrowly. The phrase has been located either in the conscious analogy drawn by the author (Mann, Joyce, Proust) between their thought-processes and musical composition, or as a critics' language to designate prose whose formal side tends away from the mimetic structures traditionally associated with Realist fiction. These are valid arguments and I am not attempting to shift the usage, merely to suggest that even Realist prose is musical in that it operates according to a logic different to that implicit in its subject-matter. The gap between narrative prose and music is anything but unbridgeable. Without considering the Formalists' complete taxonomy of prose – which includes rhythm, onomatopoeia and the other more obviously musical devices a writer might use when describing – we can recognize the literariness of all artistic language, even when it is applied to unambiguously prosaic objects, such as the printing press. Without descending to the onomatopoeic – such as the *clickety-clack* rhythm of the machines (it could be argued that, having shaped the structure of his writing musically, Balzac has only contempt for the externalities of music) – Balzac creates musically, no less than Henry James, in whose prose units it is the arrangement of ponderous, non-expressive, bureaucratic phrases which suggest ideas of musical construction. First comes art and rhetoric, then comes genre. And with the genre of the novel, comes the centrality of plot.

Plot in the *Meistersinger*

The summary of a novel one might have read (had it ever been written):

Richard Cooper, third son of a noble line, has left home after a dispute with his family. His elder brother has just taken over the family estates from their father, disabled by a fall while hunting. There's not room for two sons in the management of the estate and Magnus' threat to kick him out of the house if he does not marry Phoebe or Agatha, hard faced scions of a neighboring family, precipitates the crisis. There's nothing wrong with these women, at least nothing which a life-time of hypocrisy, silence and renunciation – on both sides of course – will not allow to pass into acceptable routine. Worse still, Richard's father has decided that the family should make a move into the church. The second son, Edward, after a scarcely hushed up episode when he killed a poacher, took a commission in the Indian Army, and, as Richard arrives in **bridge, is fighting mutinous sepoys somewhere off the map. Which left Richard for the church. Richard is hardly impressed by the option. Canon Slime – who enjoys the living of the local church and whose lack of all religious conviction is hard to spot behind his sycophancy towards the rich, and for whom movements up and down Jacob's ladder speak not of angels descending and ascending, but merely of a one-way movement, in the form of preferment for himself – hardly offers an encouraging example. In any case Richard has been touched by two modern tendencies: a whiff of socialism, less quickly dispersed than the gun-smoke at Peterloo, and science, which has come to him on an ancient tumulus on the family estate, in the form of historical science – what will soon be called archaeology. When he refused an invitation to the hunt-ball, to which both Phoebe and Agatha had put their names, and told his father that nothing would persuade him to join the Church, the die was cast, and he went off to **bridge.

Richard has arrived at his destination, a university and market town well to the south, where he feels his lack of bourgeois qualifications and his readiness to work may not exclude him from the leading circles. He sees on a board the notice for a public lecture by a visiting scholar on the Beaker period, and – remembering his own site – Richard overcomes his inhibitions and goes into the hall. Listening to the lecture, surrounded by both the aspiring lower-middle class and a goodly section of university staff, he is fascinated by the appearance of a young woman in the audience. She shows by her enraptured interest that the topic inspires her, and yet she cannot help but show that she has noticed the handsome stranger in the audience, recognizing him as a newcomer in the circle, neither a dusty pedant nor an aspiring proletarian (little of the dust of Peterloo has fallen on her). When Richard puts a question to the speaker about the life style of the Beaker period, he feels her support, although a member of the faculty laughs out loud at his naivety in daring to speculate about what cannot be known scientifically. As the audience disperses, the young woman is still there, although it has become clear that she is under the tutelage of Mountclean, a university assistant who loses no opportunity to continue to belittle the stranger's contribution to the debate. Richard snatches a few words with her and discovers that she is Angela, orphaned daughter of the previous professor, unofficial ward of the present incumbent – and the apple of his eye. Richard integrates himself into the group, and discovers that the big event is the awarding of a special prize in the Faculty for an original essay on 'archaeology'. Mountclean is the principal candidate for the prize, determined to succeed not only for the sake of the professional advancement which the award of the prize

would bring, but on account of the prestige which he sees this conferring on him in the eyes of Angela.
Richard understands the situation as a challenge and sets to work to organize his first-hand experience of his family site into academic shape. He casts the frail craft of his life onto the deep waters of knowledge and science, hoping that the historical tide will bear him up.⁴ His response to the challenge involves frequent attacks from Mountclean, and increasingly practical help from the professor, who has noted his ward's attraction to and for Richard – and he continues to press his suit chez Angela, who finds herself strongly attracted to his apparently unconventional (but in fact conventionally aristocratic) ways. Tense, but also comic scenes follow: in pursuit of academic success, Mountclean appropriates a manuscript which he erroneously imagines to be the professor's and, in an embarrassing moment, mistakes Mary, the Departmental Secretary, for Angela, thereby incurring the wrath and physical attack of another assistant, David, who is unofficially engaged to Mary. Richard's essay wins the prize, Angela agrees to accept his offer of marriage provided he finishes his doctorate, and the professor, reflecting on the need for new blood and impressed by the environmental understanding shown by Richard's essay (as against his own, he fears, more pedantic book-learning – he speaks at the prize-ceremony of the archaeologist's need to supplement his knowledge with feeling and intuition⁵) gives up his own (distant) claims on Angela. A rosy future dawns, for Richard and Angela, for the Department and for the new science in the universities.

The [dis]credits for this supposed novel would be long – were it a film, no-one would stay to see them to the end. There's a lot of George Eliot here (though it had not rubbed off when Wagner met her in 1877), especially the praise of provincial life, and more than a touch of her doctor Lydgate, to say nothing of Casaubon, damned to pedantry because he knows no German (most characters are damned because they do have German); Stendhal and Austen offer a good line in ambitious priests (Eliot chips in with the older man – also a priest – renouncing the beautiful woman); there's some *Jude the Obscure*, and some Gustav Freytag (who devoted a whole novel to the search for a lost manuscript), certainly Wilhelm Raabe is represented here, with his interest in archaeology as a pendant to the triviality of present-day society – science, not money or law, as the true bed-rock of society; and a bit of Tolstoy, getting interested in detail, even the dry as dust work of Karenin – Tolstoy would have made Mountclean's understanding of the Beaker period more interesting and worthy of discussion than Mountclean himself could

---

4   This is one of the frequently used metaphors in *Opera and Drama*. But it achieved its greatest celebrity in Schopenhauer's unforgettable image of the individual entrusting his person (his *principium individuationis*) to a frail boat tossed on the boundless ocean of an unknowable and unpredictable universe.
5   This one of the central ideas of *Opera and Drama*, to which we return repeatedly in this book. It is not always a happy idea, for it causes Wagner's text to oscillate between being opinionated (intuitive) and prolix (knowledge).

ever have imagined. It would have had much more detail: detail is not reality, but it aspires to present itself as such, and it shows the work of the writer in assimilating such reality. (Work is the hidden ethic of all Realist novels.) But of course this unpublishable text is the story of the *Meistersinger*, imitatively transposed into the standard prose of the nineteenth century novel, and for all its clumsiness – how much better Richard Wagner would have handled the fate of Richard Cooper (somehow it seems natural for opera to come from prose, rather than the other way round) – it shows some important features of the novel which Wagner knew in his own age, which he critiqued in *Opera und Drama* and which he refrained from writing.

Modesty requires me to distance myself from this novel, but – as the list of credits suggested – it is an archetypal Realist novel. Local in focus, yet aware of the wider currents of history and society which sweep the individual stories on, it is detailed and down to earth, interested in the history of institutions as well as in the happiness of individuals. It is my own *lack* of originality which dictated the story to me. But it does suggest that it is reasonable and legitimate to see the *Meistersinger* as Wagner's Realist novel. He would have written it better, with less orthodoxy; we might well have had a few of his favorite themes in there – obviously Redemption by Woman (not that the Angela-Richard relationship is without a touch of the Fred Vincy/Mary Garth redemptive elements from *Middlemarch*). But to be clearer about why he did not write it, we use the unwritten novel as an opportunity to examine the differences between the genres and Wagner's personal attitude toward the novel as genre.

In part, our novel's clumsiness, especially in the first section, is a direct product of the novel as genre. It would be all but impossible to think of a novel which did not have this kind of detailed lead-in (although it might have been interpolated during the course of the earlier sections). Because of this our novel seems heavy handed in comparison with Wagner's opera. It shows how Richard Cooper's story is dependent on a proliferation of external factors, on what Virginia Woolf was later to call 'the calico and the cancer' of life. Most obviously the novel is so fashioned as to move from external events inwards in order to place Richard Cooper socially up to the point at which the opera opens – the wonderful scene inside the church where Walter first sees Eva and love develops amidst the thunderous, yet erotically subverted chorale. 'Drama goes from the inside to the outside, the novel from outside to inside. Drama reveals the human organism, whereas the novel presents the mechanisms of history' (*Opera and Drama* iv,47). Wagner's remark seems pertinent enough to our example. Without this background there is no novel, for, as Wagner further remarks, the novel deals primarily with the past, whereas opera and drama ought to live in a magical and luminous present. Of course, not all dramas do that: it's one reason why Wagner is no friend of Shakespeare's histories, and – closer to home - one of Wagner's specific critiques of Hebbel's *Nibelungen* concerned the way in which Hebbel turned the heroic events of the Nibelungen into a past, *off-stage* story – 'his heroes go into the wings where they carry out some monstrously heroic deed, before coming back on to the stage and [...] telling everyone about it' (cit. Mueller 1991:71). This historicizing of action was for Wagner the very opposite of the spirit of opera and drama.[6]

Given this structural distinction, the actual driving forces of the two texts are not unalike. There is not too much difference in the motivation of big things – Richard loves Angela, that much is easy: most Realist novels use the force of love to kick start the core action, it is the way they treat love within the plot which is different to romance – and, despite the exclusive claims for drama which Wagner makes, the novel has no difficulty in handling those categories of human behavior which go so much 'deeper' than socio-political observation: 'youth and age, growth and maturity, eagerness and stasis, action and reflection [...]' (*Opera and Drama,* iv,74). Indeed, one could argue that good Realist novels continuously aim at generalizations of this kind precisely because they wish to underpin their sociological observation poetically. It's what stops their novels being text-books. They underline this by drawing attention to the re-incarnation in modern times of ancient stories and patterns, as we saw in Bulwer Lytton's *Rienzi*.

It is the small things which are very differently motivated. Wagner's Sachs and Richard's professor may be identical types, both coming from a class similarly defined in contradistinction to the aristocracy, and the structure of the story may be the same, – a beautiful girl caught between a sympathetic older man, a younger, brasher, more problematic type and a pedant (the renouncing older man: Mr Farebrother making way for Vincy, Goriot sacrificing himself for the worthless lovers of his daughters) – but the motivation is different, and the mechanisms radically so. Through a beautifully self-referential comment by Sachs on the lessons of Tristan and Isolde's story – before the ink had dried properly on the score of *Tristan* Sachs quotes a snatch of its unmistakable tonality –, Wagner achieves a force and a great focusing of Sachs' motivation. 'My child,' Sachs tells Eva, 'I know a sad tale of Tristan and Isolde: Hans Sachs was wise and wanted no

---

[6]   The celebrated counter-example of this technique in the *Ring* is Loge's story of the stealing of the gold in *Rheingold* Scene 2. But of course the audience has seen the event for itself before the telling, and it's only the gods who know nothing. True to this principle Wagner was ready to embark on the theatrical difficulties of the scene under the surface of the Rhine.

share of Marke's fate' (Marke, having sent Tristan to bring Isolde to him as bride, lost both friend and bride). Not for nothing does Wagner speak of the ability of drama to achieve intensification of motivation, when he says so much in two lines. Even in better hands the novel will not often manage this luminous brevity: it limps behind with references to the modernizing and self-renewing world of science. Even its Realism is something of a sham: it is not Realist enough, for instance, even to hint at matters of potential sexual incompatibility between young wives and old men.

Another telling question is why Richard and Walter leave their aristocratic circles and move to the city in order to slum it with the middle-classes. We have no idea at all why Walter's interest in song was sufficient to make him leave home: we might surmise that, for all his love of nature, he found a life of country leisure stultifying, perhaps he missed the creature comforts of the city, where not everything grinds to a halt in winter:[7] but Wagner merely offers us musically persuasive snatches of a chivalrous, but outdated life-style (and the gesture of Walter reaching for his sword when there is a threat to his eloping with Eva), and needs say no more. In contrast to the light, but intense story of Walter's arrival, Richard Cooper needed so much more heavy motivation: money, family and social pressure. Whether either approach to motivation actually *explains* behavior is another question – in that respect novelists are again like dramatists: their real concern is plausibility, not explanation –, but the one is short, the other long-winded.

The role of history in the two versions raises questions which greatly concerned Wagner in *Opera and Drama*. Here Wagner is very dismissive of historical drama, he regards history as being incapable of getting beyond the external facts to the real people involved. For that reason he is at pains to claim that Shakespeare's greatest dramas were written not from history, but from the novel.[8] But we must recognize that history was and remained a major concern of Wagner. *Rienzi* was, thematically, anything but an accident in Wagner's development, and the *Meistersinger* shares this political interest

---

[7]   It takes little imagination to hear in Walter's famous first 'aria' in Act 1 ('Am stillen Herd, in Winters Zeit') a discontent with his 'court and estate' being 'snowed up' (*eingeschneit*), thus forcing him to his books.

[8]   One element of the discussion is, to say the least, confusing. The word 'novel' (*Roman*) is used by Wagner – perfectly correctly, but within a conventional literary-historical vocabulary – to refer *both* to the archaic epic form of the romance (as in *romans de Rolland*, chronicles and even Ariosto) *and* to modern prose fiction. This renders some of his arguments still more prolix and artificial than they need be. The confusion at this late date (while there was still space in English language discourse for the undefined term 'Romance', the word 'novel' was firmly established long before the 1850s) underlines the general point that, in German culture, the modern novel was a ghost at the critics' party.

in history. It would be a mistake to imagine the Nuremberg of Hans Sachs as a mere chocolate box cover, folksy and kitschy, but unserious as history. As Peter Uwe Hohendahl pointed out, the interpretation of Sachs[9] and Nuremberg was hotly contested, in scholarship and in literary works at the time Wagner was writing – just as Wagner's *Ring* was not the only version on the market. Variants on Sachs' story included a monarchist version, another of pure kitschy nostalgia and – in the model put forward by the liberal literary historian Georg Gervinus [10] – a two-facetted version which involves the city Nuremberg as the beginning of democratic, civil society in Germany and Sachs himself as a mediator between 'high' literature and the people. Wagner's presentation of Sachs and his insistence on the guild structure of Nuremberg (to say nothing of the fact that the opera ends with the praise of art, not of the monarchy – this had been Lortzing's[11] preferred ending) is obviously political, part of the legacy of his 1848 aspirations, and no less obviously based on a reflected understanding of the historical Nuremberg. Wagner's critique of the novel – in *Opera and Drama* he claims that the novel is for the citizen and deals with the *Staatsbürger* (iv,68) rather than the whole man (in the first half of this remark Wagner was merely repeating the claims which the Realists proudly made for their own writing) – should not make us mistake his strong interest in a society which pioneered the idea of citizenship. We should not read his comment as if Wagner were uninterested in the citizen.

Our proto-novel lacked the courage to give art as central a place as Wagner did. There are, of course, many Realist novels in which the artist is prominent: Flaubert's *Sentimental Education* involves a detailed examination of the situation of the pure artist in bourgeois commercial society, Balzac's *Lost Illusions* too – as we saw in the first section – takes cognizance of a shifting understanding of art's role in society: Gissing, like countless minor German novelists from the 1840s onwards, plied similar themes, showing art as the representative of true value in an increasingly commercialized society. I was obliged to pick science rather than art as Richard Cooper's avocation as

[9]   Hans Sachs (1494-1576) was a major historical figure, an ardent follower of Luther and a significant figure in German literature.
[10] Gervinus (1805-1871) wrote a highly influential, democratically inspired history of German literature, which brought him, following the failure of revolution of 1848 and the authoritarian nature of German unification after 1871, both increasing neglect and charges of high treason.
[11] Albert Lortzing (1801-1851) is remembered today, if at all, for his opera *Zar und Zimmermann*. In this context we should note his *Hans Sachs* (1840). His political stance had been emphatically liberal (Hermand 2008:115f). A divergent view of these portrayals of Nuremberg can be found in Carnegy (2006:60f).

a more neutral vehicle of idealism and social mobility, but also because it – like the universities which became its temporary home – embodied a social structure, something which nineteenth century art so conspicuously lacked. While in sixteenth-century Nuremberg and in the figure of Sachs Germany had an historical context to allow Wagner to treat art not as a retreat into the private sphere of social outsiders but as a social institution, England lacked those preconditions. Science seemed (as to Eliot) a better choice of model. Until William Morris revived the nostalgia for craftsmanship and for art as a social form it was hard to portray the artistic life in any other than the romantic terms of misunderstood genius – and this was pretty well alien to the Realist novel, as it was to the *Meistersinger*.

Notwithstanding his negative comments on the excessive social dimension of the novel, Wagner came strikingly close in the *Meistersinger* to the patterns of behavior and concerns of the Realist novel. Neither Walter nor Sachs has any touch of the romantic artist, although Walter is proud to have based his singing on the birds and on the medieval epics – the incomparable troubadours (*Minnesänger*) of the thirteenth century, Walter von der Vogelweide has been his teacher, he proudly explains to the very skeptical assembly of mastersingers.[12] Instead of Romantic trappings, the opera devotes a great deal of attention to the structure of the guild and to its rules. Walter has to struggle to learn them – that's the intellectual *work* to which the Realists were so committed – and without them he would never have won the prize. Art is presented insistently within a social context and as something more than romantic dreaming. For that reason science can replace many of its elements in the transposition to the contemporary novel. A fully worked version of this novel would certainly involve detailed accounts of the various scientific controversies of the nineteenth-century and of the social hierarchies within which the transmission and understanding of science were embedded. These passages would be modeled on Balzac's extraordinarily detailed account of the technical evolution of printing after 1815 (in *Lost Illusions*), or on Eliot's account of medical science, or Tolstoy's understanding of the work of the state bureaucracy. The portrayal of these elements could hardly be more intrusive or more 'external' than the laborious account of rules which Beckmesser, Sachs and David all give, or the account of the rituals of the guild which is provided by the apprentices, and subsequently by Sachs.

---

[12]   Walter's name – bird meadow – was an assumed title, which would have appealed to Storzing. The Meistersingers are less impressed: 'warblers and finches' cannot teach singing, they protest, and in any case Walter von der Vogelweide is 'long since dead'.

It would be reassuring to think that the reader might accept the similar place which romantic love occupies in the two works. In neither work – despite the conventional plot device of the look 'across a crowded room' which first brings the lovers together – does love stand on its own. It is used to set in motion a story crossing the classes, illustrating social mobility,[13] and revealing the mechanisms by which society and its 'fields' renew themselves. Rather predictably, neither woman possesses compelling gifts. Angela and Eva are highly conventional figures, examples of the boss's daughter, created from externals, not from inside. The reader wonders what Richard and Walter will talk about to the women they have captured. Walter once spent the long winter evenings by the fireside reading medieval poetry – there is little indication that Eva will share his tastes, any more than Rosamund shared Lydgate's idealistic commitment to researching disease. They are all victims of the overlapping banalities of marriage and adultery, objects of male desire; the limitations of that desire are clear enough, even if the story does not explore them. Love may start a short distance outside the social norms, but it remains a clear indication of the social ambitions and limitations of the characters. Nevertheless, it soon has to come to terms with those norms, and both *Meistersinger* stories, by finishing long before such issues arise, tacitly acknowledge this dimension. Happily ever after may well apply to art, science, the guilds, a democratic citizens' society – there's little to indicate that it applies to Richard and Walter.

One Approach to the Realist Novel's Plot

It has often been observed that the nineteenth century novel, beyond its commitment to certain ideological positions, had its own default-setting, most obviously shown in the contrast between Balzac's sober structural analysis of society and the extravagant plots of his novels. Writers and critics emphasize the Realist novel's focus on the everyday lives of ordinary and typical characters and its highlighting of the 'static' powers of determinism and environment, but this observation should not be taken to imply any

---

[13]   Hohendahl points out that in Lortzing's version of the prize song it is the Emperor who intervenes to produce a happy ending to the love story. Not only does Wagner disempower the monarchy and replace the Emperor's authority with that of art itself: his plot involves an aristocrat (timorously) seeking the hand of a middle-class girl and – as the Meistersinger make clear when Storzing is first introduced to their circle – being resented by the middle-classes precisely because he is an aristocrat, a *Junker*, as they complain, who is definitely in the wrong place.

humdrum, work-a-day quality to the plots. Indeed, the opposite is generally the case.

Plot, in the shape of stories, flowed inexhaustibly from the pen of novelists, at all levels of literary quality. Few forms symbolized that huge and driving energy more than the serialized novels and the rotation presses on which they were produced, an energy reflected in the irrepressible length of the novels themselves, stories reaching out into an unknown future and back into distant origins. Similarly there were few situations which more encouraged novelists to think in stories than the openness of society to personal ambition and the general admiration for self-made success. An individual destiny could mirror its age. Another major drive to tell stories came from the exploration of the new social milieus of the urban age, the factory, the slum and from the experiences of the different world of the working-classes. Such circumstances led to a heightened sense of co-incidence and chance which an unpredictable and open environment communicated. One throw of the dice could push an individual's life into new paths: all men, in their lives and in their writings, were gamblers, spinning strategies and plots desperately in order to stay at the table. A final element to be mentioned was the extraordinary mixing of classes and characters which social mobility permitted, the parameters of novelists' plots were unrecognizably broad in comparison to the narrow circles in which Jane Austen's texts had functioned. Add to these elements novelists' readiness to build in – or their anxiety to draw narrative force from[14] – the great archetypal narratives of the past, and we have some sense of the complexity and density of the narrative energy of this time.

The critic Peter Brooks is determined to find explanations for what is for him the most significant feature of nineteenth century plots: the inexhaustible energy we have outlined. His argument is essentially psychological, focusing on the drive of libidinal energy into fictions – a process of what Freud calls *cathexis* (which we also encountered in Kramer's arguments in Chapter Four) – revealed not just on the analyst/critic's couch, but through the structure of the plots themselves. On that point it takes no sophisticated argument to see the massive drives which lead Wagner's plots forward. We cannot fail to feel

---

[14] Peter Brooks – to whose study of the narrative energy in nineteenth century fiction we shortly turn – paradoxically suggests that novelists were driven to frantic plot invention by fears similar to those we observed earlier in the Wagner-Hebbel controversy, the fear namely that 'there were no more primary narratives' (1984:261), that plots were starting to become thin on the ground and had to be fought over. Certainly there were few areas in which competition between writers and publishers was more strongly felt than in the novel and in the material of its plots.

the compulsions with which the dénouements of the *Der fliegende Holländer* and *Lohengrin* are forced through, or to sense Wagner's close observation of instinctual energy even in less predictable material, for instance in the form of that mass of pilgrims moving through *Tannhäuser*, like wildebeest on their migrations, or an ocean tide, a primal force to which Tannhäuser joins himself in the third act, just as he had joined the seething sexual energy of the *Venusberg* before the opera opens. Most obviously *Tristan* is structured round one continuous movement of desire – indeed we might reflect that music had no problems with what, as we suggested above, was a serious difficulty in the Realist program: its non-explicit attitude to sex. Long before *Salome*, opera could be more direct in portraying powerful, often deviant sexuality.[15] Brooks' arguments about energy obviously meet Wagner's situation perfectly.

In terms of plot-type Wagner's individual operas cover a wide variety. The *Meistersinger* – as we have just demonstrated – fits in closely to the Realism of the 'scènes de la vie de province'. *Lohengrin* departs furthest from this paradigm, even if it's a thoroughly modernized type of medievalism which Wagner practices here and its central idea – the archetype, or myth, of gods coming down to earth – is central to Realism's focus.[16] The *Der fliegende Holländer* smacks of an archaic type of local colour, reflected in the studied folksiness such as the chorus of girls at the spinning-wheel; in spirit it is close to the movement in German literary history referred to as Poetic Realism, a context which makes sense of Wagner's debt to the romantic legacy of E.T.A. Hoffmann – in this instance Hoffmann's Scandinavian story *The Mine at Falun* (the links of *Tannhäuser* to Hoffmann are too well known to need further rehearsal).[17] *Tannhäuser* and *Parsifal* are structured round journeys, a model not unknown to the Realists, as we have seen. The stations

---

15   We return to this matter in Chapter Seven. While *Salomé* obviously did not originate in opera and the most one could say of it was that Strauss made the sexuality much more powerful than Wilde's text managed on its own – similar relationships might be seen in comparing Wedekind's Lulu-trilogy and Berg's opera – we would have to turn to the Naturalist novels of Zola and his followers to find the extreme sexual drives portrayed in *Tristan* – as in the novel, so in the opera, according to the conventionalities of the genre. Once again the extremes – opera and Naturalism – touch.

16   It may seem far-fetched to interpret the Swan as any part of Realism, but we should not ignore Wagner's insistence in *Opera and Drama* that the 'incarnation' story, in its Greek, Christian and Germanic forms, was a celebration of the importance – not to say 'divinity' – of the human. Such ideas came from Feuerbach, whose importance to George Eliot has often been analyzed and whose emphatic secularization was typical of all Realism (cf. Ridley 1980).

17   Cf. Roden 2006:38-60.

of their journey are somewhat out of the Realists' orbit, but its structure is very familiar, especially in the case of *Tannhäuser*, where the plot not only is structured round the contrast between religious and sexual love – another shake-down from the secularization essential to Realism – but also corresponds closely to the so-called Realist novel of disappointment, a type most clearly exemplified in Flaubert's *Sentimental Education* . We return to the plot of the *Ring* shortly, but already the links to Realism in Wagner's plots are self-evident.

I am not arguing that, to the extent that he shared plot features with the Realists, Wagner was himself automatically one of their number. In any case – as Brooks' study of energy has illustrated – there are many ways to characterize plot. An extreme Structuralist approach, such as that of Vladimir Propp, would attach no weight at all to the 'non-structural' elements such as historical period or narrative style (hardly more to 'energy') and would so radically reduce plots to a few basic, archetypal structures that if any similarities between Wagner and the Realists survived, they would be uninteresting. We would be left with the observation that Wagner clothed some of the basic stories of humanity in the historical garb of his time. In a major part of his argument, however, Brooks' analysis of Realist plots moves beyond the question of narrative energy to establish the characteristic features of Realist plots, picking up structural issues less radically, at a level which preserves the importance of historical color. Choosing half a dozen types from Brooks' taxonomy – orphan hero, contract and its breach, the track of ancient guilt, the assertion of origin through ending, the repetition of event and structure, transgression as the first principle of narration – we find that we have listed the structure of most of Wagner's opera plots. Going to an earlier and more general account of the essence of the novel's story – Georg Lukács' account of its basic theme, which he calls 'transcendental homelessness' (1918:25) – we could find similar broad consensus.

There are significant differences to be respected here. Opera never evolved those forensic elements which characterize the detective story and which can be traced so widely through the nineteenth century novel. Clearly the subtleties of plotting have their limits in opera. Material clues are harder to spread through the plot of opera, discovery and revelation have to lie on a different level of detail. We return to Wagner's remark that drama *internalizes* events, that it uses them, but does not set out links between them.[18] One of the effects of this approach is to oblige Wagner to integrate

---

[18] An obvious example is the place of money in the *Ring*. While the novel keeps a balance sheet running throughout the plot, recording losses and gains in the characters' fortunes –

coincidence (as one of the more troubling manifestations of the life of things) into an inner necessity. Wagner's presentations of coincidence are usually topographical – Siegmund arriving in Sieglinde's hut, the exit which Tannhäuser takes from the *Venusberg* being just adjacent to Heinrich's hunting grounds are two such examples – but the problem is one common to all opera with its need for focus, and the solution is invariably to set up a minimum level of psychological necessity. To get Saltabaldi to kill Blanche requires no subtle plotting or forensic skill, merely to make plausible the self-sacrificial love of Blanche for the King. A novel would find it hard to reproduce this kind of structure, and would have to turn to alibis, witnesses and material causes. Opera just does it, in Wagner's case using coincidence as an illumination of deeper psychological wishes and drives.

Despite these provisos, we now turn to the most obsessively plotted of all Wagner's operas, the *Ring*. Few features could more clearly show the strength of this obsession than Wagner's hanging on to the plot for nearly thirty years, interrupting it by other major projects. An interesting counter-example is Stendhal's technique – not unlike that of the serialized novelists – of inventing most of his plot heuristically, improvising from the position to which the action has come at any given moment. It would be as if Wagner did not know, from 1854 at the latest, the ending of the *Ring*, or kept an open mind as to whether Siegfried and Brünnhilde would have children. Despite the well-known uncertainties about the text of Brünnhilde's immolation aria – that is, ideological openness –, Wagner's plot is largely stable through these years. It is clear why Thomas Mann compares him to Zola: the genealogies and determinisms of his novels demanded similarly careful advanced planning. We are struck by the great similarities in the handling of plot which Wagner's *magnum opus* shares with the mainstream of Realist fiction.

The unity of the opera, across three evenings and the prelude, is the story of one individual coming to maturity in his society. We shall look at aspects of the psychodrama of his story in Chapter Seven: here we focus on the plotting of the story, and in particular on seven distinct aspects of it which meet entirely Brooks' general observations on Realist plotting:

1. The central story is seen historically, against the background of distinct historical eras. Just as the hero, Siegfried, moves out of the mythical world of origin and childhood into selfhood and love, and then into the

---

not for nothing was Freytag's best-selling novel entitled *Soll und Haben* (Debit and Credit, 1855) – the Gods' accounting system is less detailed: in short, it is concerned with money as a moral and psychological force.

world of society, so the world evolves. Siegfried's story – to misquote Flaubert's preface to the *Sentimental Education* – is 'a story of passion such as can only be told in this day'. The rather surprising jump into the world of the upper bourgeoisie in *Götterdämmerung*, represented by Gutrune and Gunther, remains true to this sense of historical development. The plot is both genealogical (to use a word much in vogue with novelists at the end of the nineteenth century) and historically conscious. Another obvious example of this, sharing the social focus of the novel, is that the Nibelungen experience their oppression by Alberich as *historical* and recall the happy days before Alberich had forged the ring.

2. Siegfried is the fatherless child searching for identity and – no less passionately – for meaning in a world which seems to have surrendered all claim to authority. Wotan, who might have been expected to play the role of authority, has abdicated: he is not only the Wanderer, he is on the run. The new generation must break his spear and make its own way.

3. Within a world which governed by determinism – the deep spirit of the earth, Erda, knows what will happen and insists on the observance of her laws –, chance and coincidence affect the individual, and even the Norns, spinning the fates of all humans, make mistakes and their thread breaks. Contingency rules, while individuals remain puppets, briefly and deceptively achieving autonomy. Behind contingency and apparent freedom, however, determinism holds sway.[19]

4. Absolutely true to the spirit of nineteenth century Realist novels is the dominance of contracts, fulfilled and broken. Wotan's contract with the giants, the stain of Alberich's stealing of the gold, a transgression which is made good only in the last moments of *Götterdämmerung*: all the while the action stands in the shadow of the contract which lays down that Alberich in choosing power will never love. We have the solemnity of contract and we have Loge, cleverly playing with its conditions and talking like a lawyer. These are the very pillars of Dickens' or Balzac's world.

5. The plot is built round a wondrous richness of levels, constructed so as to reflect a strongly stratified society, forced for the first time to confront its divisions because of its own transgressive behavior. The arrival of the giants in the home of the gods – the laboring classes arrive to build a

---

[19]   This parallel causes Adorno to level at Wagner the most conventional of the criticisms leveled at the Realist novel: 'over-motivation' and 'determinism' in handling the plot, as a result 'aesthetic insufficiency' (xiii,137).

castle – sets in motion a series of border crossings between these otherwise separate worlds. (Can anyone imagine that the gods cared about the existence of these other worlds or would have had any dealings with the Giants – let alone with the lowest strata – in normal, non-transgressive situations? They appear to read about the lower classes in their newspapers, nothing more.[20]) The descent into Nibelheim is not only a musical *tour de force*, no less dazzling in its theatricality than the most glitzy Broadway show, but is the exact equivalent of the precipitous contrasts on which novels after Sue built their plots and of the structural function of the slumming by Sue's hero in *Les Mystères de Paris* (1843), Rodolphe de Gerolstein, and his numerous successors.

6. The plot totally depends on repetition; structures and events are repeated, central stories are retold to different audiences, journeys set out differently and yet repeat the circles which other journeys made – there is no stronger example of this than the repeated marriage of Siegfried, first in his heart to Brünnhilde, then within society to Gutrune.

7. These elements are worked into plot against the background of the central story, which concerns neither an ideological interpretation of the universe (for instance in terms of Love, or the triumph of humanity, as which it started out) nor an unambiguous historical lesson of progress or change, but instead portrays an endless, cosmic drive for material goods. The unifying force of the central story is the struggle for money and power, and this struggle affects everyone, not just Alberich and Wotan, not even just the characters who are its victims, but also those characters who set themselves other goals (in Siegfried and Brünnhilde's case: selfhood and love). They too succumb, at crucial moments, to the master-plot, as they are caught up in greed and a desire for power.

Shaw's *Perfect Wagnerite* argued from the fact of the interruption of the composition of the *Ring* to a severe critique of the ideological inconsistency of *Götterdämmerung*. Rather than critique it further, it's more interesting to note what happens to Wagner's work when the overarching ideology of *Siegfried's Death* is broken. The default-setting is a Dickensian family novel, full of chance, coincidence, misunderstanding and revenge, culminating in the collapse of the dynasty.

---

[20]   If this should seem a little fanciful, one should remind oneself of Fricka's prejudices against the *Rheinmädchen*: she regards them merely as scantily-dressed tarts and is furious that her husband should have any dealings with them (Cf. *Rheingold*, Scene 2). This is upper-middle class newspaper reading at its most typical.

In all these ways, we can see Wagner's work coalescing with Balzac's *Comédie Humaine* and with the nineteenth century novel *tout court*. Wagner's imagination matches the sweep of the novel, but shares so much of its architecture too. We can map much of his work onto specific examples of the Realist novel: if we seek parallels, we must understand the majority of his work within the spirit and plot of that novel-world.

Realism in academic musicological discussion

So far in this chapter I have approached my material with a questionable lack of orthodoxy. While it is defensible – indeed, it is essential – for the reader and for the critic to be prepared to rework artistic material as a way of discovering why it is as it is, such speculation may well be an activity which should be practiced in private, rather than expecting it to be read by others. In fairness to the material therefore, I should end the chapter with an account of more mainstream – and rather more nit-picking – approaches to the question of Wagner's relationship to the Realism of his period. One reason for the less than theoretic attempt above to suggest Wagner's closeness to Realism is that I would not sacrifice a note of the *Meistersinger* for a whole symposium of theory: if theories do not increase our understanding and therefore our pleasure in the work then they will find only reluctant admission to my text. In fact, however, the same arguments arise from more orthodox debates.

We shall be looking in the final chapter at the similarities and disparities between musical and literary and other cultural periodicizations.[21] Some of the disparities will be minor, but one significant difference should be identified in the general understanding of the culture of the nineteenth century, namely the place of Romanticism. The problem is a general issue about the history of music and is not confined to any particular country. In France and Germany literary Romanticism seems to exist within relatively clear periods, from 1800 to the end of the 1820s, in France – partly through the importance of Romantic theatre – a little longer. There are differences of ideology and weighting between Romanticism in the two countries: German Romanticism stressed traditionalist values, including those of Roman Catholicism, and was largely indifferent to the movements which hoped to liberate Germany from feudalism. French Romanticism was more

---

[21] Not the most attractive word, but it refers to the work of historians of all types and shades – from the *Annales* to the historian of the symphony – into identifying coherent periods of development. Even our naïve belief in the significance of numerical units leads to periodizations such as 'the nineteenth century' etc.

iconoclastic and – despite its historicizing – more up to the moment. It would be hard not to think of its insistence on natural dialogue and on local colour as a forerunner of Realism. In England the impulse of German Romanticism (especially Coleridge's interest in the Schlegels) took on a different emphasis, but Romanticism in literature was longer lasting, less clearly differentiated by generation and historical period: a symptom of this is the importance of a clearly Romantic poet such as Tennyson in the period of the High Victorian. But at least the tradition does contain a major Realist element, growing ever stronger from *Vanity Fair* (1848) onwards.

In musical history, in contrast, a claim is made which is hardly thinkable in any other art: namely that Romanticism was the only style of the nineteenth century. Not only is Romanticism in music credited with the break from classicism: the search for freer expression and greater subjectivity and the technical innovation which this brought to music can be claimed to have filled the entire century with the purest essence of Romanticism. A claim of this kind might just be comprehensible within literature if one simply identified Romanticism with any kind of interest in the individual – that is, with a trend so general that it could be discovered at every moment of the nineteenth century and beyond –, but even then the shifts in style and approach would be too great to be accommodated within one term. Yet just such a unity is assumed for music. From that starting-point the celebrated Wagner scholar Ernst Kurth [22] is at pains to establish two facts: the unbroken development in technique across the century within European Romanticism (and Wagner's centrality to that development), and the dependence of Impressionism[23] and Expressionism – indeed, of all modern music – on that Romantic heritage. Within such a dominant interpretation of musical Romanticism it will be difficult for the category of Realism to establish itself, especially in Wagner studies. Nevertheless the argument can be made.

A natural starting point is the study by the eminent musicologist and Wagner scholar, Carl Dahlhaus, under the title *Musikalischer Realismus* (1982, English translation 1985). Dahlhaus is concerned to modify the

---

[22]   Kurth's major work (1923) on the harmonic system of *Tristan* and its place in the nineteenth century may be old-fashioned in its Schopenhauerian understanding of music, but it is still acknowledged as the fullest account of the place of Wagner's music within Romanticism/the nineteenth century. Implicit in his aesthetic starting-point is, as we saw, the rejection of mimetic forms of art such as the novel. See also Wiora 1965.

[23]   In literature it is usual to relate the emergence of Impressionism to a number of factors: the poetic movement of Symbolism, the 'atomizing' of experience in Naturalism, especially its so-called *Sekundenstil* and the scientific revolutions of Mach and Freud. Historians of literature might normally relate only Neo-Romanticism to Romanticism itself.

accepted wisdom about musical history which we have just outlined, and as part of this modification he wishes to validate the category of Realism in the music of this period, and his theme is much wider than a focus on one composer. He identifies the relevant features of the music of the most obvious candidates for the epithet 'Realist' – Berlioz, Liszt and Wagner: in later chapters he extends the discussion to Bizet, Mussorgsky and Janáček – while at the same time pointing out the great ambiguity of the term 'Realist' when applied to these composers. To call Berlioz a Realist would be absurd, he argues, if it should involve ignoring the obviously romantic, Byronic cult of individualism which was so central to Berlioz' work.[24] While it is central to Dahlhaus' argument to test his own remarks against the discussion of Realism in literature and the pictorial arts (especially that of the French Realist painter, Gustave Courbet) he is insistent that any discussion of musical Realism should make a distinction which literary discussion too ignores at its peril. The Realism of a work cannot be tested by the degree of everyday reality which it 'contains'. Realist works are full of 'reality' (and it is often a different reality than that which was 'contained' in Romantic works), but Realist art was no less concerned to transfigure everyday reality than other forms of art – such as the classical – had been. It did not cease to be art just because it called itself Realist, just as the Nature which appears in art does not cease to be artificial just because the work is labeled 'Realist'. Dahlhaus is right to insist that what appears as nature is an aesthetically reconstructed nature, not 'real nature'. The Victorian productions of *A Midsummer Night's Dream* which placed real trees and forest animals on the stage should have no part in the discussion of Realism.

With his openness to ambiguity and his insistence on the aesthetic nature of Realist art, Dahlhaus has no problems with the common possible objections to his argument for Wagner as a Realist. The first objection is advanced by music purists, who point out with ineluctable logic that the first term of any understanding of Realism in the non-musical arts is the imitation (*mimesis*) of external reality. Of such imitation, the purists argue, music – beyond a few natural noises like birdsong, a few mechanical noises like clocks and (in extreme cases) steam engines, together with certain rhythms – is not capable. Ergo: musical Realism is a contradiction in terms, and cannot exist. Not only did it not exist, it could not have existed.

Dahlhaus' argument does not challenge this argument, although he points out that *Tonmalerei*, picture painting in sound, was less than common in

---

[24] Similar caution is called for in the treatment of Balzac's work, in which obvious 'Romantic' elements coexist with exemplary Realist practices.

nineteenth century music (in part, of course, because the Romantics despised it.[25]) But he has no hesitation in identifying elements proper to music where Realism is a valid category. Where Realism does take place and represents a major innovation in music history is in the shift from verse libretti to 'musical prose' (the phrase and the practice were Wagner's), the freeing up of artificially set verse-forms, the approximating of song to the rhythms and periods of prose speech.[26] We should not forget that Wagner saw the shift from instrumental music as essentially democratic, since for him instrumental music was indelibly marked with its function at court, i.e. 'to entertain and delight a feudal lord through the energy of his servant, the musician' (cf. Voss 1977:173).

The purists do not care for this development, out of a pedantic version of Verdi's argument, but otherwise nothing in Dahlhaus' account is calculated to make music cease being music. It is for that reason that we managed to turn the *Meistersinger* into a Realist novel only on a basis which music purists – and not only they – would properly call non-musical, namely: its plot, its milieu and finally its ideology. It takes little imagination to see the problems we would have had in applying these specific types of argument to the other significant examples of Wagner's operas, such as for instance, *Parsifal,*[27] but, no matter which opera one experiments with, more precisely mimetic features are unlikely to be found within the music.

Dahlhaus reaches a sympathetic and moderate conclusion. He believes that there is a function in using the category 'musical Realism' to describe the musical developments of the nineteenth century. Our understanding of the particular ambiguity of the period and of its significant works and composers would be impoverished without this concept. But he constantly warns against failing to differentiate between music and the other arts in its approximation to some of the elements of Realism. He would be horrified at the story of

---

[25]   A.W.Schlegel, for instance, regarded the technique as merely humorous (cf. Edler 1965:107).

[26]   See also Schmid (1981:252f) and Stein (1975:51f). Verdi – who did not go down the path to prose, but insisted on his libretti having verse-forms (and it would take some courage to call them 'artificial') – was correspondingly impatient with the slogan of Realism in his day: All good art was Realistic, Shakespeare was Realistic, but out of inspiration, not calculation. He preferred a good *cabalette* to any system originating outside music (or, for that matter, outside Italy: but that is the topic of a later chapter). Notice that Nietzsche's complaint about the lack of rhythm in Wagner's music relates exactly to this innovative feature of his operas (vi,3:416f).

[27]   In a similar way no-one could claim for Flaubert's *Salammbô* that it had much affinity with his Realism. Writers do not only develop in one direction only: they may wish to write in styles that differ from that direction.

Richard Cooper if this story seemed to imply an easy transfer from one medium to the other.

An important counter-argument to Dahlhaus' view was put forward by Martin Geck in 2001. Geck is an eminent musicologist of a slightly younger generation than Dahlhaus and editor of the standard edition of Wagner's opera texts. His title – *Zwischen Romantik und Restauration: Musik im Realismus-Diskurs 1848-1871*[28] – makes clear that Geck is writing in the wake of a significant change both in literary studies and in musicology, as well as in their interrelations. In particular, a major shift has taken place towards a greater uncertainty in classification of literary texts. In part this change is the product of a profound questioning of the referentiality of literary texts, but in part too it results from texts being read against a much wider historical background. Geck's argument is constructed round discourse theory, rather than focusing (as we have so far) on comparison with individual, complete texts. In considering the place of music within a variety of historical discourses, including those of Realism, the investigator is less concerned with overall interpretations of the objects themselves, and more with the clusters of attributions which these cultural objects received during and subsequent to their own time. So Realism is not a movement, or a category of literary analysis, but a discourse.[29] Discourses exist in historical competition with, or in evolutionary descent from, other discourses: we see this clearly for instance in the relationship between the discourses of idealism and Realism which is a marked feature of all the principal cultural systems in the nineteenth century.[30] Martin Geck's work clearly establishes and documents the presence of Wagner's work within the discourse of Realism from the 1840s onwards. Mapping Wagner's position can be compared to the establishment of a graph's line through a series of dots, the recorded historical utterances. The line of Realism clearly passes through Wagner and

---

[28] *Between Romanticism and Restoration. Music in the Realism discourse: 1848-1871.*
[29] Geck bases his method on Jürgen Link's understanding of discourse as: 'an historically specific, specialized and governed formation of utterances, which are directed to a specific and specialized group of objects. The concept of "discourse" stresses the materiality of the manner of speaking and its institutional framing conditions [...]' (2001:4). Discourses are formed across much wider disciplinary fields than those separate fields – e.g. philology, political history, aesthetics etc – which came over into the twentieth century, and to consider discourse as an entity in itself will transgress any disciplinary boundary.
[30] A well known example in English literary debate in the 1850s was the labelling of Dickens as an Idealist, in contrast to Thackeray, a Realist. To what extent those terms expressed truths about the literary figures themselves or about their works is at least debatable: that they represented clusters of discourses in competition with one another was very clear.

his work, but it is a line which requires drawing: it is not self-evident, nor does it define the dots through which it passes.

It is not cynical to look back over more than thirty years of discourse theory to suggest that the approach does not always generate insights which can immediately be used in present-day interpretation of texts. We operate today in different discourse situations that those which placed Wagner within Realism, and it may not always be helpful to the way we wish to understand a Wagner opera today to start from the past collective judgments. We can illustrate this issue generally if we take an example from a narrower segment of our field: the sound of Wagner's *Tristan*. It is easy to make historical sense of the critique of the opera which found *Tristan* tonally cacophonous and grating to the listener (a view epitomized in the popular cartoon of 1869 showing Wagner working with a hammer and chisel on the inside of the human ear – there was a distinctive discourse denoting what is painful to listen to). We can understand why Wagner's best-known opponent, the Viennese music critic Eduard Hanslick, (and for that matter Mark Twain, who remarked that Wagner's music was 'not as bad as it sounds') rejected a music so much in breach of the tonal conventions of the classical period. It is however much harder to use that information as part of a present-day hearing of *Tristan*. We have got used to more extreme forms of dissonance and chromaticism, as well as to more immediate forms of sexualized music. Past judgments serve as a poor basis for our own understanding of the work – not because they are wrong, but because they start somewhere else –, and it is all but impossible to recreate that crucial element of the music's effect. All we can do is to read back from Geck's material in order to find our own interpretative approaches to Wagner's individual works. We start by asking what aspects of Wagner's works caused his contemporaries to place them within a discourse of Realism.

A major influence on the discourse of the years in which Wagner began to make his mark was the revolution of 1848, which cast its long shadow forwards into the years from perhaps 1830.[31] Everyone knows of Wagner's short-lived participation in the uprising in Dresden and his fleeting friendship with revolutionary giants such as Bakunin, and understandably there has been debate about the revolutionary content of his dramas, most notably the *Ring* –

---

[31]   In Germany the period from 1840 is referred to by many historians as the *Vormärz*, i.e. the period leading up to the March revolution of 1848. Other historians, and historians describing other countries, handle the periodicization differently: 1830 is an important point of orientation, because of the July revolution in France and its various repercussions across continental Europe; in England on the other hand a similar organizing role is assumed by the Reform Bill of 1832.

debate provoked by the occasional manifestation of a highly political slant in Bayreuth productions (notably by Patrice Chéreau in 1976). The association with the revolution does not enhance everyone's appreciation of Wagner's operas today, nor would it necessarily involve Wagner's Realism. Today one might tend to regard revolutionary fervour rather as a symptom of youthful romanticism. Furthermore, in terms of discourse history, we need to recall that Wagner was numbered among Realism long before the *Ring* was known, and when the *Ring* was in the repertoire no-one, least of all Wagner himself, was talking about his youthful indiscretions, and no-one spoke of revolution any more. Revolutionary spirit was part of the historical cluster of Realism for very different reasons than those eventually offered by the finished product of the *Ring*. We can mention the cult of action and change in Wagner's views of society, art and – in particular – music. Realism was a frequent synonym for the desire for action, life and change – without the question of what kind of change receiving much prominence. Anything that did not reinforce either the over-comfortable philistine life-style of the *Biedermeier* period or the narcissistic cult of inactive fantasy was soon labeled Realist: actual support for the revolution was not a necessary part of the concept.

In an argument of immediate relevance to the *Meistersinger*, Geck shows clearly how the state of the music profession and of music itself was a revolutionary topic around 1848. The revolution was a catch-all time of unrest, in almost every area of society discontent identified itself with the revolution, and music was no exception. The call for the 'democratization' of music and for the removal of music from its place within a rigid and steep social hierarchy was very unlikely to be answered fully – economic realities meant that operatic orchestras were either funded by aristocratic patrons or would cease to exist – but the calls bore fruit not only in Wagner's abolition of all boxes in his Bayreuth theatre and in the introduction of darkness into the auditorium (which, as present-day visitors to Bayreuth will have noticed, made difficult, but by no means impossible, social snobbery and displays of wealth), but in the huge attention which he pays in the *Meistersinger* to organizational questions of the guild. The guild was not an accidental assembly of quaint musical amateurs but a configuration of a democratic musical fraternity. We saw above that the vision of Nuremberg was politically conceived by Wagner, and did not come off a *Lebkuchen* packet. Its 'national pride' was strongly democratic. The understanding that democracy meant music turning to the people, to the *Volk*, put into the discourse of Realism aspects of Wagner's work which present-day judgments might more easily ascribe to nationalism and, by being ideological, regard as being less than 'Realist'.

Other features intrinsic to the music which were labeled 'Realist' in their day were notably the search for greater clarity of expression. Dahlhaus reminds us that characterization was, first and foremost, part of the Romantic legacy of local colour (for which Victor Hugo's *Préface de Cromwell* was the most notable literary expression), and as a Romantic heritage characterization quickly turned into unnatural exaggeration and non-Realism. This did not prevent the revolutionaries of 1848 hailing it as the abandonment of an elitist musical inwardness. It was not just in writing songs for the barricades, or 'chorus-ballads'[32], that composers followed some of the expectations of revolution and Realism: clarity of expression in itself [33] (even if, in the opinion of some critics, that word meant little more than the 'singability' of melodies) and the simplification of the musical portrayal of character and social interaction stood in the closest possible relation to both revolution and to Realism.[34]

Another important element in Wagner's Realism merely reflects the polemical nature of discourse systems. His friends and mentors spoke of him in terms which made him a Realist, but no less significant was his good fortune with his enemies. In France, for instance, the principal advocate of Realism – the journalist Champfleury[35] – strongly championed Wagner, comparing him to the lodestar of Realism, the painter Gustave Courbet. Whether or not Wagner had, by that stage of his career (1855), written any work which 'qualified' for Realism in the way Courbet's work did, was less

---

[32]   This was the development in Robert Schumann's work which caused his work in the 1850s to trespass on the practices called Realist, as Geck shows (2001:79f), even if other aspects of his work obviously belonged with idealist discourse or – in other terms – with Romanticism.

[33]   Another general area in which this increasing clarity of expression can be seen is that of a greater precision in the production of musical effects, whether in terms of instructions to players included in the score (a procedure first introduced by Berlioz) or in terms of the greater focus on conducting. In such ways the cult of the personality of the individual conductor could paradoxically be seen as an element in musical Realism – certainly Wagner's own conducting skills were aimed at exploring the reality of the music, not just at self-glorification.

[34]   One of the ironies of the period is that Realism was identified not only with the revolution, but – and perhaps still more strongly – with the disillusioned acceptance of the failure of revolution. Theodor Fontane's famous pages on Realism (1853) – which have an important place in Geck's account of contemporary attitudes – explicitly define Realism as an overcoming of the heady idealism of revolution. Readers of Emerson would recognize many of his emphases in essayistic writing of this kind.

[35]   Champfleury (*nom de plume* of Jules Husson) was, with Louis Edmond Duranty, editor of the short-lived periodical *Le Réalisme* in 1857.

important in Champfleury's praise than the fact that Wagner had been attacked by the critic François-Joseph Fétis, one of the principal opponents of the Realist movement in France. Sharing enemies (as we saw in Wagner's tempestuous relationship to Hebbel) can be more important than sharing ideologies or aesthetic ideas. Something similar happened in the case of Wagner's critic Eduard Hanslick. His best-selling study of musical beauty (*Vom Musikalisch-Schönen*, 1854) took on the function of being a rallying point for the values of 'idealism', and put him in opposition to Wagner, simply because of the discourse field in which Wagner moved. As we mentioned above, discourse fields exist in distinction to (often in direct conflict with) other discourse fields, and invariably there is a high level of interdependence. Without the other camp, the actual categories would not have been created; without the idealist Hanslick, there is no Realist Wagner.[36] By this degree of polarization it had become all but irrelevant what Wagner had actually written. This is shown in the comments on Wagner by Julian Schmidt, the critic most involved in the campaign for Realism in Germany. In 1856 Schmidt wrote of Wagner in his journal *Die Grenzboten*:

> In its motifs this music is admittedly extraordinarily spiritualist, but the means which it employs – and that is the ultimate question in art – are entirely based on materialistic features, and it is only on account of this talent that Wagner's music had such a big impression on the people (*Volk*). The people delight in the clear painting of Richard Wagner, a painting which outdoes reality: it takes no pleasure in his highly romantic subjects. (Quoted Geck 2002:187)

Few more polemical approaches to the issues of Realism can be imagined than this absolute separation of form and content and the arrogance with which Schmidt claims to identify popular taste.[37] By such processes, however, artists got assigned to one or the other camp. Advocacy and deliberate factionalizing played a significant role too.

---

[36] It is in structures of this kind – rather than some psychopathology on behalf of the critic – that Hanslick's split attitude to Wagner's music makes sense. His famous description of himself as someone listening in the hope of liking Wagner – 'surrounded by the entranced masses, whose joys one would so gladly partake of' (2007:66) – (echoed in many of Nietzsche's comments on his erstwhile mentor) is not only poignant: it raises a clear issue of the way in which critical divisions come into existence.

[37] Of course, Schmidt was anxious to keep his campaign for Realism in touch with conventional aesthetics, as the 1855 – positive – review of Hanslick's *Vom Mukalisch-Schönen* makes clear, even if he does insist on the 'ultimate test' of any theory to be 'its relationship to the practical endeavors of its age' (1855:475).

Why does Wagner's Realism matter?

There is one final source for the initiatives within musicology to make Wagner a Realist. In common with many other critics, I have been concerned here with the *status* of Realism (again as distinct from any *definition* of Realism) in literary discourse, a question of some importance not merely in the second half of the nineteenth century, but in the period after 1930 and again after 1960. In the nineteenth century anyone wanting – and at that time everyone *did* want – to create in their culture a *national* literature of quality looked towards Realism to achieve that. Whether the desire came in the form of looking for a new Shakespeare, or a new Tolstoy – American, Socialist or whatever –, Realism, however vaguely understood, was the touchstone of the maturity of national literature.[38] Critics were anxious to establish for their own national culture the kind of legitimation which Tolstoy gave to Russia, or Balzac and Stendhal to France. Two types of argument were frequently encountered in these ideas. In an age of ironclads and railways, foreign conquest and frenetic industrial and urban expansion, it seemed grotesque – and for the critic and historian embarrassing – to have on offer a national literature concerned with fairies, escapist medievalism,[39] or with cultural values borrowed from other nations. If literature (or music) had a function, then it had to relate to the conditions of its day: if it had a national identity, then it could not ignore what was happening within the contemporary nation. It was not only those dangerous people, the 'cultural politicians', who argued in this way: the artists themselves joined in. The Realists wanted to matter to national life: if they did not, their aesthetic creed could hardly be taken seriously. Affirmation or critique of national policy was less important than simple relevance to national life.

The search for Realism was repeated in the 1930s, especially among Communist intellectuals. The desire was not only to develop a Realist literature in the Soviet Union (without it, literature would not be seen to match up to the greatness of Stalin's achievements), but to show Communism as the culmination of a tendency of progressive bourgeois humanism, enshrined in Realist writers' skeptical approach to the evolution of capitalist society in the nineteenth century. Not only the category of Socialist Realism, but also 'bourgeois Realism', and 'critical Realism' were much discussed. Foremost among the critics was Georg Lukács, who devoted a lifetime of

---

[38]   This desire was particularly strong in Germany and in the United States of America, as my own comparative study (2007) makes clear.
[39]   That some medievalism was anything but escapist – for instance, serving the myth of the new nation – is evident. Cf. final chapter.

critical work to establishing Realism as the one acceptable style of the novel, leaving behind both some of the monuments of critical encounter with the novel and some unfortunate compromises with political expediency. With the emergence of the 'New Left' in the 1960s the Realism debates were taken up, and far from uncritically at that. The critique of Stalinism made critics of the centre and the left careful to avoid authoritarian models of Realism, but the search for Realism in national literatures was hardly less frantic than in the nineteenth century. Books and articles on Realism came out in profusion, and a not always over-reflective sociology of literature swamped the academy.[40] It is hardly surprising that there was a Cold War element in such debates, especially in Germany, where socialist theories of Realism formed a significant part of the scholarly output of the East German academy and universities and were less than welcome in some West German critical circles as a result.

If Stalinist theories of Realism had been highly influential in the 1930s – one only has to look at the career of Shostakovich to see its effects – music development and musicology were strongly influenced too in the 1960s, and even the slight generational difference between Dahlhaus and Geck is on its own sufficient to cause significant differences between their positions on Realism, and not just in the methodological issues we referred to earlier. It would be wrong to call Dahlhaus' work conservative, for it contains radical and positive insights into the modernization of music and music practice in the nineteenth century. His understanding of the 'progressive' effects of the technical improvements in the orchestra[41] is remarkable and close to the materialist music theories of the Brecht circle in the 1920s. In general Dahlhaus reveals a well-founded impatience at any random application of half-baked theories of Realism to nineteenth century music: he has read widely in the canon of Realism, and shares more of Geck's position than their differences might allow them to recognize. Yet there is one tendency in Dahlhaus' account which Geck identifies for criticism and which matters to our understanding of Wagner. It's a well known type of reaction to irritating political debate: to retreat into an excessively unpolitical stance. Dahlhaus has some wonderful illustrations of the irritation, not to say fury of the political agitators of the *Vormärz* over what they perceived to be the general indifference which music – both as an art and as a profession – displayed

---

[40]   Becker (1963) and Hemmings (1974) were classic volumes, much used across universities to underpin courses on Realism.

[41]   Having reminded his readers of Berlioz' credentials as a Byronic, romantic type of artist, Dahlhaus writes: 'However, the emancipation of the orchestra, the increasing tendency towards technical sophistication, was anti-romantic' (1982:53).

towards revolution. Playing in tune seemed a metaphor for their reaction to politics. For every musician like Wagner breathing the fire of revolution, there were thousands whose concerns went no further than their sheets of music. While art-forms such as novel, lyric, drama and painting greedily soaked up the fervor of revolution, music seemed largely impervious to the events going on about it. 'Music is not interested,' wrote Louise Otto in 1845,[42] 'in the life of action, it cares nothing about the nation or the new age. All it cares about is its own rules, which no-one but composers and music experts are entitled to hold an opinion about.' It appears to Dahlhaus that there is some wider truth in this observation: 'It seems as if the *Zeitgeist*, despite its claims to universality, kept out of music', he comments dryly (1982:65), in a drastic application of the default-setting hypothesis.

It is this sense of the detachment of nineteenth-century music from contemporary political and historical currents of which Geck is critical (2001:199). Dahlhaus' conclusions share something of the affection with which Thomas Mann constantly emphasized music as the ultimate expression of the 'unpolitical' German.[43] Not only does Mann himself offer opinions with which to counter his own view: it is continuously challenged in explicitly political stagings of the *Ring*, in every attempt to show Wagner's irony and the breaks in his monumentality, and – I hope – in the focus of this book on techniques and understandings which Wagner explicitly shared with the Realist novel of his day. We should not confuse Dahlhaus' gentle irony with a lack of commitment to Wagner's importance in the world outside music, but Geck's insistence on the actuality of Wagner and his music does represent a conscious attempt to break continuities of understanding of the German nineteenth century – and with that ambition one must wholeheartedly agree.

It is worth discovering this actuality in each generation, since the debates on Realism show a particular understanding of music – and of all culture – shared by critical positions both in the second half of the nineteenth century and in their revival in the 1960s. As we read the debates, we constantly encounter what can only be called an *anthropological* understanding of culture (and therefore of music too). Rather than discussing culture within the exclusive context of aesthetic principles – what Otto called 'its own rules' –,

---

[42]   Die Nibelungen als Oper, in: *Neue Zeitschrift für Musik*, 1845 (cit. Dahlhaus 1982:65). Louise Otto was a well-known revolutionary novelist and campaigner, i.a. for women's rights. The role of women in music during the century is a topic in its own.
[43]   This is the principal theme of Mann's highly political *Reflections of an Unpolitical Man* (1919), in which Wagner appears with Nietzsche and Schopenhauer *affirmatively* as part of the three-fold constellation (*Dreigestirn*) of German culture in the nineteenth century.

artists and critics strove to create an art which might be the expression of the identity of a national, social, or ethnic group.[44] From the eighteenth century on the ancient Greeks and Romans, like Shakespeare, had been discussed in these terms in all European countries. Each emergent social grouping tended to identify itself in the culture being produced, or in the already extant culture, in which it could claim to see its own greatness reflected. Hence the search intensified for Italian and German national culture to match the attainment of political nationhood; hence the search was engaged on behalf of the middle-classes to achieve their own, non-aristocratic culture to replace the previously canonized functions of traditional culture for the aristocracy (later in the century the Naturalists would use similar arguments to extend art to the industrial proletariat); hence it became generally fashionable to discuss the culture of 'the English-speaking races', 'the Latin races', the city-dweller, etc. While concepts of nationhood and identity had clearly changed radically – and by no means for the better – the relationship of art to these social groups had also been radicalized, and these trends constantly informed the debates about musical Realism.

We return to these issues – somewhat more lightly – in our final chapter, where we are concerned with the ability (perhaps also the necessity) for opera in Italy and Germany to take over leading functions in the task of national culture at the end of the nineteenth century. As Geck reminds us, however, opera shared these functions with other artistic forms and our present understanding of Wagner's work is not free of expectations derived from our own 'anthropological' assumptions about it. We may not ask questions of the *national* quality of cultural products with the urgency that was once widespread, but we certainly ask continuously who opera is for, what function it serves in society at large, and – with seat prices in national opera houses soaring: air-travel, but not opera, being the subject of price-led 'democratization' – we ask where, apart from snob value, its importance and appeal can lie. It is a feature of the literature we call Realist that it tackled these issues centrally, in 'anthropological' terms, and Wagner's political concerns with art and the nation were no different. Geck himself, having admirably conducted the Realism debate in a way far removed from the value-judgments of the present, allows his own priorities briefly to emerge when he remarks that not only did Wagner's operas find entry into Realism

---

[44]   We may call this anthropological since it sees the justification of culture neither on a hierarchy of aesthetic quality, nor within aesthetic criteria at all. If aesthetic qualities do happen to be identified, these are subsumed in ethnic or social identity. Contact with other cultures, especially those of the non-European world, reinforced this view – often disastrously.

because their plots and their music 'were the result of exact observation and analysis' (2001:158) but the artistic quality of Wagner's works was a *result* of Wagner's participation in these movements: he speaks positively of 'Wagner's surrender to the Realist Zeitgeist' (2001:199). In these features of Wagner's work we may discover therefore not simply another element in the historical justification of the epithet 'Realism', but a source of the operas' possible appeal to present-day sensibilities. Such as view, as we have seen, is related to the Formalists' theories of the progressiveness of art (although it does not contain their restriction to formal methods alone); it is closer to Gregor-Dellin's understanding of 'intelligent music'. In essence, however, such attitudes reflect an insistence on the modernization process at the heart of Wagner's work and the refusal to permit his works to be buried in archaism and parochial tradition. This purpose is shared with Dahlhaus, and is the central concern of my book. All wish to celebrate an art-form which combines musical beauty and human significance of plot with intelligence, observation and penetrating understanding – we must claim Wagner back from some of his ideologically suspect admirers, and we must on occasion claim him back from himself.

6. Questions, Answers and Body Language in Wagner and the Realist Novel

> 'The basic position of the Enlightenment and its way of thinking is tied
> to no particular age. In the moment that in the face of any king by divine
> right, any holy father, any holy book or holy nation some figure asks
> "What's supposed to be holy about that?" – in that moment, if only
> for a second, the mythological world falls apart.'
> Peter von Matt (1995:147)

To those who do not know them, Wagner's operas are bombastic, declarative monologues. Nietzsche complained that every character sounded like the statue speaking (in *Don Giovanni*: vi,3:421) – in a word, inhuman. To those who know them, Wagner's operas are full of division, tension, dialogue and questions. Even with regard to actual questions a negative reaction is more usual: everyone knows about the question you should not ask, such as Lohengrin's instruction to Elsa never to ask him where he came from, how he came and what his name is. It is too nearly funny, too certain to fail – a suburban adulterer's charter – for eyebrows not to be raised at the counterclaim that dialogue and the answer to questions structure the operas. And as if that were not enough, Wagner's detractors point in his operas to those long explanations, which seem to lack a corresponding question, as when a page asks Gurnemanz to tell him 'what happened when...': thirty minutes later he is still being told: Hanslick complained of Wagner's 'frightful long-windedness' (2007:62). To those who do not know them, Wagner's operas are like their author: opinionated, pushy, intolerant of other opinions, not letting anyone else get a word in. The opposite case must be made, as Dahlhaus comments:

> In the teeth of the all-but ineradicable prejudice which wishes to see him as a musical
> demagogue, Wagner was less anxious to persuade – let alone anaesthetize – his listeners,
> than he was fundamentally to be understood. For that reason he was an inexhaustible
> *raisonneur,* who could never give up the hope of making himself understood. (1996:164-65)

I shall waste no time fighting a prejudice which even Dahlhaus finds insuperable. To do so would come close to instructing other people to *like* Wagner. But it is worth showing how committed he is to open dialogue and to the rational understanding of relationships. In doing so we establish another profound affinity with the Realist novel, which – as a glance at any text will show – is constructed round clear interaction in dialogue, critically presented by a narrator who wishes to get to the truth and is as skeptical of individual characters as of ultimate authority. It was a marked feature of the Realist novel to move away from stilted and poetic words and their artificial, rhetorical arrangement. Dialogue was therefore part of its program. My aim here is not simply to claim Wagner's works to be entertaining – after all the Realist novels which used the same techniques as Wagner's are not to everyone's taste either. Instead, I want to show dialogue and questioning as part of the apparatus of the Enlightenment, devices challenging both set opinions and established authority. The fourth section will look briefly at how Wagner's rationalism handles myth, and the final section attempts to compare opera and the novel at one of their most widely separate points: the treatment of the body.

Dialogue as an Instrument of Reason

An obvious place to start is the scene in *Rheingold* which introduces Wotan and his wife Fricka.[1] Not only is the scene one of ordinary domestic conflict, but it totally lacks the formality and grandeur of traditional conflicts between the high-born. Its material comes from the Realists – obviously Ibsen would be a place to look for parallels – but in fact Flaubert's minute observations of the banalities of marriage (*and* adultery) come to mind. Not even Balzac bothered to show us the actual conflicts between the philanderer Baron Hulot and his unfortunate family: we see only the momentous results. In contrast, Wagner gives us the conflict itself – over breakfast! – in all its banality. Wotan and Fricka are arguing about money, how to pay for the luxurious castle in which they have just awoken. From the earliest drafts the scene contrasted Wotan's dream-like satisfaction with Valhalla with Fricka's wide-awake *scolding*.[2] She complains that he is proud of his prestige residence, and that only she worries about the price to be paid. She comments bitterly on the fact that she, as a woman, has been left out of the major decisions

---

[1]   Wagner's preference for the domestic introduction is clear when we note that the early drafts had Wotan bathing in the river and thereby observing the theft of the Rheingold. The change from the first drafts shows the importance to him of a less mythologically charged approach to his story.

[2]   For a detailed account of the construction of this scene cf. Darcy (1993:127f). It is amusing to note that Brünnhilde describes Fricka's arrival in *Walküre* Act 2 Scene 1 as a storm (an image which Wotan immediately adopts). Compared to Fricka's scolding the Ride of the Valkyres is a stroll in the park.

concerning the house: her husband's unreliable friend, Loge, knows more of it than she does. Wake up, she urges Wotan, and start thinking. Otherwise the cost of the castle will be the happiness of the family, in particular that of Freia, Fricka's sister, whom the giants will demand in payment for their labors. (One gets the impression that Wotan could have been more easily reconciled to trading in Fricka: he may have lost the sight of one eye in his wooing of Fricka[3], but it is Freia who offers eternal youth – certainly not Fricka.) Wotan enjoys pointing out that he built the castle only because Fricka wanted it, to which Fricka replies that the whole plan had been a strategy to tie her husband more strongly to domesticity and keep him out of mischief ('I may honor women more than you care for!', Wotan concedes) – in any case, she didn't get enough furnishings ('wonniger Hausrat')[4], the building came out too war-like, too concerned with male prestige. With foreboding she hears Wotan insist that, even in 'their' new home, he is still a god and will wish to conquer the world and not be tied to the house, in which she is gradually recognizing the start of their misfortunes.

Whatever else the *Ring* tells – it has started with the crime of Alberich stealing the Rheingold –, an important element after this opening is the domestic conflict over money. While we could not claim that the language of the scene is naturalistic, the confrontation is direct and the more poetic language comes from Wotan, in keeping with his lofty plans: Fricka is much more down to earth. The *Ring* develops as domestic tragedy. Audiences would be mistaken if they did not accept this. Of course, there have always been approaches which prefer not to see Wagner's characters as flesh and blood, but they are untrue to the real Wagner.[5]

---

[3]   One of the unsolved mysteries of the *Ring*, and one of the few aspects of the story which are not fully explained. In this scene, the missing eye seems to be a reminder to Wotan that he has reduced his vision of the universe by marrying Fricka – surely he would have given details of any heroic deed of which his injury was the result.

[4]   I give these quotations to show that it is not my text that reduces Wagner's scene to the level of a kitchen-sink drama, as Brecht did when he transformed Elizabeth and Maria Stuart into fish-wives. It is not just a domestic conflict, it is a conflict about domesticity, and the language is, in its time, not far elevated above the domestic.

[5]   An anonymous author (HLWC) in a theosophical pamphlet of 1909 under the promising title *Brünhilde [sic] A psychological study*, claimed indignantly: 'one of the most common errors into which people fall in describing Wagner's characters is that of treating them as ordinary man and women' (p.3). If s/he is right, then not only a large number of post-war producers of the *Ring* are wrong, but Wagner himself. We suspect that Fricka is right when she describes Wotan's high-minded sentiments as a mere cloak for further domestic-sexual deceits (*Walküre*, Act 2,2).

For our next example we move to the wonderful Scene 4 which precedes the dramatic dénouement Act 2 of *Walküre*. Although it is pitched at a level far removed from arguments about money and furniture, its use of dialogue is both supremely human and in its closeness to the rules of conversational pragmatics emphasizes its proximity to literary Realism. The conversation arises as Siegmund cross-examines Brünnhilde, who has come on her father, Wotan's, instructions, to collect Siegmund and conduct him to that club for dead heroes which Wotan maintains as personal bodyguards somewhere beyond the rainbow. The scene is interesting enough for the ideas it contains, for they are very close to the original impulse of the *Ring* – the anti-metaphysical, anti-authoritarian humanism of *Siegfried's Death* is nowhere more touchingly illustrated than in this scene. But it is its structure which will first strike us here.

Siegmund is waiting for Hunding – his sister-bride's husband – to come out and fight him. Judging by the story he told Sieglinde when they first met – fleeing from Hunding after the previous day's skirmish –, Siegmund is sanguine about his chances, yet he is surprised to find Brünnhilde standing on his path. Her explanation of her presence does not disconcert Siegmund, who starts asking the questions which shape the scene.

Will he be there alone? Siegmund asks, thinking of Brünnhilde's visit as an invitation rather than a summons. No, Brünnhilde replies, the hallowed band of the dead heroes will greet you. Will he meet his own father? – a major question this, for Siegmund knows nothing of his family: he is another of the orphans and foundlings of the *Ring* and meeting his father would do much to reconcile him to death. Yes, he will. Siegmund's next question begins a crescendo of concerns which may surprise those who see Wagner's heroic ideals as unfeeling: Will he be greeted in Valhalla by a woman? Brünnhilde's answer is not only more fulsome than her first answers, it is accompanied with increasing passion by the orchestra, the harps stressing the beauty and paradisiacal state of having the wish-maidens (*Wunschmädchen*) passing round drinks. (This picture of these maidens seems – from the composer of *Tannhäuser* – to be remarkably free from erotic charms. Only later do we understand where the opera's real erotic charge is to be found.) Valhalla is a place of great sweetness and dignity: it is the heart's desire for mortals wishing to associate with the gods. Siegmund appreciates this, he formulates his next question carefully in terms of conversational pragmatics: flattering noble and holy Brünnhilde – 'hehr und heilig' –, he goes on to ask if his sister and bride Sieglinde will be in Valhalla to meet him. No, she must still breathe the air of this world, Brünnhilde replies, the music making clear the sweetness which she knows Sieglinde's breath to hold for Siegmund. But even she is startled by Siegmund's response, for Siegmund – in another very carefully formulated utterance – shows where his heart lies and what he thinks of the gods and their organization of the world. Sending his greetings to Wotan, to the dead heroes, to the *Wunschmädchen* (in other words, meeting all conversational politeness) – Siegmund declares his rejection of Wotan's summons. He will not follow Brünnhilde, but will stay on earth with Sieglinde. You have seen me, she replies: you have no choice but to follow. She tells Siegmund that the freedom which he proudly claims for himself is meaningless: death can and will compel him. Who is to kill me? Hunding, it is decreed, says Brünnhilde and Siegmund's protestations, his insistence on his own independence, his reliance on the sword which he took from the tree are as nothing, for Brünnhilde explains that he who made that sword (Wotan himself) has taken away its powers. Even then Wagner's handling of the conversation remains naturalistic, as Siegmund rebukes Brünnhilde for talking so loudly that she might wake the sleeping Sieglinde, and the scene is over. A scene of great power, wrenchingly human and normal – despite its defiantly anti-naturalistic basis – but entirely dialogic, constructed on the counterpoint of question and answer, following the logic of normal conversation. Not even the gods are monolithic here, for that relentless fate which Brünnhilde has come to announce is about to be subverted, and by Brünnhilde herself, favorite daughter of Wotan. Progressive logic, dialogue, the power of argument, unnatural setting but totally human conversation – these are the stuff of *Walküre* Act 2 Scene 4.

If Siegmund shapes this amazing scene by asking questions about the future, other scenes are constructed around questions about the past. As we saw with our prose version of the *Meistersinger* in the previous chapter, opera and drama start with characters already formed and placed. Novels need to start with the background, operas start at the point of action. Wagner knows this explicitly – he had discussed it at length in *Opera and Drama* –, and he turns into the mainspring of some impressive scenes the process by which characters establish themselves and show how their past has made them the people they are. Wagner thus uses dialogue to make up for what he felt to be the deficiencies of the prose text. Sometimes, in a way not far from Brechtian theatre, characters tell of themselves in words, either directly – their character a kind of subscript to their action – or indirectly, with music underlying the gestures characteristic of the class or place from which they come. Sometimes, often indeed, Wagner uses once again the structuring device of question and answer to drive this process forward.

The scene in Act 1 in which Parsifal is first brought onto the stage is a powerful example of exposition through dialogue. On the holy lake at which the Grail Knight Amfortas bathes his wound and seeks purification, a holy swan has been brought down by Parsifal's arrow. Outraged, the knights capture the perpetrator and bring him to Gurnemanz, who relentlessly cross-examines Parsifal about his action, his person and his background.

Parsifal is at first proud of his action – it was a good shot, he does not miss. He is shown the dead swan, its inert wing, its clouded eye, the congealing blood. The sight brings him to silence, he covers his eyes to wipe out the sight and cannot speak. Slowly he is prodded into speech. He did not know his action was wrong; he does not know where he is from, he does not know who his father is, how it was that he came through this part of the woods. His name then? Here a moment of lyricism from the orchestra, a flash-back to the joys of childhood: he once had many names (he must be referring to the endearments of his mother and the pet-names she used for him), but now he knows none of them. Gurnemanz – muttering angrily about Parsifal's stupidity: only Kundry is as obtuse (itself a revealing piece of anger, for Kundry clearly knows more than Gurnemanz) – returns to the cross-examination. You must know something, well, what's that? What do you know, however little it may be? Parsifal remembers his mother Herzeleide, the woods and meadows of that childhood, and once more the orchestra – a narrator filling in details lying beyond the immediate conversation – tells us with what warmth he remembers but cannot speak of the pain of loss. Kundry joins in now: after his father's death in combat, Parsifal's mother had brought him up to avoid weapons and chivalry. Now Parsifal remembers the knights he wanted to be like, and whom, defying the direction of his education, he followed blindly when he left home. He is no Kasper Hauser brought up by the wolves, but in fact deeply formed by chivalry and imitation of his father. Exposed by Kundry's story (for, again like the Realist narrator, Kundry never lies, and it is she who tells of Herzeleide's death) the boundaries of Parsifal's past are made clear in reaction and interruption, Parsifal has been presented fully and the action in the present can continue.

The dialogue here is less symmetrical than in *Walküre*, for Parsifal knows nothing, indeed the conversation peters out as the action develops, and at the end of the act Gurnemanz is exasperated to notice that Parsifal – in whom he had lost interest, as more important religious duties called – is still hanging around. Unceremoniously Gurnemanz sends him packing, and we are left with a scene perhaps of great psychological depth (is it possible that authors, whether of novels or of operas, never quite know when they have *achieved* psychological depth? depth is perhaps a matter of reception, rather than of production – more of that later), but certainly a scene of pure revelation through question and answer interwoven with narrative. Of course, drama is good at dialogue – though opera less obviously so – the question is how it uses its skill.

With this question in mind it is interesting to compare the writing in this scene from *Parsifal* with that in an opera first performed some sixteen years later, but sourced in nineteenth-century French fiction, rather than in medieval myth and legend. Just about the most popular scene in Puccini's *La Bohème* is at the end of Act 1, as Mimi and Rodolfo introduce themselves to each other. The audience knows little about them at that point, certainly individual character is less marked than their vocal range (soprano, tenor – probably enough to identify Rodolfo as the hero among his otherwise similar friends). Clarity in the relationship is not furthered by the erotic atmosphere between Roldolfo and his *importuna vicina*: lighting candles and dropping keys have a basic symbolism which needs no sharper focus. The self-presentations of the two insist on their communicative intentions – *le dirò con due parole chi son [...] Vuole?* asks Rodolfo, while Mimi interrupts her presentation with the question *Lei m'intende?* – yet their actual words are anything but communicative. Rodolfo swaggers, stylizes himself and his happy poverty (one word strongly stressed in the music is when he claims to be in spirit *milionaria*), while Mimi – or Lucia – passes over the basic information that she is an embroideress, otherwise speaks of her love of poetry, *d'amor* e di *primavere* and tells Rodolfo that the flowers she embroiders have no scent. It is very beautiful and the tiny frozen hand justly popular, but what separates it from Wagner is not quality, but technique in dialogue as well as in music. The scene is written and played for identification, for a sentimental love-story in *una bianca cameretta*, the music serves up the story with all Puccini's magical theatrical skills. But we know no more of the characters than we did before – indeed at times the musical line smudges the divisions between thoughts and conversational steps and makes the stages of the conversation harder to follow. *La Traviata* at least confronted the social issue of the soubrette, *La Bohème* confronts no issues, it turns away as quickly as possible from any of the social or psychological interests of its story and enjoys itself as pure feeling. *Parsifal* is different, not for its mysticism, but for its rationalism, shown in dialogue.

An even more striking example of Wagner's revealing use of dialogue can be observed in *Tannhäuser* – indeed, the example forms the pivotal moment of the opera. The hero has dragged himself away from the day and night erotic activity of the *Venusberg*, fleeing the 'excessive charm' of his lover, Venus. Few partings were more ambiguous and took place amidst more mixed feelings. Tannhäuser reintegrates himself with that 'cold' world of courtly society and claims to have forgotten the forbidden world of his erotic adventures. An 'impenetrable forgetting has fallen between today and yesterday'. Like Walter von Stolzing he finds himself taking part in a singing contest, at which the saintly Elisabeth is the princess and perhaps too the prize. Tannhäuser must – again like Stolzing – sing in a particular style, this time praising courtly love within the strict framework of chivalric rules.[6] But Act 2 Scene 4 reveals how the competition, the interaction, enters his heart and as the contest gets under way his ardor asserts itself and the formal discourse of a prize song starts to slip. When Wolfram praises the 'purest essence' of love, Tannhäuser goes one better and insists on its 'true essence'. When Walter von der Vogelweide (Walter von Stolzing's model for his early songs in the *Meistersinger*) sings that love can be tasted by the heart, not by the senses, Tannhäuser is driven to assert that love should be a pleasure (*Genuss*) – this claim already well surpasses court etiquette and causes affront. Biterolf sneers at this concept of love: compared with that noble impulse which makes him as a knight take up his sword to defend 'a woman's honor and her high virtue', he argues, Tannhäuser's idea is cheap and unworthy. This drives Tannhäuser to proclaim the praise of Venus and to tell Biterolf that, if he wishes to understand love, he should move in with Venus. This provokes outrage, putting an end to Tannhäuser's courtly career – nearly to his life – and to his hopes for Elisabeth.

The one thing Tannhäuser should not have said, he has come out with. The 'impenetrable forgetting' shows itself to have been an illusion, a superficial repression of something he has in no way forgotten. The revelation which brings him down is not triggered by external agency, some souvenir of the *Venusberg* – as we suggested earlier: (Desdemona's handkerchief aside) opera as genre is not very good at the use of forensic devices – but it is the result of a repression re-emerging in conversational interaction.[7] We may consider other features of the scene to have Freudian overtones also, but the return of the repressed is unmistakable, Jensen's *Gradiva* [8] had appealed to Freud precisely because it traced in literary mode

---

[6]   Mary Cicora gives a full account of the medieval practices to which this competition is (rather distantly) related and which Wagner researched in and behind his sources (1999).

[7]   While what I call the 'forensic' contributes to those qualities of novels which cause them to be labeled 'page-turners' (how will the details work out? where did the money come from? etc), psychological tension is no less effective and ultimately no less analytical (will Anna survive with Vronksy? will living with Casaubon destroy Dorothea?). Music can heighten – though hardly analyze – the first, but it can explore, indeed *create*, the second, and that is what Wagner's operas achieve.

[8]   Freud devoted a whole work (including Jensen's text) to *Dreams and Illusions in Wilhelm Jensen's 'Gradiva'* (1907). The story concerns an archeologist who – repressing an early

a case of this phenomenon, and Wagner's scene is constructed on exactly the same principle.[9] The material of the opera may show clearly Wagner's debt to Feuerbach's materialism and sensualism (Tannhäuser's praise of *Genuss* is clear proof of that), but the treatment of sexuality looks forward strongly to psychoanalytical thinking. And this all happens naturalistically: not through the poetic ghostliness of Zoë's appearance as a revenant in Pompeii, but in dialogue. Writing in 1861, shortly after the excitement of the Paris 'failure' of *Tannhäuser*, Baudelaire was clear-sighted enough to see that the essence of Wagner's skill in the opera lies in its dialogue:

> There is beauty in the dialogue, such as we can frequently find in Wagner's dramas, saturated with primitive magic, enlarged with ideal feeling, and whose solemnity does nothing to diminish its natural gracefulness. (1925:227)

What Baudelaire underestimated was the cutting edge of that dialogue, nor – prescient as he often was – did he sense the modern purposes to which Wagner put his devices of revelation: conversation, challenge and answer in language. But – over the noise of cat-calls and booing, and behind the lure of the bordello music – Baudelaire heard the huge importance of that often-neglected element.

Dialogue as a revelation of truth

We have suggested that not all answers to questions are necessarily accurate, that Wagner was a master of the process of teasing out truth by questions, stripping off the layers of ignorance, illusion and deception. Somewhere in Wagner's scenes, like a wise narrator in the novel, someone tells the audience the truth. Nowhere is this more clear than in the second half of *Siegfried* Act 2 Scene 3. Mime – having grudgingly brought up Siegfried, a rather dangerous cuckoo's egg dumped in his nest – has just about reached his goal in life: he has got Siegfried to kill the dragon Fafner (who has been sitting on the Nibelung treasure since killing his brother Fasolt, just after they have been paid for their labors on Valhalla), but all his planning is spoilt when

---

love for a girl in his circle, Zoë – encounters her during her work in Pompeii but takes her for the spirit of someone killed in the eruption. (See below, p.169n).

[9]   It is striking that Graf's work (1911) – which has claims to be the first Freudian account of Wagner's work – is blind to this element. One is tempted to think that the Freudians were so insistent on analyzing the authors that they had no time to consider their actual works – something Freud clearly and generously does in the case of *Gradiva*'s author. (See the following chapter, *passim*).

Alberich turns up and makes clear that Mime will get nothing of the treasure Fafner had been guarding, because Alberich has priority. In the previous scene Mime, thinking of his two enemies, Siegfried and Fafner, had expressed his desire humorously: 'Siegfried, Fafner – I wish they would kill each other': now he is reminded that he has three enemies, not two, and that only one of them is dead. He must make new plans fast.

Siegfried may or may not be the most charming of Wagner's heroes in the *Ring*, but he certainly is not the most clever. What he is good at needs a wise woman to guide him: that need will cause him a bigger problem later, but even here it could lead him into trouble. He hates Mime and says so with dangerous regularity, but Mime is no fool – with enemies like his, he has needed his wits to keep alive this long, and no-one would back Siegfried to outthink him. He plans in a limited and unimaginative way, neither knowing nor risking enough to become clear-headed, like Alberich (with his single lapse of judgment). We have therefore the characteristic situation of so many nineteenth century novels, where two characters interact without possessing between them enough insight (or fair-mindedness) – whether about themselves or about other people (the blindness of egotism is a common theme of the Realist novel) – for the action to be visible to the reader without external assistance.

This is one of those situations where the narrator invariably intervenes, not in order to manipulate the characters, nor to pass judgment on them, but to fill in the details by pointing out what was really meant across the chasms of ignorance and egotism, which are too broad for the characters to communicate across. This narrative input is so important that even Flaubert, for all his celebrated *impassibilité* – his insistence on holding himself out of the narrative – intervenes in that celebrated scene (1856:203f) when, on a starry night just before their planned elopement, Rodolphe and Emma Bovary nearly, but not quite, understand each other and nearly, but not quite, express their feelings. If they did manage either of these, the scene would not be realistic, for neither of them possesses the necessary degree of self-awareness or verbal skill: if they were silent, the poetry and the pathos of the scene would be lost for good, and the narrator has to rescue them. Irony is not just a literary device, it is – as Flaubert himself points out in a well-known letter – a fundamental truth about life, and he wishes his novel to express it. For that reason the narrator insists on showing us behind the clichés which his characters use the basic problem they confront: like all human beings they are caught in the inadequacy of language, even where they touch beauty and search for a language to move the stars, as indeed the stars have moved them, all that they come out with is banality, a tune hardly good enough to make bears dance. This type of authorial intervention is essential to Realist novelists in creating their objective world and in conveying understanding. To be *objective* requires the active involvement of the otherwise seemingly impartial author. These techniques form the basis for those conclusions about people which Wagner missed out on in *Rienzi*, where he failed to base the final judgment on Rienzi (i.e. that he could not love) on any foregoing analysis – we hardly understood how that could be true of him, and were more than a little surprised that Irene had not noticed that feature of her brother before. By the time *Siegfried*, however, Wagner has learned his trade. In Act 2 Scene 3 he uses two devices that clearly follow in the footsteps of the Realist novel's narrator.

The first, unsurprisingly for an opera based in its superficial outline on dragons, dwarfs and the magic *Tarnhelm* which makes the wearer invisible, is the logic of the fairy story, as it were, a magic powder which falls on the characters and makes them – in this case Mime – actually speak the truth. Mime suddenly moves into a discourse in which even Siegfried can see what he is about. It is as if the narrator's voice has been externalized, spoken by the characters themselves, rather than whispered by the narrator alone. 'What I wanted you for', Mime remarks complacently, 'is what you've just done for me. Now all I have to do is get the treasure off you, and that won't be difficult, you're so easy to fool'. A few moments later he gives Siegfried the poison he has had ready for this occasion and explains exactly what he plans to do after Siegfried has drunk it. Siegfried, as if he had been reading the narrator's sub-text, rather than using his ears, re-phrases what he has heard (to rephrase direct speech is another characteristic device of Realist narrators – Flaubert's *style indirecte libre* was one of their most celebrated features and Wagner's text is written on the very edge of this dividing line between direct and reported speech[10]). He asks: 'you mean you're going to murder me?' and he takes the appropriate action. Without the narrative device, Mime and Siegfried might have muddled along together for a while. Perhaps circumstances might have frustrated Mime's murderous plans too, but Wagner wishes to move the plot forward and uses dialogue for that purpose This is clever dialogue, an ingenious inversion of realistic narration, in one sense funny, but actually concerned with the pursuit of truth (as, in fact, good humor invariably is).

Again, as in other scenes Wagner shows himself a master of the pragmatics of dialogue, a skill without which no decent novels would be written, but beyond that skill he shows himself to be, in Freud's phrase, a

---

[10] Žižek extends the comparison to Wagner's general use of *Leitmotiv* (1999:24).

psychopathologist of language, showing how language repairs lapses, hides motivation and yet reveals itself through lapses – often to the discomfiture of the speaker. This device makes the scene even more impressive, and still more clearly shows the subtlety of narration which Wagner aims at, and which he achieves.

For it is not only Siegfried who hears what Mime says and is appalled. Mime too hears himself telling truths he wishes to conceal, and is appalled at himself. 'What am I saying', he exclaims in acute embarrassment, 'I didn't say that, you're misunderstanding me'. 'Open your ears and listen carefully' he admonishes Siegfried, as if he hasn't got the message already; yet shortly afterwards he has to repeat his self-rebuke: 'did I say that?' he asks, more of himself than of Siegfried. He is desperately trying to stop deep truths coming out, only he has lost control of the devices of repression. In other words we are in the world of Freudian slips and of conscious and unconscious utterance: Mime is like Dr Freud's patients telling him that they see their uncle only *in flagranti* (when what they 'meant' to say was *en passant*), or like Freud himself telling a patient that he is pleased to have such a *durable* (i.e. curable) case. We're with Flaubert again, showing his readers what lies behind the banal utterances of his intellectually restricted characters, with Balzac and the extraordinary diminution of language through psychological disorder and passionate excess which he studies in Goriot. Freud writes of his own lapse: 'The speech blunder spoilt the intent and laid bare my dishonesty, in which I acknowledged more than there really was to confess' – well, in Mime's case, it revealed everything there was to confess, and that is why Mime did not live long enough to appreciate the subtlety of Freud's admission.[11] Although the music playfully highlights these excesses, the revelation happens directly, in the language, in the text. It is not hidden, buried in a drama which requires empathy to experience its real action, into which Brechtian alienation would need to be introduced to create that distance without which there is no art. The alienation is there in the basic concept of the scene. Wagner builds his text on seen and unseen levels of truth with the self-understood naturalness of the Realist novelist. The true currency of legend and fairy tale is rationalism, and dialogue its chosen form.

Another scene showing mastery of conversation tactics and pragmatics (a mastery which includes much detailed *observation* – in itself a surprising feature of mock-medieval tales) is the opening of Act 2 of *Lohengrin* between Ortrud and her partner Teleramund. Of course there is a delicious irony in the fact that an opera known for its wedding march contains not

---

[11]   All the examples come from Freud's *Psychopathology of Everyday Life*.

merely the milk and water Elsa (yet another not over-bright bride-to-be), but Ortrud, who certainly fights above her weight and whose showcase scene makes the point that – as so often – the devil has the best lines and sometimes the best music.[12] Teleramund has just been defeated in the contest fought by Lohengrin to defend Elsa's honor, which had been impugned by Teleramund at Ortrud's prompting. Strikingly, the first act has ended neither with the triumph songs of king and retinue, nor with the swooning ecstasies of Elsa – 'take everything I am' she exhorts Lohengrin – but with the defeated parties Ortrud and Teleramund slinking off to regroup. Teleramund has not only been beaten in swordplay, but his life was spared, with the instruction to spend his remaining days in contrition. No wonder he feels humiliated, obsessed with the salvation he thinks he has probably forfeited and the irreparable damage to his social status – who knows in which order. Ortrud – 'experienced in the darkest arts' – responds to the set-back with extraordinary rationality: who is this person who has defeated him? she asks: 'Am I going to give up?' The opening of Act 2 answers that question forcibly.

Teleramund wants to flee and return to the dark woods in which he and Ortrud live. One confrontation is enough and he cannot face another. Ortrud is made of sterner stuff. She wishes to suck the poison out of their situation and put an end to 'our disgrace and their joys'. Teleramund blames Ortrud for everything: of course he does, men do that, Rawley blames Becky Sharp for working in their interest – it's a good way of avoiding responsibility for his own actions. He even blames her for marrying him. More plausibly he blames her for the lie which she told him about Elsa – i.e. that Else was supported by magic and has killed her brother. Who lied? Ortrud demands angrily. Teleramund resorts to his favorite discourse, that of religion. God proves that you lied, he retorts – that's why Lohengrin defeated him. God? Ortrud is not impressed by the argument. How horrible God's name sounds on your lips, ripostes Teleramund, determined to keep his ethical credentials in place. But he has no answer to Ortrud's rejoinder – which Ortrud could have found on almost every page written by Stendhal or Eliot (let alone Nietzsche, but only forty years later): 'Do you call your cowardice God?' This is not just a bull's eye in their argument: it hits the audience too, just as the Realists wanted their readers too to feel uncomfortable at the general truths which the novels played out in front of them and of which their characters' fates were an illustration. It should be as difficult for the audience

---

[12] Certainly the most advanced, harmonically in the case of Ortrud and Teleramund. In a similar way Beckmesser produces technically quite extraordinary musical outbursts as he tries to make sense of the song he has purloined and thus anticipates – as Ernst Bloch (iv,208f) showed – some of the avant-garde music of the twentieth century.

to keep faith with their comfortable hypocrisy as it is for Teleramund. Later in the conversation, as Teleramund again provokes Ortrud's scorn by claiming that he was fighting against 'God's power', Ortrud reveals her plan to confound Lohengrin. There's no magic in this, but an acute psychological intelligence – and a further example of the tendency of the Realist novel to make its beautiful heroines stupid, and only the plain girls smart. 'Sharpen your mind' Ortrud tells him, understand that what in Ortrud herself her husband Teleramund calls sorcery can also be seen in Lohengrin. (This is hardly a great insight, but no-one else in the opera has said so – Ortrud has just asked the question Peter von Matt referred to at the head of this chapter.) Despite the stark contrasts between Ortrud and Teleramund's dark music and the ethereal lightness of Lohengrin, the plot makes clear another truth insisted on in the Realist novel: that good and negative qualities are present in all people. Ortrud's strategy works perfectly, and very soon after this, rather than speaking of God's power, Teleramund is cursing Lohengrin for his 'trickery and magic'. Ortrud's relationship with 'the most secret arts' shows itself to be little more than an ability to hear and speak in the voice of reason. Teleramund has soon been programmed to pursue his revenge on purely rational grounds. The scene ends with an uncanny evocation of the 'sweet joys of revenge' and, as Elsa sleeps in her innocence, the night is given over to *Unheil*, an evil in which Ortrud and Teleramund are united in the closest of harmony. This consensus is not given in their character, for, though they have the capacity for evil, their characters are open, positive moral qualities are mixed in. Living in the nineteenth century, one feels, Ortrud would have run a salon and written novels rather than slumming it in the woods. The consensus they reach is the product of discussion, argument and a conversation expertly handled, both by Ortrud and by Wagner himself.

Myth and Psychology

We have seen so far a double structure: a mythological background and the instrument of reason applied in and through dialogue. In different guises this combination can be seen everywhere in the nineteenth century – it's a matter of taste whether we prefer the non-mythological realist background and the romanticizing dialogue such as we saw in *La Bohème*, or the combination which Wagner arrives at. One way or another Wagner shares with his age both this general ambiguity and the particular combination he arrives at. We go on to consider a final example of this combination, in a scene which grows directly out of the earlier scene involving Brünnhilde, which we examined above: the scene of Brünnhilde's confrontation with her father Wotan at the end of *Walküre* Act 3. She has disobeyed Wotan and tried – in vain – to support Siegmund against Hunding. When Siegmund is killed, Brünnhilde takes Sieglinde and hides her in a forest where Wotan is loath to go. Wotan chases her across the skies in fury – that's the famous *Ride of the Valkyres* – and finally catches up with her.

We have something of a Cordelia-Lear situation: a cherished daughter's refusal to obey a demand of her father which she knows did not come from his true heart. Her claim is to love her father as he truly wishes to be loved, rather than to obey his unnatural command that she should quantify that love and thus destroy its essence. In both situations the daughters' disobedience has immediate consequences.

Disobedience and rebellion is traditionally left to sons, but in this scene Wagner reverses the tradition and gives evidence of an acute sensitivity to women, as well as a remarkably prescient explanation of the nature of father-daughter relationships.[13] The figure of the iron father is well known in nineteenth century literature, from Kleist's imperious Kurfürst, condemning his son to death for disobeying orders in battle (even though his disobedience caused the battle to be won) to Kafka's unbending father in *The Judgment*.[14] Even where they do not have a kingdom to rule, these fathers believe that their son's rebellion threatens the entire political order. Wotan, with the universe to govern, takes the episode much more personally. He faces a favorite daughter, the one to whom exclusively – in his so-called narrative in Act 2 ('Als junger Liebe Lust mir verblich') – he has revealed his innermost fears and weaknesses, but the scene shows up weaknesses he did not know he had. Like the rebellious sons, Brünnhilde and her sisters have been brought up to be 'brave in battle, with hard and strong hearts': Wotan's problems start when Brünnhilde begins to be brave in her relationship with him. Like a parent bringing a child up to be independent – but only as far as he permits – Wotan's strategy is utterly inconsistent. He is forced to admit his attitude of *ownership*: that she was nothing but what he wanted; she was *his* wish, *his* order, *his* protection, and if she rejects that she will be nothing. Brünnhilde's pleading with him is not in the language of sentiment and tears. When her sisters try that tactic with Wotan he dismisses them contemptuously as a 'bunch of soft-hearted women'. Brünnhilde is far tougher, and shapes the

---

[13] This general argument I owe to Germaine Greer in her BBC introduction to Act 3 in their complete showing of the *Ring* some thirty years ago.

[14] Peter von Matt (1995) gives a wide-ranging account of these connections in classical and post-classical literature.

conversation out of her intelligence and deep understanding of how her father sees her. Wotan's opening claim – 'It is not I who punish you, you created your own punishment' – reveals his weakness and lack of certainty in punishing her. And the means of punishment are hardly more intelligently chosen. Brünnhilde will be set out on a hillside for any man to acquire (we recall the mythical tradition of putting out children in this way – Orestes for instance). Wotan seems to have forgotten that his 'great thought'[15] is based on the readiness of man – admittedly, heroes – to restore by their free actions the sanctity of treaties and to solve the gods' problems. He, to say nothing of Wagner himself, with his anthropomorphic view of the evolution of religion, knows that only a link between gods and men can save the world. The Valkyres are stupid in their horror of becoming human, but their obvious stupidity reveals the emptiness of Wotan's threat: he does not believe in it himself. He has not made a good start.

In fact, however, Wotan is not just weak and foolish in dealing with Brünnhilde: he is outright sadistic, poking fun at the husband who will win his daughter's favors (again the sexual element in this is unmistakable: if you won't have me, then think what will happen to you), a husband whom she will obey, as she sits at the spinning wheel 'the butt of jokes and mockery'. The implication is clear: he, Wotan, alone is worthy of his daughter.

Once Brünnhilde gradually regains her confidence and her simpering sisters have been sent away, Wotan's attitudes become clearer still. His 'farewell' (as the last section of Act 3 Scene 3 is often called) reveals the unambiguously erotic nature of his relationship to Brünnhilde. Jealousy as well as sadism dominates his behavior. While he admits that Brünnhilde had understood him – 'I thought you had understood me and I punished that knowing defiance' – it makes him angry to think that her understanding included an insight into his sexual humiliation at the hands of Fricka. While he was indulging in his 'eternal grief in the ruins of my world', Brünnhilde was tasting, albeit vicariously, a draught of human love. This is clear sexual jealousy, and, out of the same motivation as his blustering gives way to a readiness to compromise, Wotan agrees to Brünnhilde's request that she be surrounded by fire so that only the most noble of heroes can possess her, saving his pride by finding a sexual partner for his daughter worthy of her father's love for her. He would humiliate *himself* if he threw her away sexually. So the punishment is fixed, and unsurprisingly all his parting

15 Wotan's 'grosser Gedanke' is mentioned at various times in the *Ring*, most recently in conversation with Brünnhilde. She of all people knows what major designs he has in mind.

memories are erotically charged: riding together, her passing the mead at table, her shining eyes. Like Emma Bovary's dying kiss on the crucifix, the kiss with which Wotan 'kisses divinity from [Brünnhilde]' is anything but a merely ceremonial action (cf. also Žižek 2005:324).

Wagner therefore has taken the myths and done something with them of which any Realist novelist would have been proud. He has not only brought the myths down to earth and domesticated the gods, but has operated through the narrative devices of dialogue and questioning. At the end of the process we have an extraordinary portrait of a nineteenth century father, striving to hold on to his family and his authority. And though many of the trappings of the Realist novel are there – from broken contracts, adulteries and the longing for power – Wagner's scene includes a dimension from which so many realists held back: sexuality. In doing this he anticipated – in a way we look at more closely in the following chapter – the work of Freud and the pioneers of psychoanalysis. One of these - Otto Rank – devoted fifty pages of his study of *The Incest Theme* (1912) to the relationship of father and daughter 'in literature and legend'. So many elements of the myth background are repeated in *Walküre*: the daughter as negotiable property (Wotan, we recall, had initially traded in another female relative – Freia this time – to finance his new castle[16]), the sadism, the sexual jealousy which devises ever harder tests for their daughter's future suitors. Rank's explanation of Wagner's achievement is interesting: he refers equally to the poet's 'intuitive grasp of the tradition represented by the myths' and to an ability to learn from 'the poet's personal complexes' (1912:592).[17] But Wagner's achievement is to have grasped the dominance of sexuality in family relations in a way to which – some forty years later – Freud and his circle would return. Scientific questions lead to scientific answers.

Before examining Wagner's relationship to Freud more fully, we need to discuss the relationship between the physicality of characters in both opera and the novel. This involves a consideration of Wagner's relationship to the body in terms of its language, expressed both in formalized gesture and in the physical being of his characters on stage.

---

[16]   Behavior of this kind appears 'sanctioned' by history. Cleops, as Otto Rank mentions by way of direct analogy, sold his daughters into prostitution to pay for building his pyramid.

[17]   Rank's remark is focused on a diagnosis of sister-brother incest, and the complexes to which he alludes concern not only Wagner's problematic relationship to father-figures but his particularly intense relationships to his four sisters – foremost among them Ottilie and Rosalie.

Bodies on stage and on the page

Gesture in its broadest sense is of central importance to drama and opera – so much so that one might question whether there really is a distinction between formal gesture (such as specified in the stage-directions) and an actor's sustained body-language during the performance. In the novel, even when characters are taking part in a scene, their body is not visible; either another character or the narrator has to draw the physical presence of another character to the reader's attention. As Goffman commented in one of the classic texts of the 1960s: 'Although an individual can stop talking, he cannot stop communicating through body idiom'.[18] When a narrator fills in this 'body idiom', however, the body is much more dependent on the readers' imagination and more absolute than is possible in opera and drama. Short of filming the text, no-one can alter the author's data. But for the overwhelming proportion of the time bodies remain unseen. In drama the opposite is true, with the result that stage bodies are at the mercy of the actor/singer/producer and, while they are the abiding impression of a theatrical evening, bodies in drama and opera are paradoxically hard to analyze without reference to specific performances. This is especially so when we recall Freytag's account of the appeal of the theatre to the young writer in the mid-nineteenth century, for this clearly involved a physical appeal, the bodily sensation of presenting one's ideas in corporeal form, including ultimately the accolade of the author being pulled in front of the curtain to be surrounded by the physical presence of the characters one has created and to be applauded in person. In comparison to that experience, whether or not the novel or the drama is the road to fame, the creator of prose seems to work in a more ethereal medium. His bodies may be absolute, but they are far less tangible.

In practice the gesture in drama or opera seems to exist outside the story, as a physical dimension which can be added to any text and which with scenery and lighting can, within the ensemble of a production, create a major element in audience response. The dismay of recent Metropolitan Opera audiences at the replacement of Zefferelli's production of *Tosca* – not a note has changed in the score – makes the point eloquently.[19] Apart from affecting

---

[18]   *Behavior in Public Places* (1963:35). Goffman's insights drove the sociologists in Malcolm Bradbury's *History Man* – which mediated those insights to one generation of general readers. Over recent years, however, Pierre Bourdieu has become more prominent on the question of body-language, in part because of the wider historical range of his studies.

[19]   For different reasons, the continuation of the 1984 production of *Tosca* by the Staatsoper in Berlin makes an extraordinary effect, for the present-day audience cannot escape the sense of how the action stands in the light of the practices of the East German secret police. The

our immediate experience of a piece, gesture and the style it reflects offer a significant key to theatrical history. The importance of Naturalism at the end of the nineteenth century, for instance, makes full sense only if we recall that its style was imposed on the theatre's whole repertoire. It was the time of *Midsummer Night's Dream* with rabbits on the stage, under the motto: dream about anything, but leave the theatrical devices naturalistic.[20] This makes generalizations about Wagner's use of gesture problematic, and while I am suggesting arguments here I must refer gratefully and continuously to Carnegy's fine history of the staging of Wagner's oeuvre (2006) for more detailed guidance.

Historical style is only a small part of the argument. Cosima's efforts to make the Bayreuth style (which included acting gestures) obligatory for all Wagner productions was not only foolish (for Wagner himself was anything but happy with those productions), but they threatened to condemn the work itself to anachronism – as indeed had already begun to happen until the revivals during the Weimar Republic and in the 1970s under Wieland Wagner. But gesture is more than the clothes horse of changing historical fashion: it is also a pivotal aspect of the communication between text and audience, reflected in the actors' own view of the part which they are playing. In Wagner we think of the classic *Lohengrin* joke – when there is a mechanical breakdown in the swan, the actor turns to the audience and asks what time the next swan leaves – but the anecdote wrongly suggests in Wagner an unusually unsophisticated anxiety to preserve (on one level) the theatrical illusion of reality. In so many other scenes, as we have seen, there is a multiplicity of perspectives *within* the action: illusion is broken deliberately. In other words, to consider gesture within opera presupposes both an awareness of theatrical history and a set of fundamental assumptions about theatrical representation.

The importance which Wagner attached to gesture was evident from the start of his writing, as a study of the sketches and drafts for *Rienzi* make clear (Deathridge 1977:16). Even much later in his career, critics regarded

---

body language of the Stasi and its victims were so well-known that the secret policeman Scarpia seems naïve (in other ways it makes him seem *sophisticated!*). (Cf. reactions to the film *Das Leben der Anderen*). Such questions hardly separate from the experience of the opera itself. Carnegy gives an amusing account of audience reactions to the production of the *Der fliegende Holländer* in the Kroll opera in 1929, and in particular the negative response to two physical features: the Dutchman did not have a beard, Senta wore a pullover! (2006:256).

[20] Ludwig of Bavaria made his grooms perform elaborate equestrian feats in his private performances of the *Ride of the Valkyres*: such was the theatrical literal-mindedness of a believer in Divine Right of kings.

Wagner's attitude as unusual and excessive. One Viennese review complained of 'the multitude of nuances he wants to be conveyed, almost every step, every movement of a hand, every opening door is "musically illustrated"' (quoted Carnegy 2006:62). Wagner's own writings on gesture are found in his theoretical texts, such as *Opera and Drama,* also in the more practical language of his various autobiographical writings, as he comments on his own theatrical experiences, and finally in the considerable detail with which he identifies gestures in his libretti. Given that he could not control the physical appearance of his singers,[21] Wagner really did set out to establish his actors' movements and gestures. Hofmannsthal, as we saw, correctly recognized Wagner's commitment to this aspect of opera, and we shall need to return to his aspiration that '[...] the music must literally force the singer into good and correct acting, as Wagner so beautifully succeeds in doing'.[22] To recognize this skill, despite a historically changing theatrical practice which certainly will not have always made it visible in performances, suggests the centrality of these ideas in Wagner's oeuvre. And the idea of music 'forcing' the singer to act well is not only at times attractively utopian, but it's always highly intangible, since gesture cannot be expressed in language:

> The gesture of the body, articulated so as to show in the significant movement of the most expressive limbs and of the facial expression an inner feeling, is something inexpressible, in that language can only describe it and interpret it and only the limbs or facial features can actually express it. (*Opera and Drama,* iv,174)

Wagner's further comments on gesture in *Opera and Drama* fall into two categories, both of which are capable effortlessly of creating confusion in the reader. A consistent element is Wagner's awareness of the historical context of theatre practice, which in *Opera and Drama* focuses particularly on Shakespearean theatre. Wagner's comments here resemble his account of history and the novel (*Roman*) which we looked at in the previous chapter, in being both dogmatic and arbitrary, the arguments arbitrary and interchangeable. Shakespeare is merely wheeled out as a name to add weight

---

[21]   This was something of which Wagner was constantly aware. The casting of Wilhelmine Schröder-Devrient as Adriano in the premiere of *Rienzi* – indeed the part was conceived as an alto for that reason – was a case in point. Wagner's huge admiration for her – which began when he experienced her Leonora in *Fidelio* in 1829 – based on her ability *to communicate the text.* By 1842 (when she was only 37) her suitability for Adriano was not reflected in her appearance.

[22]   David Lewin builds an interesting argument concerning the gestic quality of operatic music, from Mozart onwards, and its ability to offer 'cues for actors' (1992).

to the case Wagner is trying to make – any familiarity with Shakespeare's plays is of little help to the reader. The more important discussions concern the basal relationship in stage performance between hearing and seeing, hearing music and hearing text and seeing gesture. The extensive passage which I quote below requires an unreasonable effort from the reader, but in fairness to Wagner we should point out that its high level of abstraction is constantly redeemed by Wagner's obvious concern for something entirely pragmatic: that interdependence of the separate elements of opera if the production is to succeed as a whole. Such concerns are common to any artist who wishes to see a work adequately realized on the stage: the music and singing expressive, the scenery stable, costumes acceptable and the acting passable. If such an artist were to theorize about this very natural feeling it might come out as follows:

As a message directed necessarily to the eye, gesture expressed what word-language could not express – indeed, where word-language could do that, gesture became superfluous and distracting. The eye was excited by gesture in a way which was not matched by a balancing message to the ear. But such a balance is essential if the impression is going to become entirely understandable to the audience's feeling. Poetic verse, which had been intensified to the point of becoming melody, converted the rational content of the original message into feeling, but this melody did not yet contain the element of communication to the ear which perfectly matched the gesture. But – to the extent that it was an *intensification* of verbal language – melody contained the *reason for wanting* the gesture itself to be intensified, and the melody *needed* that strengthening element, because it lacked the perfect equivalent of that strengthening which creates gesture. Verse melody therefore contained only a need for *formation* of the gesture: i.e., the justification of gesture in terms of feeling – in the same way that the verse language was justified by the melody, or the melody by harmony: or rather, they are *clarified* – such clarification is beyond the capacity of the melody, which proceeded from the verse-*language* and remains orientated, indeed tied to word-language through an essential part of its being (*Körper*). Word-language cannot express the special quality of gesture, so the melody called on gesture for assistance in order to communicate to the ear, for the ear is anxious for an equivalent in its own domain. The element of gesture, which is inexpressible in the word-music language, can however be communicated to the ear by the language of the orchestra – a language totally abstracted from all word-based language, and this communication corresponds to the message which gesture gives to the eye. (iv,175/76)

You need an ice-pack on the head to read this kind of passage. Its horrible paratactic structure (which I have tried to relax a little in the translation) is like the small print on guarantees, where the reader is always unsure whether they have the right referent for the relative pronouns or the right sequence of conditions. The reader is tempted to follow the instructions with which Brecht prefaced one of his early plays: don't worry about the details, fix your eyes on the finishing-line. For the finishing-line of Wagner's text is clear enough. He is not interested in a use of a gesture which merely illustrates the voice-melody and with it the written text. Antithesis (as in 'To be or not to be', for instance) should be articulated *within* the melody, rather than outside. i.e. in gesture. Yet, conversely, he is not interested in gesture without musical equivalence, gesture stuck on, so to speak, as decoration: he thus gives the orchestra the double function of bearing the voice-melody *and* filling out the stage gesture. Gesture is clearly shown to be a separate communicative system, corresponding to the physicality of the stage. Theories of the *Gesamtkunstwerk* are always thought of as synthesizing elements: we need sometimes to remember that Wagner also emphasizes the separateness of these elements. In an amusing passage in *Opera and Drama* he ridicules the idea 'that for instance in an art-gallery, surrounded by statues, someone should be reading a Goethe novel out loud while a Beethoven symphony is being played' (iv,3f) yet his arguments here have an entirely practical background. Wagner is outlining the interconnection between the elements of opera, in the name of envisaging the harmony which they will achieve in performance. What does it say of wider relevance to our search, and how can those remarks map onto prose?

Striking here – in everything but the *style* in which he himself writes – is Wagner's concern with communication. All the arguments of *Opera and Drama*, and not just those on gesture, are concerned with communication. Other potential elements of art, such as self-expression or the autonomous beauty of the art work, receive no mention.[23] Art-works are not there to *be*, they are there to communicate. The ambiguity lies in what is being communicated, and even in the passage above there is a potential conflict between feeling and clarity as the content of communication. Whereas it is possible to think of communicating clarity *about* feeling (we look in the next chapter at the way in which literary and scientific psychology can perform that task), it does seem that Wagner thinks of feeling as something experienced through empathy – which would make the gesture an invitation to the audience to identify with the individual character – this we saw in Mimi and Rodolfo. Yet at the same time Wagner makes clear – and his later comparisons with the gestures of wordless acting, such as pantomime, underline the point – that gesture is a collective, social language rather than a key to individual feeling. He shares the insights of the novelists on socially

[23] Adorno – in an underplayed part of his argument – points out that the psychological insights of Wagner's operas (which he does not rate as being particularly profound or fully developed) are diametrically removed from inwardness, being acted out and shown on stage. This is exactly my point here: Wagner's use of gesture is the opposite of the inwardness which Brecht so disliked – and ultimately Adorno even admits that (xiii,112).

conditioned body-language. Not even in the communication of feeling does Wagner think like a soap opera. His realism in the theatre is to be based on stylization of gesture rooted in an observation of 'the social nature of man', not on the copying of the everyday – he is in that sense, like Brecht, clearly an opponent of Stanislawski's Method. Wagner writes:

> Gesture, as befits the character of drama, is not simply a monologue, the body language of a single individual. Gesture is, so to speak, multiple and polyphonic, distilled from the typical and significant meetings of many people. (*Opera and Drama*, iv,178)

Even when he is speaking of feeling, therefore, Wagner contextualizes to the generality. To convey feeling it is not just to be emphasized and intensified in a private world into which the audience is invited. It is to be made clear in the process of being displayed, objectified in cooperation with the social observations of the audience. It is not a series of fossilized and dusty poses carried through by actors in search of self-glorification.

What is interesting, finally, in Wagner's rather obscure account of the interrelation of gesture with other aspects of opera, is that he holds on to the idea of language as rational. Not only that, but even the musical language which supports and intensifies the text is thought of as rational. That's part of what Gregor-Dellin meant by the 'intelligence' of Wagner's music (cf. Introduction). It's for that reason that the melody accompanying the voice is deemed to be as incapable of expressing gesture as the word-language itself. An irrational view of language would have easily bridged that gap – irrational language can do anything, even express gesture. Wagner does not argue for the non-rationality of all aspects of his music, indeed he does the contrary, and even the orchestra is involved in the business of showing and explaining. We stress throughout the book the function of the orchestra as commentator and elucidator of the action. We note here that it takes over another rational function: the task of making gesture more fully communicative.

If we have managed to show the closeness of Wagner to a rational practice, we have now briefly to map out these practices on the writing of fiction.

Literary Realism began in an age (or at least a literary climate) which professed to like the body. While German classicism had devoted its attention to spiritual beauty, the *schöne Seelen*, who – as Kipling commented about the anti-corporeal attitudes of a later Aesthetic generation – 'moo and coddle about their precious souls', the Realists arrived as materialists, to whom the body was both real and important. This was marked in the characteristic style of the physiognomic studies around which early *feuilleton* writers built their portraits of the life of the city. They portrayed the household figures and the trades-people, locating them geographically within the city and also locating within their appearance the marks of the city and of their particular trade. Balzac's short piece *The Grocer* (1840) – together with its accompanying engraving (by Gavarni[24]) – captures what is perhaps the most significant feature of these pieces: the body language of the grocer, in which is expressed not only the physical conditions of his work, which mark his body and determine his gestures, but the class relations of the society as a whole shown in the servility which it imposes on him. So the portraits create not one grocer, but the essence of all grocers, as Wagner remarked 'distilled from the typical and significant meetings of many people'. The observation is of what Bourdieu calls *Habitus*. Studies of this kind, from major and lesser-known writers, ranged across portraits of all levels of society (for instance it's interesting to note how the early portraits of the stock market in Berlin created the physical type of the stock-jobber from the stereotyped *physiology* of the gambler: an idea not without contemporary relevance[25]). By the time phrenology had become fashionable – and its still more disagreeable associate, racism[26] – the corporeality of writing was both universal and verging on the inhuman. The paradox is illustrated in one of the high points of the trend: Sherlock Holmes – true successor of Balzac, who wrote with the bones on which the great anatomist Cuvier conducted his investigations in front of him. Holmes' greatest skill is that forensic look which deduces everything (job, residence, past history, moral condition) about a visitor from physical appearance. Few better examples could be found of Adorno and Horkheimer's (1944) vision of Enlightenment as liberation turned into *tyranny* and totalitarian control.

For all this, the body is rather absent from nineteenth century Realism. The principal characters tend to live cerebrally, each one a separate consciousness moving among other bodies but hardly inhabiting their own. Because so much of their action takes place within society – that was their

---

[24]   Gavarni was the working name of perhaps the best known of the illustrators, Sulpice Hippolyte Guillaume Chevalier (1804-66). The practice was widespread in England and Germany also, where Bulwer Lytton's significance for German writers first emerged. This topic is covered in its European ramifications in Martina Lauster's exciting study (2007).

[25]   Apart from being right about so many aspects of capitalism, Marx's striking achievement in *Capital* was to physicalize money and its behavior. He was – like so many others, including of course Wagner – intelligently moving on from the common positions and metaphors of his period. The issue of what ideological baggage Wagner brings with him as part of these common positions is brilliantly identified by Žižek (2005:318f).

[26]   A racism practiced not just towards the peoples of what we now call the Third World, but very active in the classification of Europeans according to their 'ethnic' origins: Celtic, Germanic etc. – and Jewish too. Beddoes *The Races of Britain* (1862) offers a case in point.

conscious program, after all – the Realist novelists portray the body masked by more than seven veils of convention, and glimpses of stocking are all too rare. And the gestures which mark their principal characters are correspondingly bounded, despite their powers of observation. For of course no-one imagines that Balzac actually wrote novels about the grocer subjects of his 'physiological' sketches, any more than Victor Hugo would have written about an ordinary court jester. In their art, both looked for tragic greatness in their figures – that greatness was the poets' reward for their strenuous journey into the social underworld. Ordinary grocers line the streets down which Balzac's heroes pass on their more important business, but it takes the sort of massive intensification which Flaubert brought to Yonville's dreadful pharmacist Homais for him to feature at all in the *dramatis personae* of the novel. And the caricature elements are so strong that Homais gives up his physicality almost completely. Physicality is focused in the bungled operation Charles carries out on Hippolyte's club foot. Seldom indeed does the physical presence of Realist characters stick in the mind, except perhaps with a sense of regret: regret that the charms which Lydgate (whose 'spots' are on his character, rather than on his complexion) perceived in Rosamund were so shallow, or that Tony Buddenbrook's beauty fades so quickly into coarseness. Only Tolstoy seems to break the mould, and many readers of *Anna Karenina* remember not only the aching muscles after Levin has spent hours working in the fields but the magnificence of Anna's white shoulders above her ball gown. These are bodies we can inhabit as well as desire, but they are exceptions.

In trying to line up opera and novel in the use of gesture, we shall not be helped by further impressionistic, generalized surveys of the Realist fiction. They would do no more than reinforce the observation that opera is much more physical, more body-centered, than the novel. Wagner might hide the physicality of the orchestra under the Bayreuth stage, but the physicality of singers' production of the notes can never be hidden, even by radio and CDs. And while the observation is true, it has nothing to say of the distinctiveness of Wagner's work. The actual composing of an opera is no more physical than the writing of a novel. Wagner's love for Senta can be no more central to creating her music than Tolstoy's often remarked on love for Anna dictated the text of his novel, and the real corporeality of opera-work – pushing people around on stage, teaching singers how to show off their bodies – is as vicarious in this medium as for prose writers whose manipulated figures are merely on paper. It would be a mammoth and unrewarding task to give a taxonomy of bodily gesture in Realist fiction: that would be hard enough even on the basis of *filmed* Realist classics – Garbo's

Anna, Hanna Schygulla's Effi Briest –, where the director has already made a selection from the printed text. But since I want to suggest how Wagner's compositions can be mapped onto the novel and that what he does on stage is entirely conceivable within the covers of a novel, we shall take a sample of 'gestures' from the first hundred pages of *Madame Bovary* and, I hope, see their striking affinity to Wagner's practices. I pick Flaubert because his Realist practice is embedded in aestheticism, whereas often for Balzac those practices are embedded in a range of Romantic gestures. Of course we would find affinities there too, but they would merely confirm an existing picture of Wagner and contain no surprises.

Charles Bovary first meets Emma Roualt in the house of her father (a farmer-patient). Charles observes the whiteness of her nails standing out against the rather coarse, work-a-day hands: the bold candor of her eyes, 'eyes that came to meet yours openly'. He observes her rich hair, with the whiteness of her ears just visible through it. These are observations conducted by the character, but Flaubert has some gestures of his own: 'she shivered as she ate, revealing something of her full lips, which she had a habit of biting in her silent moments'. Flaubert has sensitized his readers to her postures by explaining those which she has consciously practiced, after she has discovered them in the cheap fiction she reads: a way of kneeling at confession, lying on a sofa with an open letter beside her, and these postures are well established as moments of self-stylizing. But a recurring posture which only Flaubert sees and which shows the erotic and its place in her *vie intérieure* is more directly – if still metaphorically – suggested. Emma's nervous sensuality is summarized in an image which opposes her white skin with the world of passion indicated in moisture and drops. On an early meeting with Charles Emma puts up her parasol as protection against the water dropping from the melting ice on the roof (this image is in Turgenev territory: passion melts the snow) and 'smiles in the moist warmth beneath it', listening to the drops of water on the taut silk. Later as she sits between the hearth and the window – between domestic security and the lure of the world – 'little drops of perspiration stood on her bare shoulders'. At the ball she is at her dressing-table beneath a picture of a rose on a fragile stem on the tips of whose leaves dewdrops tremble, and after the ball – as she looks out of the window into the night – drops of moisture form on her eyelids. It took a Nietzsche – because he hated the novel, and never managed to separate the art of a novel from a plot which he reads with extraordinary literal-mindedness (an error he repeats in his ludicrous judgment on *Parsifal)* – to describe Wagner's heroines as 'spitting images of Emma Bovary' and to mean that as an insult (vi,3:28).

As we read these pages we marvel at Flaubert's artistry, his gentleness of touch, the minuteness of the devices, the consistency with which he builds his effects. The depth of Emma's eyes, the carelessness of her dressing-gown – all these will culminate in scenes of shocking carnality. But they are very small physical details, static not only in the sense of an action frozen in immobility, but even more strikingly because there is no action; even in the postures of her literature-inspired dreams action is at a minimum, the transitive action (reading a letter) is replaced by *lying* with the *already opened* letter beside her. The absence of transitive verbs de-corporealizes the narrative. It's Charles who has a body: it is his legs which ache after the ball and he who falls asleep in the chair, his hair inelegantly disordered; it is Charles who feels sick smoking the cigar he picked up on the aristocrats' estate. It is the aristocrats who are characterized by socially indicative gestures, their faces showing 'the complexion of wealth', their 'nonchalant glances reflecting the quietude of passions daily gratified', behind it a 'brutality inculcated by dominance in not over-exacting activities'. Flaubert knows what Balzac can do with gesture, and – explicitly referring to Balzac in the text – quietly shows that he can do it just as well, that he observes *Habitus* no less precisely than his great predecessor, but Flaubert's artistic heart lies elsewhere. He too was a 'miniaturist'.

It's easy to see why these gestures cannot be directly reproduced in opera. For all their passionate inwardness their detail and externality has a kind of forensic quality which dramatic action cannot copy (though TV and film can). They are not verbalized by the characters. Also they fall in moments for which drama has no time: their static quality is not to negate time, but to represent huge and repeated chunks of it, stretches when nothing happens – Mann refers to it as *Ewigkeitssuppe* ('the soup of eternity') in the *Magic Mountain*. These are the times as Emma waits for Charles to respond to her readiness for passion, as she regrets seductions which have not taken place. Such time can and does, however, exist in opera – the repetition of sexual conquest in *Rigoletto*, the sense of a suddenly arrived at old age in *Rosenkavalier*, the endless evenings Siegmund had *not* arrived at Hunding's residence, the glimpse of passing time which suddenly, when Freia's apples have gone, leaves marks on the gods themselves – and it is this which Wagner puts into his gestures.

For this reason it is striking to note how strongly Wagner's use of gestures overlaps with Flaubert's. Both artists have big actions, yet gesture is so often reserved for the small. We know how much importance Wagner, when rehearsing, attached to gesture and body language, insisting on his actor/singers and the production team attending a read-through of the opera before any rehearsal,[27] noting the stage directions above all. Nowhere is this better shown than in the opening scene of *Meistersinger*. The elaborate stage directions here are doing two things: they describe the Katharinenkirche in Nuremberg and put the characters into position. More importantly they also give a series of explicit instructions to the actors playing Walter and Eva. In at least nine stages their eyes are to conduct a passionate dialogue of set gestures. Walter, 'at the side, leaning on a pillar', his gaze fixed on Eva, who repeatedly – in a 'dumb play of gestures' – turns round to face him from her seat at the front of the church. The type of look is explicitly spelled out, ranging from 'longing, shame-faced, tender, insistent, shy' to 'soulful'. The historical form of these looks will change with the generations, but the separation of gesture from text is unchanging. The word-language of the scene is magnificently large-scale and unambiguous, consisting of the hymn for St John the Baptist's Day, and it is accompanied by the word-melody, a stunning chorale. There is, however, in addition an unmissable but smaller orchestral voice, which overlays the chorale, sinuously and sensuously tracing the fervor of the looks Walter and Eva silently exchange. Yes, the gestures are in quick succession; what Flaubert needs fifty pages for[28] Wagner must compress into seconds, just as Walter's first visit to Pogner's house (to which Magdalene refers later in the scene) is not allowed to hold up the action, in contrast to Charles' first visit to his future father-in-law which takes up several pages of the novel. But in fact all of the gestures, poses, wordless stances, are inactive. They are looks, which become part of the text, but only due to the effort of the composer who drives them to ever greater intensity. The scene illustrates *exactly* what Wagner so cumbersomely explained in the long theoretical passage we quoted above. It combines musical richness with detail, and behind it is a patience in analyzing the stages of burgeoning love (what happens after the first look 'across a crowded room', and *how*) which amounts to a testimony to Wagner's belief in the importance of observation and *clarity* in portraying feeling through gesture. Wagner is one of the few artists who would have understood the

---

[27]   This procedure may sound routine: we should not forget the incredibly short time allocated for rehearsals both by commercial and by court theatres in the mid-nineteenth century. Wagner's insistence was far from corresponding to the cost-efficiency required of him by his paymasters, instead it reflected his deepest aesthetic principles.

[28]   The category of length is too often ignored in discussions of Realist fiction. Thomas Mann insisting to his publisher that the length of his *Buddenbrooks* manuscript is the whole point (i.e. because it allows processes to be traced slowly, across time) articulates a protest against the acceleration of perception in his day. Wagner's skill at retardation, at dissolving the headlong rush of events, is part of the secret inventory of the clever Realist novelist.

immense attention which Brecht paid to rehearsing the separate phases of a stage action – we think of the famous scene in the *Caucasian Chalk Circle* in which Gruscha knocks on a peasant's door to ask for milk. How many layers Brecht found in the simple action of opening the door, how much he focused on process rather than effect, and how this obsessive care over gesture was directed by the awareness that it is gesture which links fictional action into real society – Wagner understood all that well.

The opening of *Meistersinger* shows the wonderful integration of disparate elements which Wagner achieves. Anyone who can write that would be excused for writing the lines we quoted from *Opera and Drama* – in fact, we suspect, it is only the one which makes the other possible. But this level of integration makes it necessary to come back to an element of Wagner's realism: the often made assumption that Wagner is *really* writing program music,[29] and that his skill as a Realist (often in the *Leitmotive* too) is to be equated with *Tonmalerei*, with sound-painting. Giants walking heavily on their proletarian feet will get a plodding motif, thunder a crash-bang, and the oppressed masses of Nibelheim will bang their hammers in a distinctive, rhythmic way, as in a documentary on the early Industrial Revolution. It would be silly to deny that the misunderstanding is true up to a point. Wagner's Realism would not allow the music for St John the Baptist's Day to be the *Venusberg* music, or permit Lohengrin – even on a defective mechanical swan – to enter to the music of Nibelheim. But the program is neither the Realism nor the story, any more than St John the Baptist had anything to do with Eva and Walter's romance. We can show the difference between the two levels with the example of the re-entry of the Giants in *Rheingold*. Fasolt and Fafner return to Valhalla to collect the gold for which they are prepared to exchange Freia, their hostage. Their heavy walk is marked by brass, lower strings and percussion. This is the program, the story. But within that music, now shifted to wind and upper strings, is Fasolt's *gesture*: standing and *looking* as he thinks of the miraculous apples and the vision of youth and beauty which they open up and which he is going to lose. His gesture (which is quite different from his action, and indeed *suspends* it) is to *look*, and outside the word-melody the orchestra points up the significance of that gesture. In narrative terms the gesture is rendered meaningless by Fasolt's immediate death (which comes not from the gesture of utopian longing, but from greed), and that gesture is beautifully and

---

[29] See above, p.113f. Hapke (1927) feels that program music is the form in which Wagner's musical achievements have been (incorrectly) appreciated and built on in his day. (He is obviously thinking of Strauss' tone-poems.)

discretely identified by the orchestra, just as it was Flaubert who showed us Emma's most revealing gestures.[30]

So, for all the physicality of his world, Wagner uses gesture to create great delicacy and nuance. In the same way Flaubert holds back the physicality of his rural world and lets the too too solid flesh melt. Both Wagner and Flaubert had problems achieving these effects within their chosen genre – the reluctance and inability of characters to say what they feel is a problem in both genres; moreover their audience was constantly determined to miss the point and to read *Madame Bovary* as obscene or to identify themselves only with the big moments, specifically overlooking the ironic hollowness of the gods' entry to Valhalla just because they were impressed by the dignified tune.[31] In these ways audiences risk blotting out the subtleties of interaction and the precise language with which character is explored. But Wagner and Flaubert could have authored the other's work, and within their different genres their techniques showed great similarities.

The whole discussion of gestures, rational dialogue and the physical belongs, finally – although that is far from the intention of my basic argument –, to the contentious debate which has raged about musical development in Wagner ever since Hanslick's criticism of *Rienzi*. Hanslick argued that Wagner had used plot to solve what were in fact purely musical issues of musical development,[32] thus he had not respected the primacy of music over

---

[30] Both the example and its interpretation come from Hapke, who shows that this different voice can be articulated by a range of musical means: melodic and rhythmic, dynamic and harmonic, and also by shifts of orchestral color. From the point of view of tonality, Laing analyzes the moment as an 'extreme harmonic clash' – i.e. these are the consequences of the music resolving a double perspective on events (1973:222).

[31] Thomas Mann's *Death in Venice* suffered a similar fate, when his readers repeatedly failed to recognize the ironic deflation of Aschenbach's pomposity aimed at in Mann's style. They thought of the work as an uncritical homage to a great writer, and if readers failed to like the story they blamed *the author* for pomposity.

[32] We should explain this briefly. In the forms of music tending to prescription – we need think no further than the sonata or symphony – the form dictates not merely the horizontal extension of the music (i.e. the number of themes, their repetition and sequencing) but also its harmonic modulations, the hierarchy of related keys. Musical convention made specific demands, and the genius of the composer was to work creatively within these formal requirements. The more symphonic opera became – that is to say: the less it subdivided into musically distinct sections and the more it flowed throughout the whole story, with themes recurring during its whole length, even to the extent of the *Leitmotive* – the more the question of musical development is raised, in a form which the 'number opera' did not pose. This is a question concerning both melodic extension – program music uses the story to determine the sequence of its themes: as we suggested, a Berlioz could happily have coped with Adrian's plague journey within a radically differently weighted plot – and matters of harmonics, i.a. those shifts of key for which musicologists still search for *musical*

theatre, of the eternally beautiful over the cheap effect. The argument has haunted Wagner studies ever since. If plot leads the music, it is said, then it cannot be 'proper' music. A comparison of Wagner and the novel will neither resolve the issue nor in fact is it hoping to make *any* contribution to the debate. But there is common ground, one which has been illuminated at various moments of Wagner's reception – notably as part of the East German revivals of his works – and by the resulting focus on the inherent rhetoric common to both musical and literary texts. In particular this has shown itself in the wider use of the Brechtian concept of *Gestus*, i.e. the rhetorical trope of a type of showing based on objective observation (such as the portraits of the grocer), which, among other critics, Lawrence Kramer identifies as a salient feature of both music and poetry (1984:8), thus shifting the political focus of Brecht's idea and allowing its proximity to Wagner to appear. For Wagner's opponents there is no debate possible on this ground. For them Wagner's music merely 'serves up' and 'intensifies' the false and kitschy sentiments and gestures of bourgeois life.[33] In doing so they sweep aside his own insistence on the action of clarification. On the other hand, too many Wagnerians do not see the need (or the value) to identify this gestic feature of Wagner's work, often because they enjoy what Brecht derisively called the 'culinary' effects too much. The gestic has no conceivable place within Schopenhauerian aesthetics, and it is not often spotted, unless a critic sets clearly adversarial ideological targets or works with some principled suspicion of the artist, such as that which lies behind our default-setting hypothesis. Yet Wagner's operas depend on the balance between a dynamically developing word-language plot and the profound insights into

---

explanation in the *Ring* (cf. Laing 1973). Writing opera not only makes demands on the coherence of the drama within its own terms (i.e. for all the force of the music, if Rienzi has no *motive* for his ambition, then the whole works fails), opera also makes similar demands on the cohesion of the music, and the plot's logical and motivated progression cannot merely drag the music behind it, like a tin can behind a honeymoon couple's car. Even before Wagner's elaboration of the complex interactions of music and drama, word and note, acting and singing – there is no evidence that his ideas were fully developed as he worked on *Rienzi* – setting a drama text to music stretched the possibilities of both media and set up, for critics at least, the clash between 'a self-sufficient music logic' and 'an intrusive, text-generated gesture' (Abbate and Parker 1989:6).

[33] A classic text (from which I am quoting here) is found in Brecht's notes on the opera which he wrote with Kurt Weill, *Mahagonny*. While there's no doubt that these notes – like the opera itself – are conceived in direct opposition to Wagner (though the opera itself seems to refer more to *Fidelio*, certainly in its ending), it is not clear that Brecht and Weill either were (or wanted to be) fair to Wagner. Their relationship is, however, rather deeper than the notes imply. On the East German Wagner revivals – which touched more than once very relevantly on these ideas – see Carnegy (2006:310-353).

human behavior which are more central to its purpose than wondering how Emma Bovary (or Wotan) pay their bills. They are built on the orchestral voice which darts around in between the plot and shows itself both in commenting on the meaning of the text which it accompanies and highlighting the world of gestures. Such a balance is exactly parallel to the situation in prose fiction. It is reasonable to claim for Wagner that Flaubert could have written his works, and *vice versa*. And rather than justify this claim with further argument I'll simply point to the counter-moment in Flaubert's other principal work, his *Éducation Sentimentale*.

Packed full of action and plot, development, revolutions and *coups d'état*, love, ambition, rise and fall, and disappointment, the novel ends with the hollowest of gestures. In the final scene *Éducation Sentimentale* winds down into a non-action: the memory of the heroes' failure to go into the brothel when younger, the best thing they never did. Perhaps Wagner's deepest affinity to Realism can be seen in this mixture of negation and depiction, in the relationship between the determination to understand active life and the detached observation of states of a *vie intérieure*. It little matters whether we blame Schopenhauer for the artists' detachment and negation and therefore find justification in a set of aesthetic ideas, or whether, as Adorno does, we choose to see this passivity towards the world outside as the price to be paid for any nineteenth century artist's success in capitalist society – the deep affinity is there. Wagner shares with the Realists not merely the confidence that a skilled and humane middle-class will take over from the corrupt aristocracy: we saw that message in the *Meistersinger* and in much of the *Ring*, He is, however, still more perfectly in tune with the Realist novel of despair and disillusion. Adorno highlights the paradox which arises when an artist, whose Realism has been over-dependent on some of the more common clichés of nineteenth century bourgeois society, turns against that society and negates those features on which his work had been constructed. The paradox leads him to one of his most gnomic expressions of praise for Wagner (*all* Adorno's expressions of praise for Wagner are gnomic[34]):

---

[34]   The ambiguity and obscurity comes from Adorno's extreme difficulty in coming to terms with 'the bourgeois heritage'. One may critique Wagner for sharing so many of the features of his age (and our comparison with Realism has the effect of highlighting that shared heritage), but where else does the critic live, where is the fulcrum which lies outside that heritage? My favorite among Adorno's words of praise for Wagner shows that dilemma exactly. Speaking of 'that moment at the start of *Tristan* Act 3 when the horn in the orchestra echoes – across the frontier between something and nothing – the sad melody of the shepherd' Adorno claims: 'that moment will live on for as long as human beings are able to understand the basic experiences of the age of the bourgeoisie' (xiii,140). The remark seems almost to express the hope that those experiences will *always* be understood.

If Wagner's music sets out – within the depravedly allegorical storehouse of motifs and themes – to decipher the message of nothingness, then *his* vision of nothingness – in its contrast to the nihilism of his age – works like a utopia. (xiii,142)[35]

Few words could more effectively summarize the last scene of *Éducation Sentimentale* and with it the joint heritage of Wagner and the Realist novel.

---

[35] This idea applies not only to Wagner, but to the whole of bourgeois opera. In *Klangfiguren* Adorno argues that it is precisely because nineteenth century German opera kept itself free from the social conflicts of its century, preferring to operate as 'a rest home for the bourgeoisie' that 'opera was able to reflect so directly the developing shape of bourgeois society' (xvi,33). Because of this Adorno – not just in his view of Wagner – attached so much weight to the negativity of art.

7. Wagner and Freudian Psychology

'One of the great masters of psychological music, or of musical psychology.'
Camille Bellaigue, 1909[1]

An interest in 'psychology' is never absent from Wagner's works. We noted in *Rienzi* Wagner's identification of a psychological problem – the incapacity to love – which the contemporary form of opera gave him no chance to explore further. The presentational impasse which Wagner arrived at showed that it was the problem itself, not its dramatic possibilities, which attracted him. Becker has shown that the type of hero favored in the Paris Opéra of the time was the psychologically ill-defined and hence 'vacillating hero' (1965:157f): even in *Rienzi* Wagner had moved to the presentation of characters who know themselves better and have stabilized into more identifiable personality types. The question is how far Wagner continued down this path, and how his concerns for psychological clarity appear in the light of Freudian psychology.

In the previous chapter we had occasion to refer to the work of Freud in order to characterize the type of observation of human behavior which we find in Wagner's operas. By citing Freud we did nothing more than suggest an analogy – we certainly did not use Freud as an honorific citation to boost Wagner's modern credentials. With Otto Rank's comments we moved closer to a considered parallel, since Rank came from the centre of the Freud circle, indeed from the exclusive, so-called 'Wednesday club'. In his work judgments were made about Wagner and an explicit shared context was established by Rank between the practice of psychoanalysis and Wagner's works. More explicit still is the claim Graf makes in the preface to his study of *Der fliegende Holländer* that:

> The thoughts which I put forward here were formed in the course of continuous discussions with Professor Freud and as the product of the numerous encouraging suggestions which I received during discussions in his house. (1911: Vorwort, unnumbered)

The claims for Freud's participation in the book and its enthusiasm for Wagner are not easy to substantiate. In this chapter we shall therefore restrict ourselves to an examination of the extent of the analogies and shared context,

---

[1] Quoted in Morris (2002:12)

and to understand how these might affect our search for a Wagner within the project of the Enlightenment.

It will clarify our task and its difficulties if we start a consideration of the place of psychology in Wagner's works with a brief discussion of what was manifestly of central importance to Freud: namely, the Unconscious. We preface this account with some words which Freud wrote to the Austrian writer and psychiatrist Arthur Schnitzler in May 1922. The letter elaborated Freud's surprise that he and Schnitzler had not already become much closer friends and collaborators – on the obvious basis of common interests:

> Your determinism, no less than your skepticism – what other people call pessimism – the way you are seized by the truths of the unconscious and of man's drives, your deconstruction of conventional cultural certainties, the way your thoughts circle round the polarity of life and death – all that touched me with an uncanny familiarity. (cit. Worbs 1988:179)

At no point in the following pages do I want to imply that Freud could have written these words to Wagner, however easily everything Freud mentions can be identified in Wagner's work too. More likely would have been a range of accusations, starting with vulgar exhibitionism and opportunism and culminating, of course, in the charge of anti-Semitism.[2] To the extent, however, that Wagner's relationship to Freud must include an assessment of Wagner by Freud – as we shall see later, Freud did not embrace every one of his forerunners – Freud's letter to Schnitzler is indicative of priorities. While there are evidently more variants of psychology than Freud, it is convenient to take Breuer and Freud's work in the years before 1910 as a point of comparison. It seems reasonable to look for signs of Wagner anticipating aspects of their thinking – indeed, this is the only legitimate course of action. If we were to detach the word psychology from any of its specific practitioners, and ascribe to it no more precise meaning than an interest in human behavior, then it would be hard to find any literary work which did not contain psychology. We would be like Monsieur Jourdain, surprised to find that people could be practicing psychology without knowing the word. But we do possess the word, and we cannot discuss Wagner's relationship to psychology without starting from a fixed and historically relevant reference point. For that reason we will take Freud's remarks as our point of departure. One result of this limitation is that we shall not have space for post-Freudian interpretations of Wagner's work, or – more importantly – for an assessment

---

[2]   Anti-Semitism was so common in Vienna that neither Rank nor Graf bothered even to refer to it in Wagner's world. Possibly they saw it as Freud's problem rather than their own.

of Wagner's potential closeness to (let alone his fascination for) post-Freudian psychology.

It would be helpful to have a working definition of Freud's Unconscious, as he used it in the letter. In his book tracing in eighteenth and nineteenth century literature and philosophy *The Unconscious before Freud*, a study which remains untouched by post-Freudian considerations, Lancelot Whyte offers the following: his search as historian is, as he explains in the Introduction, for evidence of 'the self-aware European becoming aware of the need to *infer* from his direct experiences the existence of mental processes in himself of which he is not immediately aware and to employ a special term for these unconscious processes' (1962: unnumbered). On the basis of that definition there would be little difficulty in identifying the absolute centrality of the unconscious in Wagner's work. And the source of this preoccupation is no less clear. Wagner's view of the unconscious came from long established traditions in German literature and philosophy, culminating around the time of Wagner's birth in the writers and thinkers of German Romanticism: Jean Paul, Hoffmann, Tieck and Herder, Fichte, and Schelling.[3] The concerns of these figures with a world beyond consciousness, and with forms of behavior and experience which signaled the reality of that other world, are too well known to need further rehearsal.

Schopenhauer's philosophy reinforced the interest in the unconscious started by the Romantic writers. His insistence on the importance of the Will was not just a metaphysical account of the world, but involved an understanding of human behavior in which the conscious self was often little more than the plaything of deeper and unseen forces, which Schopenhauer called the Will. That was the implication of the famous image of the individual sailing a frail boat across raging seas, which we mentioned earlier. Alongside his major work, Schopenhauer was the author of numerous aphorisms laying bare the inadequacy of humans' understanding of their own behavior, but for Wagner it was the link which Schopenhauer established between music and the unconscious which offers the quickest access to his view of the unconscious. Rather than plough this rich furrow in Wagner's own writings, we see his position efficiently by looking at almost any page of Kurth's book, from which His Masters' Voices boom forth clearly. Having claimed at the start of the book that musical harmonies are 'reflexes from the unconscious' (a view which goes back to Schopenhauer's familiar claim that

---

[3]   To this list Whyte explicitly adds Hegel – one of the inspirations for Wagner's generation's active engagement in history. While the judgment is understandable, Hegel's importance for Wagner would not normally be seen as related to the unconscious. Cf. also Marquard (1968).

music was a direct representation of the Will, rather than of the world of appearance), Kurth goes on: 'All melody has its origin in the unconscious, as does by far the greater part of all life activity'. So even before Wagner has found themes, in which his idea of the unconscious could be embodied, or living proofs of the 'existence of mental processes [in the self] of which he is not aware', his whole work as musician could be – and generally was – understood to be focused on the unconscious.[4] And he certainly used a special word for these processes: indeed, it was his proud self-description in *Opera and Drama* that he was a 'knower of the unconscious' (iv,128) – a phrase deliberately emphasizing the cognitive role of the artist. At times Wagner's understanding of the 'unconscious in human nature' and the need to 'bring it to consciousness' (iv,66) has a political emphasis, but he means in essence nothing different to Freud's awareness of the repressive effect of society on individual development – indeed, as we shall see later, they share a (somewhat over-flexible) radicalism in these opinions.

It's not surprising in view of his self-description that Wagner's works focus repeatedly on situations and characters in which the unconscious plays a central part. In the scene we examined in the previous chapter, Mime emerged as a victim of his unconscious self – even if it is not obvious *why* his unconscious self forces him to tell the truth, except that he is driven on by the sadistic pleasure of anticipating killing Siegfried and owning the treasure.[5] In that respect he joins a long list of characters driven by the unconscious: Senta, the Dutchman himself – although he blames the devil (not an unusual explanation of neurotic compulsions) – Kundry (a clear example of lucidity alternating with compulsive, seemingly irrational behavior) and Erda herself, in *Siegfried* Act 3 Scene 1 the sleeping figure who understands and participates in all events ('my sleep is dreaming and my dreams are thoughts' she says), primal mother and Delphic oracle.

This scene reveals a striking feature of Wagner's take on the unconscious: its insistent rationalism. Just as he insisted in *Opera and Drama* on the rationality of language, so here Wagner is determined to portray the unconscious – when it is finally brought onto the stage in person – as

---

4   Salon conversation in Berlin around 1870 – reported the novelist Friedrich Spielhagen – linked Wagner's works to Eduard von Hartmann's study of the unconscious (*Die Philosophie des Unbewussten*), a work which Nietzsche mocked in his early essay on David Strauss (cf. Gabriel 1998:7).

5   Almost uniquely among the characters of the *Ring*, Mime does not appear to be driven by any world pessimism or death-wish (which might be another possible explanation of his behavior). He genuinely wishes to be left alone to enjoy life and the treasure, free from the attentions of Alberich and Siegfried. Self-immolation is not on *Mime's* agenda.

cognitively structured. Fascinating in the portrayal of Erda is not only that Wotan foolishly imagines his individual will to be mightier than Erda – an illusion of the type that Schopenhauer enjoyed puncturing and which the whole plot of the *Ring* shows up as little more than a pathetic illusion on Wotan's part –, but that she sees through Wotan rationally: 'You are not what you call yourself'. The scene also reveals in Erda a belief in the rational skills which her daughter, Brünnhilde, possesses. Why consult me, she asks Wotan, when you can ask your daughter? (A question to which there are several answers.) Such a remark does make explicit the co-existence of both unconscious and rational energies in Wagner's plots. We cannot simply label the Unconscious with the poetic terms of Romanticism – such as the Daemonic, or the Irrational. It is part of a rationally explicable picture of the psyche – as Ackermann argues, in a work strongly orientated towards Adorno, Erda illustrates Wagner's efforts to prove that Enlightenment is itself part of myth (1981:81) – an idea central to Adorno and Horkheimer's *Dialectic*.

In all these figurations the dimension hidden behind consciousness is made clear. In addition, the potions which play such a central part in *Tristan* and *Götterdämmerung*[6] are obvious theatrical instruments to articulate unconscious wishes in the character. We have Fafner bringing to consciousness only in the moment of his death the identity of the man who has killed him, and in the classic Freudian model we have the dream. For something unseen the unconscious seems pretty omnipresent in Wagner's works, and Wagner is continuously anxious to articulate it.

Clearly we must return to a number of these topics, as well as to the other elements mentioned in Freud's letter to Schnitzler. Two further prime interests of Wagner's – the *Leitmotiv* (properly called the motif of remembrance) and repression – play a massive part within the context of Freud's ideas, and require more detailed consideration. But such matters will not necessarily help with the crucial questions which must be raised about Wagner's ideas in relation to Freud. First we must ask whether a preoccupation with the unconscious, being, as we saw, a common property of Romanticism, accords with the Realist novel onto which we have so far mapped Wagner's ideas. Secondly – perhaps the answer will help with the

---

[6] This argument which follows is general in the Wagner literature, and it bases on the reading by the psychoanalysts of a compulsive drive within Wagner (and, by extension, within his characters) to be the third in a relationship, to disrupt an existing dual relationship – hence the necessity for a device such as the potions. Clearly the Freudians – notably Graf (1911), who most confidently outlines the theory – related that unconscious drive to an Oedipus complex within Wagner.

first question – we need to be clear what Wagner actually *does* in his handling of the material of the unconscious. We need to examine to what extent his approach to it is itself in any sense intellectual or analytical. When these matters have been clarified, then we can look at the other fascinating elements in his relationship to Freudian thinking.

Psychology among Wagner's Realist contemporaries

'Let wakefulness reign where once deep sleep enfolded all'
(Siegfried Act 3 Scene 1)

A quick assessment of the relationship between psychology and the Realist novels would be that the novels' focus lay elsewhere. The Realists' deepest interests lay with understanding the motivation of human behavior within society, rather than with taking their readers into private areas of the soul, whose activities are otherwise not manifested publicly. To the extent that the unconscious manifests itself in social interaction, opening the observer's eye to hypocrisies and the inauthenticity of much social behavior, the Realists participated in the general interest of the Romantic period. However, the Realist novel generally reveals a tendency most clearly shown in Ibsen: to start with social problems (for instance, the drinking water scandal in *Enemy of the People* in the 1870s) and only much later, in the mid-1890s, to move on to studies of socially detached, unusual individuals outside society (for example in *John Gabriel Borkmann* and *The Master Builder*), i.e. subjects which demand an approach closely allied to psychology.[7] For the main thrust of their writing the inner workings of the unconscious are less interesting to them. Tolstoy, for instance, clearly shows the social effects and resonances of Oblonsky's serial adultery, but what his author or his friends do not themselves observe[8] and what he fails to explain wittily to those friends

---

[7]   This later Ibsen offered Thomas Mann one of the strongest links to Wagner. Mann explicitly compared *When we dead awaken* to *Parsifal* (x,227f). It will be clear, incidentally, why we have not included Dostoiewsky in the list of Realist writers. The importance of the present topic to Dostoiewsky is one of the reasons why he seems so much more a figure of the post-Realist generation.

[8]   *Anna Karenina* starts with that wonderful comment on society that 'happy marriages are happy in the same way, unhappy ones differently unhappy.' There's not a sniff of 'psychology' here – in fact, behind its dazzling commitment to general truths, one must question whether the comment is actually even true. Tolstoy's pathological dislike of

(even after a full meal, runs Oblonsky's celebrated *bon mot*, one feels like eating 'a fresh roll') does not get said – namely the nature and origin of his drive. If there *are* psychological explanations for serial adultery, Tolstoy will not explore them. His novel opens everything out to scrutiny and understanding except what is hidden deeply within, and which tends to stay there. That is a further feature of the novel which provoked Wagner's judgment on the novel – 'Drama goes from the inside to the outside, the novel from outside to the inside' –, indeed Wagner's observation is probably truer about the Realist novel than, for instance, about the sentimental or epistolatary novel of earlier periods. Wagner's comment ceases to be true only with the modernism which really does start *inside*: inside the mind, inside the memory, even inside the mouth (in the case of Proust's famous *madeleine*). In the century before that, explanations of behavior in Realist novels are social, rather than psychological. Furthermore, a reduced interest in psychology is in part the reason why the Realists paid little attention to childhood – a topic whose importance to writers and psychologists at the end of the century can hardly be exaggerated.

Differences of emphasis do exist, of course, between the various novelists. Turgenev, Flaubert and Stendhal devote real attention to the interior life of their characters, and it would be absurd to deny that Balzac's studies of obsession in novels such as *Cousine Bette* or *Le Père Goriot* were engaged on a serious enquiry into psychopathology, even if the emphasis remained firmly on the social effects of psychological states. Thus the more psychological writers of modernism could build on the interests shown by novelists in the earlier period, for whom psychology was part of the legacy of the Enlightenment (so, for instance, Proust's consciousness of the legacy of Balzac is a continuous feature of his great novel): that is to say: an extension of the drive to understand human behavior in society more deeply than the superficial motivations offered by religion or convention, and to look to science – rather than superstition or traditional 'lore' – to understand individual and collective psychic problems.[9] In trying to relate Richard

---

Wagner's operas (expressed in the hilarious appendix to *What is Art?* (1895), which describes an evening wasted at *Siegfried* – or, for that matter, an evening of *Siegfried* wasted on Tolstoy) – suggests either that he did not suspect any psychological truth behind the action, or that, suspecting such a truth, he did not care for it. Above all, Tolstoy cannot abstract from the shallow conventionalities of opera (he is, for instance, obsessed with Siegfried wearing tights!) to other types of truth which the work might contain and to which Tolstoy remains stubbornly blind.

[9] We have only to look at the tradition of the aphorism – from La Rochefoucauld in the seventeenth century through into Schopenhauer and Nietzsche – to see the strength of this Enlightenment tradition.

Wagner to the Enlightenment we can as little exclude his approach to 'psychology' as we can that to the Realist novel. To neglect psychology as one of these methods shared with Wagner's contemporaries – even at this rather banal level – would be an action worthy (to quote Freud) of the Russian censorship.

An important element in the psychology of the late nineteenth century was not only the interest in the psychic situation of infants and children, which did not get the attention of the Realists (still less did infant sexuality), but the general place of sexuality in the adult personality. This theme clearly cannot be described as one of the Realists' principal focus-points. Its lack of prominence is often simply a question of taste and convention: it should not be mistaken for restraint, or lack of interest.[10] So it is less significant to note the absence of explicit scenes of sexual activity in the Realist novel, for in the process of *not* finding such scenes we constantly discover between the lines unmistakable allusions to explicit sexual action. Leon and Emma Bovary in the closed cab, urging the coachman not to slow down; Anna Karenina having just experienced 'that which for Anna had been an impossible, horrible, but all the more enchanting dream'; Effi Briest's letter arranging her love-tryst in the dunes with Crampas – these are powerful scenes proceeding from sexual activity, and even if we see nothing with our eyes our imagination will not fail to fill in the details.[11] It's hardy surprising that Thomas Mann at the end of the Realist novel parodies these scenes in the uncertainty which all the characters share during the long pauses in the music room, where Gerda Buddenbrook is practicing with the handsome Leutnant von Trotha – practicing what, all the members of the household outside the music-room door ask themselves, is it a sex scene or the pause between Adagio and Presto? Robert Musil (notoriously hostile to the writing of his contemporary, Thomas Mann) was both accurate to complain that Mann's characters were 'like statues: without genitalia' (1976: 722,819) and surprisingly insensitive to the graphic power of what it left unsaid.

---

[10] The wonderful work by Peter Gay (1984) has told us enough for the 'restraint' not to be called prudishness. Apart from anything else, the literature contained sufficiently clear metaphors and tropes for readers to know exactly what was happening. A small example of this is given in Peter de Matt's reading of a poem by Annette von Droste-Hülshoff – a poet whom generations of students have read with 'modern' eyes without thinking that sexuality was one of her themes in that poem (1995:177ff).

[11] The least clothed – and in its time most notorious – scene from these years comes from Gutzkow's *Wally* (1836) in which the heroine, unable to marry the man she loves, shows herself naked to him on the night before his wedding. Maximum flesh, minimum sexual impact – but of course the novel was banned anyway. The sexual scandal came more from *not* reading the novel rather than from its details, but it did briefly impress Wagner.

Sexuality is present in the Realist novel therefore, transposed into pauses of social life, but it has shape only as an occasional coupling, around which social decencies more or less successfully have to arrange themselves. By the end of the century the understanding of sexuality has changed radically, it has become less focused on individual objects, it is now a drive. Zola's Nana and Wedekind's Lulu (and, before that, his *Spring's Awakening*) have moved into new territory. In comparison, Emma Bovary seems simply to be a woman who made mistakes in finding an object worthy of her desire, rather than the incorporation of a cosmic sexual drive. Even her sexuality is not seen 'as a persistent force within the personal subject'; instead, in Lawrence Kramer's phrase, as 'an ardor which visits' (1990:137). Indeed, it is Kramer's thesis that only music – and in particular, Wagner's music – can express that radically new concept of sexuality. Its other true home was, of course, psychoanalysis.

We should look to science, rather than prudishness, for explanations of the restricted place of sexuality in the Realist novel. The Realists were proud to swear allegiance to the great names of innovative, systematic nineteenth century science – Balzac acknowledging the anatomist Cuvier as his model, Eliot acknowledging her debt to the social historian and anthropologist F.H.Riehl, Zola modeling his work on the theoreticians of genetics and heredity, ultimately on Darwinism. In their day, systematic psychology had no scientific status and did not offer itself compellingly as an interpretative model to these writers. Where it had the best track-record – the de-masking of religious hypocrisy, for instance – they used psychological insight continuously, but there was no reason to extend this use to sexuality in a way which would have foreshadowed Freud. Indeed, they were, in terms of their science, in a different camp. The materialism of their method had put the Realists close to that school of medicine which, in its stress on heredity and determinism, Freud's new science had to overcome.[12]

Briefly turning our question on its head (i.e. asking about Freud's perceptions of Realist writing), we may observe how seldom Freud refers to the Realists in his works. As we know, like Marx – and hardly surprisingly in view of their similar backgrounds – Freud continually illustrated his scientific theories with supporting material made more persuasive by reference to the reading of the educated middle-classes. It remains a major pleasure of reading the works of both men to find in the wealth of literary quotation and

---

[12]   Freud never lost the ambition to find a material basis for the phenomena he studied, but in order to treat the conditions such as hysteria he had to move away from traditional materialist explanations and treatments. In this sense the difference between him and the Realists was clearly generational.

reference not only a breadth of mind and human experience but an understanding which anchors their theories in wider historical contexts. In his use of literary quotation, however, Freud went a step further than Marx, in that he claimed for himself a higher level of understanding than that possessed by his literary sources.[13] Freud explicitly distinguished between the 'raw material' which literature offered him and his own scientific insights: 'The poets and philosophers have opened up the unconscious to me', he remarked, going on with a characteristic sense of superiority: 'my discovery was the scientific method' (quoted MacIntyre 1958:6). Literature involved poetic imagination and empathy with psychological states: the psychologist alone was able to abstract from individual cases, to be systematic and analytical. We must ask why, for all their scientific pretensions, the Realist texts were so little valued by Freud even as 'raw material'.

It would be incorrect to relate this omission to our observations above, to the effect that the Realists were more interested in the social than the inward self. As author of a *Psychopathology of Everyday Life*, Freud's interest was – at least in part – in psychological states which surfaced in real social situations, and the Realists offered such situations in abundance. Nor is it sufficient to point to the traditional aesthetic taste which Freud, as a typical member of the educated upper middle-class, the *Bildungsbürgertum,* had cultivated and which never quite involved the novel (we observed above that Wagner took over elements of this judgment too – probably from the Hegelianism swirling around in the Germany of his youth, rather than directly from Kant or Schiller's aesthetic writings). Of much greater importance in Freud's approach was a division of labor between science and literature on which he strongly insisted. That was a principal reason why he disapproved of so much of the *fin de siècle* literature in Vienna, written as it obviously was in the modish shadow of his own early writings on psychoanalysis. When, for instance, around 1910 Freud critiqued a recent Hofmannsthal play, he made a characteristically programmatic judgment: 'The art of the poet does not consist of discovering and treating problems. He should leave that to the psychologist. His art consists rather of creating from

---

[13]   Marx tends to allow his references to speak with their own voice. Only occasionally – for instance in his account of Eugène Sue's best-selling novel *Les Mystères de Paris* – did Marx critique literary works, or show how social and economic understanding was being either only half perceived or directly perverted by the literary text. Most of the time he was happy simply to have quotations which he could make rhetorically effective and to leave literary criticism to the specialists. Cf. as always Prawer's classic study (1976).

these problems artistic effects.'[14] Just this attitude is likely to have caused him to be suspicious of the Realist writers: they tried – more genuinely perhaps than Hofmannsthal – to discover and treat the human condition, rather than merely poeticizing it. In any case, all new scientific disciplines, though they are often inspired by the activity of enthusiastic lay people, begin to establish themselves by jettisoning their dilettante begetters,[15] and psychoanalysis was no exception. Often it has been felt in particular that Freud's apparent neglect of Nietzsche[16] is best explained by reference to this process. It may well have been the closeness of the Realists to Freud's interests which led him to make no reference to their work.

Yet, in one of his most focused accounts of a literary work, Freud envisages and explicitly welcomes a wider function for the literary writer in the process of psychoanalysis. Wilhelm Jensen's story *Gradiva* contains, alongside its characteristic and familiar features,[17] something which Freud is completely persuaded by: a figure who systematically interprets and tries to unravel Hanold's confusion. The young woman Zoë tries, in the cause of love but with the devices of play and reason, to take Hanold out of his illusions and get him to recognize that it is really she whom he loves. In his praise for this story Freud recognizes for literature a secularly redemptive, therapeutic function, one closely allied to the work of the psychoanalyst. Freud's metaphor which we quoted above simply does not work here: in this one

---

[14]   Quoted in Worbs (1988:265). See also for the literary background Urban (1978) and Schorske (1968).

[15]   Literary science and anthropology are obvious examples in the nineteenth century (cf. Ridley 2007:36f and Bendix 1997).

[16]   While Freud's early disciples were enthusiastic readers and propagators of Nietzsche (we need refer only to Havelock Ellis, one of the earliest advocates of Nietzsche in the United States), Freud's books and essays are extraordinarily empty of references to Nietzsche. It is not conceivable that this gap can be explained by ignorance on Freud's part, and – especially when Freud turns his hand (not necessarily with great success) to cultural-political issues, as in *Civilization and its Discontents* (1915) – the silence is deafening, for Nietzsche's writings had dominated that field for over twenty years. As ever Harold Bloom's *Anxiety of Influence* offers wonderful insights into the paradoxical forms in which the fear of 'influence' expresses itself. Silence is pre-eminently such a form. On the general topic of Freud and Nietzsche cf. Marquard (1968).

[17]   The story of an archaeologist (Norbert Hanold) who, while excavating in Pompeii, believes that he has met a local girl who was buried in the eruption and has returned to the ruins as a ghost. That belief is so strong as to be a pathological illusion. In fact the girl whom he meets in Pompeii comes from closer to home. She, Zoë, is the daughter of a colleague in the faculty and Hanold's near neighbor, to whom he was once strongly attracted, before abandoning girls in favor of his archaeological studies. It is striking that not even Freud's interest has done anything to persuade later readers to explore Jensen's other stories and Jensen's extensive oeuvre remains as forgotten as ever.

case, literature is a mine which forges its own steel and cuts its own diamonds, as well as digging them out of the earth as raw material. Perhaps it is because Freud did not further develop the ideas in his essay that Freud critics have paid increasingly little attention to the *Gradiva* story,[18] focusing instead on Freud as a producer of texts himself, without the authority of a theory standing outside texts and therefore above literature. It is Freud's own literary practices which have now come to be under scrutiny. But that is far from the original reality.

It was important to establish something of Freud's attitude to Realist fiction. It blocks a line of argument which would take Wagner out of Freud's world just because Freud does not mention him. The answer sharpens our question as to what Wagner did with the potential 'raw material' of psychological observation in his works, and – a still more primary question – what that material was (not 'the problems' and their treatment, but 'the poetic effects' developed from those problems). We start our answer to this question in four simple points.

a. Hunting the causality of neurosis

> 'The track of this ancient guilt is hard to detect'
> (Freud: Wolf-Man)

When Thomas Mann compared Wagner to Zola – this a more sustained comparison than that with Ibsen, which we briefly mentioned above –, he had in mind principally their shared passion for tracking down the distant sources of guilt and transgression. Their search was historical in both cases, for Zola in the form of genetic tracing, for Wagner the outworking of curses and injustices. Nowhere is Wagner's obsession more clearly shown than in the *Ring*, which follows the history of man from the first glimmerings of the gods and the birth of heroes, and for which Freud's phrase above is more than appropriate. Another such history, equally blatant if far from transparent, is contained in *Parsifal*. Indeed the question of long-buried guilt overflows the opera. While Amfortas' guilt is of recent origin, and certainly traditional in nature, and while Parsifal himself feels guilty for the transgressions in Act 1 (no-one is quite sure what he means: it is both an inevitability and, he feels, a

---

[18]   Meisel's excellent study – even under its title *The literary Freud* (2007) – sees no reason even to mention this text of Freud.

personal fault to have been a fool when first hearing of Amfortas' problems), the deepest guilt is Kundry's. She bears on her shoulders every historical guilt, since sneering at Christ on the cross. Guilt is ancient – and probably imagined –, yet it affects individuals in the present. Not just eccentric figures outside society, such as Kundry, with their obvious personality disorders, but more everyday types, for instance Wotan with his deepest, manifestly human, psychoanalytical question to Erda: 'how can the god conquer worry?'. The track of these problems is long and laborious to trace.[19]

Despite the Christian ambiance of *Parsifal*,[20] there is no reason to think of these guilts – any more than those of the *Ring* – as being approached in a moral way. They offer instead reflections on the deep questions of unhappy individuals and a world where cause and effect, though profoundly connected, appear to have got out of kilter. Kundry is haunted by the memory of these transgressions, which, as an individual, she can have committed only in the same way that Hamlet dreams of repeating Oedipus' guilt – by repetition. While critics are divided about whether or not she was to be classified as a hysteric in the Freudian sense,[21] it is evident that the problem is not adequately met by the act of forgiveness, but only by a working-through of her guilt in suffering. Nor is it possible to see the other patient we have just mentioned, Wotan himself, as passing through any moral process: his fading from the action in *Siegfried* Act 3 (he does not appear at all in *Götterdämmerung* – something Shaw might have more fully commented on) makes clear that the momentum of his story is not contained in the person, but moves outward from him, just as we see happening to Alberich's curse.

---

19   Žižek argues strongly against moral readings of these complex interpersonal transactions and finds in Lévi-Strauss' anthropological reading of them as *exchange* a more plausible set of criteria to evaluate them (1999:7f).

20   I hope to be forgiven for putting into a footnote my skepticism about the meaning of *Parsifal* (cf. Heftrich 1975:81f,241f).. Nietzsche's crude attempt to pin it down to an orthodox Christian view has rightly been discredited, though some critics still manage to take it seriously. There's hardly an ideology which has not been pressed into service to explain the opera's plot – Robert Gutmann's colorful account (1972) acts as a reminder of some of these, while Jost Hermand's willful and witty essay on vegetarianism as the best thing in *Parsifal* (1993) may not find agreement, but will always be welcomed in its profound skepticism about any other explanation of the opera. Manfred Frank however is successful in showing Kundry's integration in a long literary-theological tradition of negativity, in which her problem seems personal to her rather than to Wagner and her closest affinities are to some of Kafka's characters (1979:58f).

21   Bronfen (1999) tends not to think so, Dettmering (amongst a veritable cloud-burst of psychological conditions which he diagnoses) has no doubts in labeling Kundry in that way (1976). 'A modern type of woman' is Graf's more moderate verdict on all such Wagnerian characters (1911:9).

Wagner is not concerned with guilt as a question of personal morality, but as a feature of history and in its generality a cause of blighted lives. The situation of the individual is the site of the processes which interest Wagner. Here his closeness to Zola's studies in heredity is unmistakable.

The form in which Wotan's guilt moves out from his own person is typical both of Wagner and of the Realist novel. It illustrates, in Wotan's case with particular clarity, the most significant area in which the nineteenth century novelists pursued their affinity with psychology: the portrayal of the family. When the Romantic hero externalized himself and his fantasies, it was in nature, the wilder and more lonely the better, the less marked by previous significations. When writers of that period wished to indicate the uniqueness of their individual characters, nature was the favored backdrop. This was true of the heroic heroes, and of the more domesticated, like Goethe's Werther. But the Realists and their predecessors in the early nineteenth century placed their characters within the archetypal unit of bourgeois society, if not of human history in its entirety – namely, the family. It was the bourgeois family too which provided Freud with his well-known examples – similar to Greek tragedy in being taken, as Aristotle remarked, from the stories of the 'best families' out of which the ancient dramatists fashioned their dramas. In the same way the Realists set out to discover within the microcosm of the family the same passions which passed through the Atrides, or the Capulets,[22] and Freud did the same. It was within the family that the primal scenes of human socialization – the *Urszenen* – took place and here that the focus of nineteenth century fiction and of early psychoanalysis lay. Without this focus, Freud's work could hardly have found resonance in his generation.[23] In registering the individual psyche, the family acted – in Friedrich Kittler's phrase (1995) – as an 'inscription system' for personal experience and psychological understanding.

The majority of Wagner's work clearly fits into this general classification. After *Rienzi*, which – apart from Irene's final comment to Rienzi – stays

---

[22]   Not just a programmatic goal of the Realists, this idea was central to Schopenhauer's view of the supra-individuality of music, which he claimed to be independent of the milieu in which its elemental conflicts were played out, indifferent to 'whether Agamemnon and Achilles or a squabble in a middle-class family provides the material for the conflict' (2,576). Another favorite image was of the drop of water containing – for those who had learned to *see* – the same energies and storms as moved mighty oceans. The image can be most easily found in Emerson's lecture *The American Scholar* (1837), but it accompanies the whole of the Realist movement.

[23]   Kramer sets out to show 'that Freud's psychoanalysis is in part a codification of nineteenth century expressive and discursive practices' (1990:184). But even if that is so, it hardly guaranteed Freud's popularity.

outside the intimacies of the family circle, much of *Der fliegende Holländer*, *Meistersinger* and most obviously the *Ring* follow this contemporary pattern. Whether or not we follow the tradition of seeing the *Ring* in terms of a general indictment of industrial capitalism, or whether it is a story of the abandonment of authority by the gods, its principal striking feature is that these wider themes are contextualized in terms of family history. Even if we think of the *Ring* in the category of incarnation dramas such as *Lohengrin*,[24] we note that the divinity drops not into the holy family, but into the bourgeois family. In doing that Wagner gave himself the freedom to range widely and archetypically through the *Urszenen*, around which Freud's work is based. We should not forget that these were explicit choices on Wagner's part and were in no way dictated by the material he took over. They are closely connected with Wagner's affinities to the Realist novel.

b. Rebels with one cause

We saw in Realism the dilemma of a movement devoted to the lives of ordinary people, yet ambitious for the over-lifesized. Rigoletto was both a jester, rather than a king, and an infinitely greater (i.e. more tragic) figure than any king. Both the ordinary and the exceptional, what Ibsen's Stockmann calls the 'damn compact majority', and the rebel were Realism's subject. Wagner certainly follows that path, in his comedy *Meistersinger* no less than in his tragedies, but his originality lies less in any political radicalism than in the explanation of the rebellions which his works offer. We need look no further than the folksy scene which opens Act 2 of *Der fliegende Holländer*, a humorous genre-painting of the village girls at their spinning wheel. In their midst is Senta, whose bizarre obsession with the portrait of the Dutchman, hanging on the wall transforms – with the singing of her famous ballad [25] – into a passionate and absolutist break from her

---

[24] *Mitteilung an die Freunde (1851)* contains a full account of *Lohengrin* as a continuation of the ancient Greek myths, in which – among others – Zeus came to earth in a mixture of human and super-human form (IV,290). Such stories possessed no divine origin: they were receptacles of man's intense longing to revere human attributes. For an account of the fundamental difference between this approach of Wagner's and Nietzsche's understanding of myth cf. Ridley (1980).

[25] It's not fanciful to hear behind Pirate Jenny's show-stopping number *Die Ballade der Seeräuber Jenny* an attempt both to catch the powerful magic of Wagner's piece and to shift its radicalism from the inner to the political life – Brecht and Weill's pirates in the *Threepenny Opera* are anarchical bringers of justice, albeit rough justice, but the only ones

environment, as she swears to redeem the Dutchman through her love. Tannhäuser too, as we saw, provoked absolute horror in the conventional group by revealing his devotion to Venus. Few more radical ways to alienate oneself from the compact majority can be imagined, unless in Tristan's chosen way of carrying-out of a royal command.

It is here that the radical element is most evidently located in a psychological, rather than a possible political motivation.[26] Tristan differentiates himself from the group of courtiers not merely because he has fallen in love with the wrong woman, but because that love is so absolute that only death itself is a suitable context or designation for it. The dominant themes of night, death and the wound move ever closer to being the resolution of the initial *Sehnsuchtsmotiv*, that haunting motif of longing which so famously opens the opera. More surprising still is Senta's familiarity with that darker, death-centered world of passion. Immediately after singing the Ballad, she declares – to universal incomprehension and to Erik's horror, for he has just dreamed the scene – 'I must go to my death with him [the Dutchman]'. The break with the majority is close to being pathological. Something similar happens in *Rienzi*, in Irene's deeply psychological reading of her brother's conduct. By contrast, it is the absence of this death-centered passion which is so illuminating in *Walküre*. Siegmund and Sieglinde make themselves outsiders in the most blatant, if richly traditional manner – incest –, yet their action lacks morbidity. That is one of the reasons why the whole opera is so gloriously human. The height of transgression here is *not* pathological, except in the sense of reflecting an original transgression which lies beyond individuals. It is this feature which earns Rank's praise for Wagner's deeply emotional and yet psychologically enlightened understanding of myth. (1912:592) The end of Act 1 is a defiantly normal surrender to passion: 'Bride and Sister are you to the Brother, let the blood of the Walsungs blossom'.[27] Paradoxically the most

---

the poor may ever get to experience in economic and class relations, and then only in dreams. Salvation comes from the sea.

[26] Adorno criticizes *Rienzi*, arguing that Rienzi's opposition to the *nobili* is motivated only by his jealous dislike of their life-style rather than by any criticism of their political role in Rome. It's seems a little less than likely, even less likely than my own view, which stresses Wagner's growing interest in psychological aspects of Rienzi's ambition.

[27] Hofmannsthal shows Jokaste and Oedipus's wilfully embarking on incest in a much more deliberately 'wicked' way, enjoying the shock their actions will provoke – but, as Mann's celebrated story which rewrites Sieglinde and Siegmund's love, *Blood of the Walsungs* (1907), makes clear, writers' acquaintance with early psychology had turned these long tabooed practices into something very interesting to polite society and easily exploitable for a frisson of forbidden pleasure (cf. Worbs 1988:317).

pathological action in the *Ring* is treated as the most normal, but precisely that feature suggests the psychological perspective.

c. Making the inner visible

'What wonderful dreams enfold our minds' [28]

At various points in the discussion I have spoken of the difficulty of opera to be forensic. In comparison with the novel, the plots of opera will be less at home with material clues and chains of evidence. Comparing the landlord Benoit's role in *La Bohème* with the function of Lheureux in *Madame Bovary* makes the point clearly – the one drives Emma to suicide by the accumulated debts which the narrator has carefully documented; the other joins in the four friends' parties, even though they have problems paying the rent. And though the *Ring* starts with worries about money, by Act 2 of *Siegfried* no-one is thinking about money any more – whatever else Siegfried takes from Fafner's cave it does not appear to be the treasure of the Rheingold, which had been so carefully piled up on stage at the end of the first evening, and the treasure is not mentioned as being thrown back into the Rhine at the end of *Götterdämmerung*.[29] But the tracing of a line of guilt is, as we saw, central to Wagner's plots, and it is here that the forensic dominates. Among the devices used to explain his characters' behavior – the externalizings from which the audience comes to an understanding of their actions – none is more important than the dream.

There is a clear progression in Wagner's use of the dream, although the function of dreams – to make external the hidden minds of the characters – remains constant. Elsa's famous dream ('Einsam in trüben Tagen') in *Lohengrin* – she dreams in her distress of a knight with bright armor, on whom she calls to defend her honor – contains little psychological subtlety. On the contrary, its nature is philosophical, for, as Wagner himself explains, it shows how the gods are a creation of human longing, projections of human

---

[28]   The opening line of the fifth song of the Wesendonck cycle.
[29]   As David Blackbourne showed, part of the effect of the industrialization of the Rhine during the late eighteenth and early nineteenth century was that the gold which used to found in it ceased to appear (2006:105). So there is probably an ecological message in the *Ring*, on top of all the others.

wishes.[30] The only element of Elsa's character that is reflected in this dream is the intensity of her desire. There is nothing else to tell about her, and her dream is therefore easily contained within a traditional aria structure – indeed, it is little more than a traditional operatic 'number', while the orchestral voice has no function except to accompany. The place of the dream in the plot is to prepare for Lohengrin's entry and nothing more.

Erik's famous dream in *Der fliegende Holländer* has two distinct functions. 'As I lay dreaming on a high cliff', Erik tells, he saw a dramatic scene on the shore – a scene which he fears, but cannot know, is about to be played out in front of us. Senta's father arrives ashore with a stranger, whom Senta embraces and with whom she then flees out to sea. The scene is as such a very standard Romantic (and medieval) device: a premonition of future events, a *Vorausdeutung*. In fact, however, it is really Senta's dream. She has fallen into a 'magnetic sleep'[31] and the stage directions tell us that 'it is as if she too is dreaming the dream Erik relates' – an idea easier to realize in film than on the stage. And it is during Erik's *arioso* that Senta comes out with the revealing line which we have already quoted: that 'I must go to my death with him'. We are clearly dealing here not just with anticipation, but with the revelation of hidden and profound character traits in dream and trance.

It is in this context that Sachs' much quoted lines make sense, when in Act 3 Scene 2 of *Meistersinger* Walter tells Sachs that he has dreamt a beautiful dream. 'My friend', Sachs replies, 'that is the poet's task, to read and mark his dreams. The truest imaginings of man are shown to him in dream, and the art of verse and poetry is only true-dream interpretation'. As Walter proceeds to sing of his dream (it forms the penultimate version of the Prize Song) Sachs' comments are 'only' formal, but Sachs has read the dream more deeply, he has come to understand the depth of Eva and Walter's love and has drawn his own conclusions. The final scene has been prepared, and with David and Magdalene they all join in the stunning quartet with the striking title: 'die selige Morgentraum-Deutweise', *the blessed morning dream interpretation song.*

The *Meistersinger* is a comedy, but the thoughts are serious, and from then on into the *Ring* and *Parsifal* the many dreams – day-dreams rather than

---

[30]   'Who else,' he asks in *Mitteilung an meine Freunde*, 'had invented the meeting of Zeus and Semele, but man in his most human longing [...] man who is able to express in the object of his deepest longing [...] only the essence of his pure human nature' (iv,290).

[31]   Sleep, trance, hypnosis – all part of the tools of Wagner's trade and, as Erda remarks, always 'a knowing sleep'. Nowhere is this more tellingly displayed than in the amazing opening to Act 2 of *Götterdämmerung*, with Alberich speaking to the deeply sleeping Hagen and winding him up for revenge.

night dreams – which punctuate the action are used for the revelation of the deepest truths. Siegfried's dreams of father and mother, the wood-bird – these are the 'dream-interpretation songs' of tragedy. And in these dreams, continuously, irrepressibly, the voice of the orchestra explains, adds information and reminds the audience of those features which make up the dream. Sachs' conventional account of the poet's work has become a tonal version of the interpretation of dreams. They are more than poetic moments: they are the action of analysis made apparent.

d. The sources of love

The argument here will be the most familiar to the reader. It relates to a particular dimension of the understanding of Wagner's principal themes within familial relationships. It was Thomas Mann (1933) who first identified this central insight of Wagner's works and used it to align Wagner with Freud – so the argument participates in a broader effort, not to rehabilitate Wagner, but to place him more accurately in artistic and intellectual history. Since then it has become standard. We will use Mann's own examples here.

In one of the most dramatic scenes in *Siegfried* (Act 3 Scene 3) the hero comes across the blazing hillside on which Brünnhilde lies sleeping, on the spot where Wotan's punishment left her at the end of *Walküre*. Brushing Wotan aside,[32] Siegfried braves the fire and starts to uncover the sleeping figure. Not surprisingly he assumes a man to be lying beneath the armor, and in a moment of revelation which would have given Nestroy more chance of parody than most of Wagner's other operas put together – small wonder that Wagner was anxious about the congruence of text, music *and* staging – Siegfried suddenly realizes that a woman is sleeping under the armor. His desperation, his instantaneous experience of fear (something which neither dragons nor gods had been able to teach him to feel) make him call out – to his mother. 'Mother, mother, think of me.' A heart-felt call which he repeats. Effortlessly, within the fantasy world of myths ancient and modern, Wagner has shown up the relationship between sexual love and the love of mother and child. Something similar happens to Parsifal, when in Act 2 he rejects Kundry's kiss. He has already called on his mother for help, and Kundry tells him that it is his mother who, 'as the last greeting of a mother's blessing of

---

[32] This scene, in which Wotan's spear is broken, represents one of the early moments of the *Ring*'s conception. Whether this event is interpreted as man's pursuit of equality with the gods, as rebellious assertion of the rights of individual feeling and love, or in pursuit of individual self-knowledge, the multi-layered quality of Wagner's use of myth is impressive.

love', gives him a kiss, which to her surprise awakens him and makes him 'see the world clearly' (*welthellsichtig*). Kundry then shows what she is made of – and offers justification of those who call her hysterical and neurotic. Listening to Parsifal recoiling in a vision of the sufferings of Amfortas, she ripostes: 'if in your heart you feel only the pains of others, then feel mine.' Here the story gets lost rather – at moments like these, Jost Hermand's sense that vegetarianism is the only good thing in the opera's plot is understandable. But unmistakable, before this moment, is once more the close link Wagner sees between maternal and sexual love and that insight is, like Realist analysis, intended for the audience.

In the previous chapter we heard Parsifal searching in his memory for his mother, and we wondered at the source of Kundry's knowledge of her, for it was she who had informed Parsifal of Herzeleide's death. In the same way Siegfried had wondered both about his father – it was impossible for him to accept Mime in that role – and his mother. He has seen in nature that animals have mothers, yet he does not know his own. It's still more impossible for him to believe that Mime is – as he claims – both: 'You must believe what I am telling you: I am your father and your mother as well'. Forced by Siegfried, Mime tells the story of Sieglinde's arrival in his place. This leads to the forging of the sword, and those magical conversations with the wood-bird, in which – in some of the most naturalistic music Wagner ever wrote – the deep truths about himself, his mother and his life are told. It remains hard to claim that Wagner – any more than the Realists – explored the worlds of childhood and infancy, and the occasionally grating naivety of the characterization of both Parsifal and Siegfried remains something of a blot on both operas. Nevertheless, in scenes of this kind Wagner makes clear that his interests involve the relationships between adulthood and infancy, and that the only language available to him to articulate them without embarrassment is music.

Our illustrations suggest that the 'psychological' content of Wagner's operas is anything but 'raw' material. It is actively handled to form the plot and the turning points of the operas, Wagner's use of the material was certainly not the passive reception of a Romantic legacy: not only in his work on the successive drafts of his operas, but in his own development an increasingly active and explanatory approach can be observed. Unformulated, not rationalized – in Freud's words we would have to call it something more substantial than 'creating from these problems artistic effects' – Wagner's approach to main-stream psychological themes is not accidental. Without necessarily sharing the judgment, we can understand why the Freudian Graf praised Wagner 'for always looking with the eye of the doctor on the passionate waves of his emotional life' (1911:3). It is true that Graf has in mind Wagner's approach to his own neuroses, but – characteristically for Freudian thinking in general at this time – no real distinction is made between the 'life reality and imaginative reality' of the poet.[33] At this point – where life and art are beginning to entwine and the artist, rather than his artistic creations, is on the couch – we must return to Freud.

A mess, but not a case

Since the purpose neither of this chapter nor of the whole book is to offer any overall psychological readings of Richard Wagner, whether as man or artist – to offer partial readings is simply inevitable – we shall be little concerned with more profound 'Freudian' readings of either. There, at all events, the emphasis will not be on the work. When Freud, loftily gesticulating over the lengths of his shelving containing Goethe's complete works, commented: 'All this was used by him [i.e. Goethe] for the purposes of self-concealment', he expressed a profound arrogance and superiority towards the artist on behalf of the psychologist, an attitude which his subsequent writing did little to diminish. Indeed, it became common for the relationship between psychology and literature to be thought of as primarily biographical, hardly more than the reduction of art to a device for the concealment of psychological breaks and neuroses, which the psychoanalyst smugly drew out of a hat and named. Freud's lack of subtlety here has been the subject of much subsequent questioning. 'Why', Meisel's study asks directly, 'was Freud such a poor psychoanalyst of art?' (2007:170) And why should we follow Freud down that path? After all, among the non-Freudian paths which psychology took, and of which we shall be saying nothing, was a Jungian psychology much more sympathetic to Wagner, both generally as an artist and in particular. Jung continuously criticized 'the reduction of art personal factors' (1930:93). For him the interest of the psychologist in art lay in the identification of archetypes, and he often discussed Wagner positively for his insights into the nature of archetypes and the functioning of myths.[34] But these developments came later, on the other side of the Enlightenment

---

[33] In regard to the precise examples we have discussed, Graf both accepts as given Wagner's exploration of the erotic aspects of son-mother relationships and their rooting in infancy, and at the same time he offers numerous examples from Wagner's life of this constellation of circumstances (1911:37ff). Wagner is both a diagnostician and a sufferer.

[34] It's worth noting that post-war psychological stagings of Wagner's works in Bayreuth started with Wieland Wagner, who was well known to be a devotee of Jung.

heritage: in the early years, psychology was Freud (and, initially, Breuer too) and the eye of the psychologist took pleasure in de-masking art – a process to which not all artists would willingly contribute.

The classic illustration of this progression can be seen in Thomas Mann. His first response to Freud was panic fear, fear of having his own problematic sexuality exposed by the relentless frankness of Freud's explorations, a fear generalized subsequently as Mann protested against the 'pan-sexualism' (i.e. permissive licentiousness) which he took Freud to be preaching. Mann's further response to his fears was systematically to lie about the stage of his life when he first became acquainted with Freud's work. Ironically, therefore, the psychology closest to him was that which he rejected and denied. (This relationship can be reversed, as Bloom would argue.) Only gradually did Mann gain a sense that literature and culture could share with psychoanalysis a therapeutic effect. This was the period when he read Freud's analysis of *Gradiva*. Mann secretly used Freud's account and analysis of the story – *Illusion and Dreams in Wilhelm Jensen's 'Gradiva'* (1907) – as a model for his own dangerously autobiographical *Death in Venice* (1911) (cf. Dierks 1991). The sexuality in the two texts is differently orientated, but the repression is the same, as is the central character's illusion of living in classical antiquity – which it is the author's task both to create and to unmask, in Mann's case without the happy ending which Jensen's story finds. This period of clandestine admiration was briefly followed by a sense of affinity with Freud because of Freud's skepticism, confronting the experiences of the First World War, about the permanence of a civilized veneer in society. Mann's *Thoughts in Time of War* (1914) and Freud's *Thoughts for the Times on War and Death* (1915) share some uncomfortable reflections about civilization's relationship to the primitive. It was a period when Mann's estimation of Wagner was still positive (later it would be eclipsed by admiration for Tolstoy and Goethe) and not without concrete political sympathies. While it would not be helpful to think of Mann and Freud as advancing similar arguments, or as regarding the war in the same way, they were both close to the anti-civilizational ideology which at times Wagner also embraced. In the final phase – when Mann penned what Meiser praises as his 'extraordinary' essays on Freud – Mann portrayed psychoanalysis as a central element in the fight of reason and humanity against barbarism and the forces of darkness, a view greatly reinforced by the Nazis' condemnation of psychoanalysis as nothing more than 'Jewish decadence'. Mann's example helps us to see the fluid nature of relationships to Freud and to Wagner, and Freud's own fluid position in European intellectual history.

Wagner's situation is not helped by the huge credence which has been given to Nietzsche's sustained attacks on him over the last ten years of Nietzsche's creative life. In his final reckoning with Wagner Nietzsche lists famous cases, artists on whose psychological disposition he wishes to pass devastating judgment (his list includes neither Wagner nor Goethe – 'though I mean them too'). He has already entitled the chapter 'The Psychologist speaks up', so the reader is prepared for what is to come. Nietzsche writes: 'These great artists avenge themselves on the world for a secret break' (vi,3:432). While much biographical work on Wagner has gratefully taken to heart these and other insights as authors chased after the more bizarre aspects of Wagner's personality and behavior, we shall resist the inclination to 'retract art into neurosis' (Starobinski 1973). In such an approach art itself seldom gets to be discussed, although the earliest Freudian studies of Wagner to which we have periodically referred exceptionally do not bear this out. Graf's study of *Der fliegende Holländer* (1911), although it claimed that Wagner had an Oedipal relationship to his mother, was strongly marked by great admiration for the opera itself and, as we have seen, for the objective psychological insights of its author. Nietzsche was never so generous, and in any case his reductionist understanding of psychology soon became outmoded – in part, regrettably, through being turned against its originator.[35]

Something else changed in Freud's approach to the arts. We suggested that Freud's relationship to literature was adversely affected by the aesthetic tastes characteristic of his class, which meant he did not always take the novel seriously. Paradoxically it may have been a surprising result of this elitism which allowed him to devote his attention to very much inferior forms of literature. Even in the 1908 essay on day-dreaming Freud indicated the usefulness of considering 'less pretentious authors of novels, romances and short-stories'. Jung too shared an enthusiasm for writers such as Conan Doyle[36] and Rider Haggard (1930:88f) – writers who dealt in crude and massive archetypes of inexplicable and paranormal behavior. One appeal of their work was clearly the complete absence of intellectual explanation in such texts, echoing Freud's preference for texts as 'raw material' or, more cynically put, allowing the psychologists the satisfaction of producing their dazzling explanations to a spell-bound audience. Not unconnected was the greater appeal of such popular texts, to 'the widest and most eager circle of readers of both sexes' (Freud iv,149). In short, Freud clearly envied popular literature the width of its appeal and was anxious to cash in on it. In fact Freud might have added 'opera goers' to his list, for he mentions Wagner in his works only on occasions when one of his rich female patients relates an experience which happened to her when at an opera. Questions of success operate within psychology, no less than on the stage.

Nevertheless, this change of position on behalf of the Freud circle makes it hard to see in what serious way Freud might have ever been prepared to express appreciation of Wagner's work. Indeed, we wonder whether his

---

[35] English-language accounts of Nietzsche around the time of the First World War made explicit reference to the parallel between a 'mad' philosopher and his 'mad' ideas.

[36] Surprisingly perhaps, Conan Doyle can hardly be cited as an example of rational handling of psychic situations, for after the Sherlock Holmes stories he shifted from scientifically based forensic science into a form of spiritualism which makes Wagner's vision of the Grail community seem prosaic in comparison.

profoundly anti-literary position permitted him to realize the difference between serious and trivial art in their approach to psychological themes. If that were so, there were contemporary examples of the same trend. In the 1920s Bloch argued for the closeness of Wagner's work to the kind of trivial literature which had become popular with Freud,[37] but, even without the dazzling arguments Bloch uses, Freud should surely have distinguished Haggard's *She* from Wagner's operas and ought to have recognized the intellectual and technical differences between these two types of art. Anyone sensitive to racial stereotyping, for instance, (*She*, like *King Solomon's Mines* is a dispiriting exercise in 'Aryan' thinking) would have no fewer problems with Haggard than with Wagner's anti-Semitism. Replacing Jensen's sensitive and intelligent heroine Zoë with Allan Quartermain as the observer of the paranormal hardly corresponds to mature literary judgment on Freud's part, and Freud would have looked in vain in Haggard's works for the rational and therapeutic approach which Freud had so admired in Zoë.[38] Freud's tastes and inconsistencies appear systematically to have prevented him from appreciating Wagner: that these obstacles to Freud's Wagner reception were not necessarily related to anything actually contained in Wagner's works seems more likely. Perhaps the truth is more banal and Freud did not actually like the sound of Wagner's music, just as he did not care for the Realist novel.

Inconsistencies, as well as an impoverishing attitude to literature therefore meant that a shift took place in psychoanalytic literary criticism around Freud's work. This based on the recognition that Freud himself was a producer of texts, no less than the writers over whose works he wished to

---

[37]   One of the really challenging accounts of Wagner's appeal was Bloch's essay 'The rescue of Wagner by Karl May', in which the residual honesty of *Kitsch* and its function as a repository of utopia (a principal element in Bloch's understanding of Karl May, the nineteenth century writer of adventure stories) is uncovered as the only truth which Wagner's operas are able to mediate. Adorno is more critical of this kind of art and its cheap effects, and when (as he often does) he compares Wagner to *Kitsch* he means the comparison to be only disparaging.

[38]   It seems to be an unbroken rule of these stories (of which Kipling is also typical: Freud included the *Jungle Book* among a list of 'great' books, but probably knew his short stories too) that, in face of the seemingly inexplicable and paranormal, where some solution is called for in order for normal life to resume, the answer is the predictable knowing wink with which the paranormal is tucked *back* into Pandora's Box. The city clerk who day-dreams the Nordic sagas verbatim, the civilized European who starts to behave like a wild animal, the soldier who – in the phrases of the day – goes 'beserk' and runs 'amok', all have to be fitted back into civilization by the end of the story. Repression rules. So the real truth behind the deep mysteries opened up by such behavior, Kipling and his contemporaries suggest, will never be known. That's hardly a taste of Freud's for Wagner to emulate.

gesticulate so imperiously. After all, it had been Freud who was struck – and for the sake of founding his science, *disturbed* – by the fact that his medical reports on patients often read 'like short stories' (quoted Urban 1978:129). Psychologists and therapists share with writers, and with dreamers one essential element: a *story*, which links what otherwise would remain apart, and – to the extent that they use reason and individuation as their tools – they all may share in the effects. In this way, of course, from whatever source, the story relates both to details and to explanation. All literature of this type tends towards the detective story, with the forensic dominating both the explanation of the person and the interrelation of elements in society.

We can illustrate this with a final reference to the type of popular literature Freud turned to, John Buchan's novel *The Three Hostages* (1924). This novel is a characteristic (if third-rate) piece of forensic, psychological literature. A master criminal (who is, hardly by co-incidence, ethnically defined, which is to say tainted) attempts to gain power by kidnapping prominent people and hypnotizing them into playing roles in which their former selves are unidentifiable. As part of the criminal's vanity, he leaves cryptic clues to his actions, in the form of seemingly unconnected references to obscure people and places. The hero succeeds in connecting these references and thus tracing the criminal. Psychology appears not only as the alien and paranormal (for instance in the form of hypnosis), and not merely as a tool to the forensic: it is also – as the text itself reflects – a model of the process of artistic creation, in which an author tosses out seemingly unconnected facts and only s/he (or the detective working with the author's help) can reveal that they were from the start intimately connected, in a hidden narrative which – it is disingenuously claimed – only analytic work can bring to light. In *that* sense Wagner's work is not psychological, and if Freud wanted art of that kind Wagner would not have obliged. Where it deals in uncovering the meaning of puzzling actions (the sword left in the tree, or the broken sword) the audience is continually given clues. Mystification – and only subsequently Enlightenment – is not Wagner's aim. Hidden motivations are contained within simple and easily decipherable devices (the Dutchman and his picture, for instance): the real interest lies in particular states of mind and their influence on a circle of relationships.

It is, finally, neither coincidence nor compelling evidence of a shared agenda that Freud and Wagner appear most strongly to overlap – in the sense not only of common purposes, but of being accessible to the same type of arguments – in all areas which have to do with story-telling. Wagner's position is that of a writer who weaves his story both out of external sources and from within his own personality, concerned on the one hand to construct a story which may illustrate understandings which he possesses and on the other – as Brooks recognized – to give full expression to the cathexic impulses within himself. The resulting network of connections clearly enrich Wagner's art with a genuine cognitive purpose, but it also lies behind what are, in Wagner's theoretical writings, some of the more contradictory elements. We have already quoted his claim to be a 'knower of the unconscious'. We have seen how his idea of making visible the internal – the whole gestic quality of his music and of the actions to which he brings his characters – involves a notion of clarification, a process of making evident, which, we have suggested, belongs within the Enlightenment. Here, rather than in the view of the artist as someone able to bring his own personal neuroses out into the open, appears to be the route by which Freud and Wagner are brought together. Yet just as Freud is not consistent, so too Wagner. Wagner's comments about the drama of the future involving 'a return from reason to feeling' (iv,72) appear to set him in the opposite direction, just as his stated dislike of the novel for the *citizen* (iv,68) appears to contradict the emancipatory thrust of so much of his work, and in particular the specifically political comments (iv,66: quoted above) on the need to make the unconscious conscious. Our preliminary comments on the 'default-setting' were not intended to exonerate Wagner from his more objectionable opinions. It was to draw attention to the centrality of contradiction in his thinking. That too he shares with Freud.

Psychology – not scenery but landscape

> 'With the neurotic we are in a prehistoric landscape, like the Jura.
> The great dinosaurs are still roaming and the grasses are
> as high as palm-trees.'[39]

In this final section we return to the theme of Wagner and the unconscious and allow ourselves a less critical walk in Wagner's garden as I have portrayed it.

An interaction is taking place. It will be a significant one, not merely a piece of by-play organizing a shallow plot. In that respect it illustrates something which Wagner certainly did not share with the Realist novelists, namely his sense of sharp focus, cutting out side characters, in a way which

---

[39]   Freud letter of July 1938, quoted in: Worbs (1988:340).

most novelists find impossible, but with no loss of Realism. We have not only a focus on character, but a focus on the essentials of the relationships between characters. If the characters relate through kinship, the scene is about kinship; if through love, then love. External factors like class and profession will be there, but serving merely to color, not to lead – like Sachs discussing art, but using the tools of his trade as shoe-maker to beat out the rhythms, or like Siegfried, forging his fragmented identity by rediscovering his parents, while, almost incidentally, forging a sword. The scene will be fixed from the centre, but the dialogue will be linear in construction, logical and explicit, if subtle. More often than not, the everyday devices of conversation will be used to shape the scene: above all, within the context of their presentation, they will uncover what the characters most want, and the course of the scene will often frustrate their desires, as reality frustrates the ideal. They will boast and have their bluff called, they will score points and they will challenge each other. Their linguistic acts turn themselves into real actions: Alberich not only boasts extravagantly, but he has to carry out his boast, and allows himself to be captured when Loge tells him that real magic is to make himself small, rather than large. He gets caught up in his boast: the conversational ploy has to be paid for. Speech is anything but social convention alone. To match the words of the contract and to equal the value of Freia, the giants insist on the Rheingold being piled high, yet the light shining between the blocks shows Wotan's holding back from the promise. Action illuminates the inside, words come from within and are charged with uncomfortably revealing meaning as well as with dramatic qualities.

The settings do not always matter. We are with Lear on any blasted heath and with the Nibelungs nowhere, only down: the wonderful musical ladder between the second and third scenes of *Rheingold* is suspended in featureless space. Yet, where it matters, the setting has a message: an utopian Nuremberg, a medieval society where kings and nobles mediate the divine in man – in contrast to *Tannhäuser*, where only the artificiality of courtly society is real –, a Norwegian village, where the cultural norms of 'the damned compact majority' leave available only one type of exit (until the last minute, a Scottish landscape: so the local color is relatively casually tacked on – Wagner's interest lies elsewhere). Yet whatever the scene, nature is always there. However much Kurth tried to protect Wagner's music against the suggestion that it portrayed nature, even he has to admit (he is talking of *Tristan* Act 2): 'Never before was a music created from which the breath of nature flowed with such intensity and expectancy' (1923:400). We need only compare Schumann's 'Rhenish' Symphony (no. 4) with Wagner's Rhine music to see what Kurth means: Wagner cuts out the public, bustling thoroughfare of the Rhine at Düsseldorf, the surface ripples of the moving water, and – as a major cultural reference – the newly completed Cologne cathedral (subject of Schumann's long third movement).[40] Right from the start Wagner goes for the symbolic river, an elemental rather than a social force, for he is tracing the long trail of guilt, rather than celebrating national events. Like the forest birds and the synaesthesia of the Nuremberg lilac, the natural objects are taught to speak a different language. It is at one level, of course, the so-called pathetic fallacy of Romanticism: winter gives way to spring as the passion grows in Hunding's hut, the door that opens abruptly for spring to enter is the door to the human heart; or that scene in Act 3 of *Parsifal*, where the meadows celebrate their day of innocence, they rejoice (here the concreteness of Wagner's vision asserts itself again) 'that no man's foot will crush them today'[41] – even his idealism is materially expressed. All nature, all the environment has personal meaning, and the narrator uses natural features of the scene to populate the space, to make it familiar to his listeners. For the present experience becomes memory, the 'motifs of remembrance' transform the scene (in Baudelaire's phrase) into 'a country which resembles you'. Yes it is new, but I have been here before. It is strange, but the strangeness is within me.

As if this were not enough – and if it had been enough, we would have works of quite different quality – these are not merely aesthetic experiences. They are saying something about the world of the unconscious: that it is the true world and that all experience is caught up in it. The unconscious is a world of memory traces, what we experience we have known before. 'Hysterical patients suffer mainly from reminiscences', Freud remarks (MacIntyre 1958:9); but the experience of reminiscence is normal, it is the stuff of all experience, both normal and pathological. It links the real and empirical with the imaginary and the mythical. There is more than atmosphere here, there is an argument. 'Richard Wagner uses the *Leitmotiv* interventions of the orchestra', Gabriel remarked, 'just as a psychoanalyst has recourse to scansions, in order to punctuate what the patient is saying' (1998:93). Wagner is doing more than Hofmannsthal and the other writers who transferred into drama and prose their readings of a fashionable Freud. He is not drawing 'artistic effects' from psychological 'problems', he creates

---

[40]   I am grateful to Dr Michael Charlton of Christ Church University, Canterbury for pointing out these differences to me.

[41]   That Wagner saw a nature restored to its full self – as men would be when the gods have passed on – is either very high class theology (and before its time at that: the vegetarianism certainly fits here) or a sign that for Wagner the only redemption is in art, in the sublime music.

a world which is a sounding board to the unconscious – Schnebel calls Wagner's works 'psychic seismographs' (1972:101) –, and within which profound truths can be inscribed. What makes his crude anti-Semitism so appalling is the subtlety and enlightened intelligence of the mind from which it comes and which expressed itself so freely and humanely in so many features of the works. For whatever reason Freud neglected (or rejected) Wagner, he closed his eyes on a significant forerunner. It took the literary work of his contemporaries to bring that affinity into the open. Their work deserves to be matched by the efforts of critics.

8. Opera, Novel and the Nation

It's a sobering experience to watch the consequences when artists get caught up in national politics. On and off stage, as creators of art and as managers of their fame, they assume inappropriate roles in the affairs of the nation and say and do things which are unworthy of them. This tendency was strongly present in Wagner and led to many of the serious doubts about him, about his nationalistic – on occasion anti-Semitic – remarks, his fawning to kings and politicians and the explicitly national quality of his Bayreuth project. Yet the general phenomenon is universal enough for us not to be surprised, least of all in the context of the various deep animosities and constant shifts of frontier between France and Germany throughout the century, especially after the watershed of the Siege of Paris. It would be difficult to distinguish Wagner's attitudes from those of his French counterparts at the time. From west of the Rhine came the sound of Debussy's *En blanc et noir* illustrating the musical 'defeat' of *Ein' feste Burg* at the hands of *La Marseilleise* (Kelly 2008:67), and Romain Rolland insisting that French musicians had a sense of revenge no less strong than that of the French army (ibid.:69). Musicians showed as little restraint in what they said and as little distance from the ignoble passions of the moment as any other group of the population, and Wagner was no exception. What was commented on in the revolutionary years of 1848 – that musicians seemed indifferent to politics, humble servants of the notes on the sheet and unmoved by non-musical causes – had changed, and not necessarily for the better.

Political aspects of the reform of music

Or had it changed? The crassness and clumsiness of so many artists' political behavior suggests that they were still behaving as artists: their other-worldliness remains apparent throughout their excursions into reality. Indeed, one of the fatal elements in the history of music in these years was the way artists mobilized political arguments in order to press for artistic change. We can see this most clearly in the movement rejecting modernism in music in several European countries. The issue was largely one of aesthetics, concerned to shift the emphasis of music away from expression and back towards form and simplicity,[1] yet the debates moved all too readily into questions of public morality and then – invariably – of national identity. In most countries, if with slightly different emphases, opposition to modernism focused on the figure of Wagner. The defeat of 1871 gave particular venom to the movement against Wagner in France. Inevitably he was presented – for instance, by the composer Saint-Saëns – as 'a war machine against French art' (cit. Schmid 2008:79), and even if the revival of seventeenth century French music (for instance, of the composer Jean-Philippe Rameau), which began in these years, did not in all cases stem directly from hatred of Wagner, it certainly reflected a nationalistic return to the 'pure' springs of French culture. It remained convenient to blame a foreigner for the situation to which national music had come – after all, Wagner was blamed in his own country for many of the excesses of modernism and it was natural that he would be blamed outside his country. If Walt Whitman's *Leaves of Grass* praised his work as 'honeyed morphine', it could hardly be surprising that more conservative terms such as decadence and degeneracy became frequent in public debate.[2]

In Italy too the work of prominent critics such as Fausto Torrefranca aimed to use historical music 'as an antidote to the opera of verismo' (Nicolodi 1991:116). Torrefranca attracted most attention with his sustained attacks on the music of Puccini, whom he denounced – in the language of extreme nationalism, including anti-Semitic and anti-feminist arguments – as fundamentally unItalian. The state of national music was more important than the success of an individual composer (cf. Mila 1973:854). Again it would be hard to blame these attacks solely on dislike of German culture – partly because so many of Torrefranca's arguments came from north of the Alps, partly too because of Germany's status as a model for Italian musical criticism (Wilson 2007:125f,59f). The real enemy was the modernism which Wagner reception had allowed to come into Italian music, and the real dilemma for conservative critics lay in the popularity which that modernism

---

[1]   One German word for this pervasive Romantic aesthetic was *Ausdrucksästhetik*. In prose the Realists would have shared the negative approach to this style, though for different reasons.

[2]   There were some French critics who ignored nationality and argued for a return to Bach – a movement which was mirrored in Italy, and of which Verdi rather unfortunately remarked: 'we descendants of Palestrina commit a musical crime by imitating Bach' (letter to Faccio, cit. Phillips-Matz 1993:701). Giusti called on Italians of genius to 'contract a strong and full marriage to Italian art and shun the wanton lust of foreign liaisons' (ibid.:207). Classical and antiquarian movements were well known in Germany too. Wagner may have been associated with a certain type of musical chauvinism in Germany, but often those who championed him neither shared his musical taste nor – if they noticed it – welcomed his effect on German music. It has not just been his detractors who would not listen to him.

had achieved.[3] Maffei, writing in 1834, anticipated the dilemma neatly. While believing that Italian music was characterized by 'simplicity, grace and truth', he could see that the tradition of Italian song was in danger of suffocating the development of national music (1834:994,992). As Suzanne Aspden, writing on 'National opera in eighteenth century Britain' comments: 'the concept of a truly homogenous "national" music sits uncomfortably – indeed, is nearly impossible – at a time when part of the process of establishing national culture, for men at least, involved eschewing refined musical sensitivity' (2002:211). It was not just on the Continent that nationalism in music had difficulties with the actual taste of the nation.

The composers themselves took various stances during these debates. Quite apart from the moments when, under the pressure of a compelling shift in public opinion (such as the outbreak of war brings about), they became directly partisan, artists tended to want to get on with their music and were less concerned about the labels which others attached to their work. Ravel for instance saw no problem in taking much of his inspiration from American music (he was, he commented, being influenced *as a* Frenchman!). Wilson argues that it was Puccini's publisher, Ricordi, who turned him into an explicitly *Italian* composer, while Döhring shows in detail how strongly the influences on Puccini's work were not Wagnerian, as his detractors repeatedly claimed, but French, indeed anything other than Italian – Verdi being the one composer who never influenced him. Even Verdi himself – although in fact we have at various points, and with much restraint, quoted his rather simplistic views on national culture and on his own relation to the Italian people – has to a surprising extent, as Parker showed,[4] been deliberately constructed in various generations as a popular mouthpiece of *Italianità*. So much so that for Dellamora and Fischlin Verdi's name was virtually synonymous with Italian nationalism (1997:1). In any case, with or without falsifications of the type Parker highlights, national tradition is highly problematic. It was all very well for Vaughan Williams to argue that it was 'reasonable to suppose' that music was national, in view of the

---

[3] Torrefranca claimed that Puccini's 'decadent psychology' was 'commercial speculation on a mass taste alienated from the national spirit' (cit. Döhring 1991:124). The case of the conservative, 'restorative' composer Respighi (1879-1936) would need more detailed consideration if these arguments were the real focus on this chapter.

[4] Parker's study (1997) is of one Verdi aria – 'Va pensiero' from *Nabucco* – and it deconstructs the alleged links between it and the national cause with which it has been so continuously linked. It is a welcome call to skepticism.

importance of tradition to composers,[5] but such attitudes are predicated on the existence of one unifying tradition in a particular country. The lack of such unifying tradition was just the problem other cultures faced in the nineteenth century, as surely Britain did too: only Wagner's enthusiasm for national art could have led him to believe that '*Rule Britannia* contained in its first notes the whole character of the English people' (cit. Apsden 2002:195).

I suggested above that the outbreak of war created situations which pushed musicians into ill-considered political statement. But it should be remembered that throughout the nineteenth century there were other situations no less capable of provoking extremism, indeed on an everyday basis. We have to think how many countries were undergoing radical change and modernization, their society re-structuring in such a form that the very identity of the nation was felt to be thrown into question. This was true of the newly united nations such as Germany and Italy; the Italian politician and artist Massimo d'Azeglio is said to have remarked in 1861 (the year of Italian unification) 'we have made Italy; we must now make Italians' (cit. Wilson 2007:11). He will have had in mind, among other things, the lack of a generally understood national language – which had actually done much to hinder the development of a national opera in Italy (cf. Kimbell 1991:415). The need to 'remake the nation' can also be observed in France, as the country tried to rediscover its identity after the crushing defeat by Prussia in 1871 and after the social divisiveness of the Paris *Communes*. The desperation and the tendency to extremism is no less intense at such times than in war; regardless of their previous political orientation, artists and intellectuals feel driven to make their contribution to nation-building and the excitement of being listened to by the public (a public which had invariably shown itself capable of ignoring their voice when they spoke within their own art) ensured that their views often came out extreme. The cause of national identity (invariably equated with national literature, national music etc) is taken to justify such positions. Commenting ironically on the drive for a Soviet national literature in the 1930s, the Russian poet Osip Mandelstam remarked: 'Poetry is respected only in this country – people are killed for it'.[6]

---

[5]   He might more usefully have discussed nationalism in those cases (are there any *other* types of case?) where composers tap into foreign traditions (Elgar comes to mind). Vaughan Williams' essay 'Should music be national?' looks for affinities established between people 'who share our life, our history, our customs, our climate, even our food' (1987:9). In a more polarized society such remarks would be harshly judged.

[6]   Quoted in Nadezhda Mandelstam: *Hope Against Hope* (Harmondsworth: Penguin, 1975), 190.

His comment was aimed not just at Stalin, but at the ranks of artists and intellectuals eagerly working in the cause. In less totalitarian circumstances, Melville writes in 1850: 'this matter of national literature has come to such a pass with me, that in some sense we must turn bullies' (ix,248). With hindsight, his readers might wish that, rather than being pushed into bullying, Melville had adopted the stance of his famous character and echoed his remark: 'I prefer not to'. For the cause of national literature and with no external compulsion, he instead opened his mouth too wide.

We have suggested that it was initially his publisher, Ricordi, who was responsible for turning Verdi into a national composer. While this was – to a considerable extent at least – a matter of commercial calculation, Ricordi's attitude testifies to the fact that artistic products were needed to bolster the self-value and cohesion experienced by the nation. Nations may be created in wars, forged in blood and steel, but once they exist they have take on less material forms of identity, and here art comes into its own. The works of art which serve that function will sometimes post-date the national unity. We see examples of this in Twain's Huck Finn stories embodying the spirit of the still young state, or in the remark of the music journalist Pietro Cominazzi 1862: 'We appeal to Verdi to rescue our art, just as we appeal to Garibaldi to save our homeland' (cit. Capra 2001:127). More often they pre-date the political structures to which they offer justification. A celebrated case was the importance of the chorus 'Guerra, guerra' (from Bellini's *Norma*, written in 1831) which came to be associated with the liberation of Sicily in 1848 and was used frequently at political rallies of the time. Ricordi was therefore one of a series of voices laying claim to (and putting his money behind) the prophetic quality of art, and of music in particular. Daniel Auber's opera *La Muette de Portici (1828)* was, as Wagner himself remarked in his memoir of Auber, universally 'recognized as the clear theatrical forerunner of the July revolution' (ix,58),[7] and the logic was that, in countries still awaiting successful revolution, other works were sought as fore-runners of political events yet to come. So the Italian patriot and revolutionary Giuseppe Mazzini 'prayed for the emergence of a young, Italian artist who would give voice to the aspirations of a nation that did not yet exist' (Phillips-Matz 1993:190f).

---

[7]   Apart from his personal appreciation of Auber (1782-1871), Wagner makes clear that only this one opera was deserving of such high praise. The opera's relation to the July revolution is not made explicit until 1860 – in his essays from the early 1840s Wagner was more careful with such remarks (e.g. in the essay 'Über Meyerbeers 'Huguenotten' (1840), i,72). Auber's opera was known for its spectacular theatrical effects (culminating in an eruption of Vesuvius), which influenced the conception of *Rienzi*'s staging (cf. Carnegy 2006:28).

Artists' works may have an important political function even before they are written. The idea was no less common in its inverted form. Big events need celebrating; (not just) in the old days verse was felt to be appropriate, but when the events are really big and really change society (a Revolution, the Birth of a Nation etc) something monumental seems to be the order of the day, and in a strange way there's a one-to-one relationship envisaged here, the idea that an age might have just one work expressing the unique greatness of the historical moment. Wagner was attracted to the idea when writing in 1840 on Meyerbeer, of whom he says that the task of genius is 'to express the most perfect ideal of a period',[8] and he expands the idea in his extraordinarily fulsome praise for Auber's *La Muette de Portici* – 'a national work, such as every nation has only one of' (i,165). While Wagner clearly had the ambition to write that one work for his own country, his operas cannot be accused of being written to meet the inverted form of monumentalism – the requirement for the newly established German Empire to be celebrated in art, for, of course, all his operas except *Parsifal* were written long before 1871. The dangerous expectation of the state for its great deeds to be celebrated in a monumental work was present during those years, and there are occasional pieces of Wagner's which responded to the expectation, but only the reception of his operas could be classified in that way.[9] That ambition for the monumental drove Stalin on to want to 'produce' 'the red Tolstoy' in the early 1930s, and its paler, more humane shadow could be recognized after 1989 as the newly united Germany began a (long) wait for *the* novel of re-unification. Whether artists can create in response to such concrete expectations – we assume that Auber's success was to some extent *accidental,* rather than the product of a deliberately planned attempt to anticipate revolutionary events in a monumental historic work – brings us back to the question of default-setting.

The idea of a national work of art is of great significance for our discussion in this chapter. We need spend no more time detailing the nationalist excesses of composers, or comparing them with the extremism shown in other cultures. It's an unedifying activity, and not just in the case of

---

[8]   (3,55). The essay is on Meyerbeer's *Huguenotten.* It is this underlying idea which helps us to see this essay more positively than as servile fawning in the cause of Wagner's self-advancement. If Wagner were to overcome Meyerbeer it would be by himself creating a work more appropriate to the *coming* period (cf. Weinland 1988:31f).

[9]   Wagner's *Kaisersmarsch* is the work in question. Brahms' *Triumphlied* (Opus 55) similarly belongs to this period – even if Beller-McKenna senses in it Brahms' *uncertainty* about the new Empire (2004:98f,104).

Wagner, made worse by a comparative perspective, for, whatever intrinsic interest the material may or may not possess, it is all but impossible for critics to remain neutral. A particularly ghastly form of Eurovision song contest sets in, point-scoring in the present by the historian added to the mindless point-scoring indulged in by the subjects in the past. Freud was right to insist that *tout comprendre* does not have to amount to *tout pardoner*, but it is nevertheless hard to achieve any level of understanding without developing special pleading such as I suggested in the last paragraph and which, by offering causes, seems to offer excuse. What is crucial, however, is the recognition that the underlying, principal aim of artists in the second half of the nineteenth century was to create – or to contribute to – an art-form in which not only their individuality and aesthetic ideas were represented, but also their national culture. This fact is as true of large countries with long cultural traditions but no structured national identity (i.e. Germany and Italy) as it is of small countries (Bohemia, for instance), or of large countries with national identity but no cultural tradition (i.e. the United States of America). And it is within this context of a national function for art – a function which is not primarily aggressive towards outsiders,[10] but aims to consolidate the national – that the final question of this book is formulated: how it was that in Italy and Germany the art form which most clearly took on this national function was opera, whereas in other countries this function was assumed by the novel. We can put the question in the alternative form: how was it that the area of national identity in which the cultural elite and the broad mass of the population met was in England and France the novel, and in Italy (Kimbell 1991:394) and Germany the opera?

It is important not to exaggerate here, and just in case some of the ensuing arguments seem over-stated I wish here to make three axiomatic remarks. First that I am not ignoring the importance of music in other traditions, notably the French. Most of the polemics we referred to in connection with Debussy and Saint-Saëns, much of the self-understanding of composers such as Fauré or Gounod, Poulenc even, depended on their understanding of the particularist nature of their experience as French musicians, the corresponding musical emphasis of their compositions (often thought to

---

[10]   A very moot point, of course. Lessing rejected French models of theatre for English ones, Mussorgsky vehemently attacked Mendelssohn (v. Motte-Habe 1991:48f) as an unsuitable model for Russian music, and of course Melville claimed to prefer the Shakespeares growing up on the banks of the Ohio to the 'foreign' bard of Avon. These were rejections of foreigners, but not necessarily xenophobic – as Lessing's choice of a different foreigner for his model made clear.

reside in French approaches to rhythm[11]) or the particularly French nature of their religious experience. In focusing on the German and Italian experience as dominated by opera rather than the novel, there is no intention of going back behind these truths. Secondly: there is a sense that the model in this chapter has more to do with perceptions of the national cultures from outside than with realities (though where objective realities might be in this field, it is hard to see[12]). This is as true of the view of the Germans as a musical nation as it is of their view of the prosaic English.[13] To the extent that this is true – and it is no argument against proceeding with the discussion – we should remember that these perceptions from outside were not hostile, indeed they were often formulated in open admiration of the riches of another culture: this was the case with Romain Rolland, for instance, despite the intemperate remarks we quoted above. In any case, which culture would not like to possess the Italian operatic tradition as its own? Thirdly: even if any of the arguments should seem convincing, then I have no interest in extending them to the present. They concern one period, which is now past. Germany – not even with the traumas associated with division and 're-unification' – cannot be described as a new nation, and no comment made about the role of culture in pre-1914 Italy offers explanation for any feature of its present reality.

Above all I wish in this chapter to avoid any question which approaches the claim to identify national characteristics. It has been so easy in the past not only to claim – as we shall see – that the Germans were 'good' at opera, but that, for instance, the English were 'bad' at it. Such claims are repeated in the view that 'the Italians' are musical (or 'the French' rationalist and prosaic, and therefore good at novels). In no time the claims of ethnicity – which we tried to dismiss in the opening chapters with regard to the nature of music itself – have taken over again, when it is the composers, or some alleged national facility for music itself, which is under discussion. Such

---

[11]   This contrasted with a German speciality in harmony and a 'natural' Italian affinity to melody.

[12]   There is little point in simply measuring the size of the output and looking for numerical supremacies. Jost Hermand (2008:18) reckons that between seventy and eighty thousand operas have been written since the seventeenth century. It would be meaningless to compare this number with the number of novels published over that period (of course, Hermand does not do that either). The matter is hardly statistical.

[13]   Such views varied from Heine's gentle ironics to Sombart's polemical war-time pamphlet *Händler und Helden* (1915). Let no-one imagine that, even in the days of heady nationalism, Bayreuth audiences were either inclusively German or made up of all classes. That selections of favorite Wagnerian pot-boilers were published under the title of *Unser Wagner* (Our Wagner), however, was not accidental: either as a recognition of the market, or of the genuine popularity of such pieces.

arguments should be alien to any civilized person when dealing with Richard Wagner; we should never admit any criterion which might potentially give space to anti-Semitic assumptions – if we can identify 'English' ethnic characteristics towards music, then why not 'Jewish' characteristics too? And who wishes to discuss whether Delius' or Handel/Händel's musicality have anything to do with their ancestry – let alone that of the acknowledged master of French grand opera, the German Joachim Meyerbeer?[14]

These approaches on the basis of nationality blur infinitely more interesting discussions: for instance the relationship between higher and popular music.[15] No-one would wish to deny the strength of the English folk tradition in music, yet it is invariably assumed that the 'musicality' of the Germans is a continuum extending from *Volkslied* to high opera, an assumption still more prevalent in discussions of Italian music – in both cases these assumptions were sedulously advanced by the composers themselves, not only by the Wagner of the 1840s, but by less political figures such as Brahms and Schubert, and of course by Verdi too. Why should popular musicality not break through into high culture? Arguments – most persuasively put forward by Michael Irwin (1991) – that it is the English language which resists the demands of operatic vocalization have to explain the excellence of the English choral tradition: it would be difficult to argue that the gap between the liturgical language of choral singing and the more pragmatic and material topics covered in opera is any wider in English than in German. It is not only the churches which are being deserted by contemporary linguistic usage. In asking why English culture in the nineteenth century culminates and is supremely represented in the novel, questions of national essentiality should concern us no further.

---

[14] Strikingly both Heine and Wagner in their portraits of Meyerbeer mention his German nationality only in connection with the circumstances unfavorable to opera which had forced him to leave Germany – as Heine says in his essay on Meyerbeer, 'the old rotten lifeless Germany with its blinkered philistines' (vi,66). It makes Wagner's later remarks on Meyerbeer as a Jew (and therefore lacking 'a mother language') (*Opera and Drama*, iii,293) still more gratuitous and offensive.

[15] Harry White's recent study of music within the Irish cultural tradition (2007) may profitably be consulted on such matters – the popular assumption encouraged by the Tourist Board that the Irish are 'very musical' needs to face up to the deficits in music's place within the high cultural tradition of Ireland. Its importance in modern Irish theatre is noticeable for bemoaning an absence rather than celebrating a presence. None of my arguments here against the concept of Jewish music are meant to deny the existence or diminish the importance of traditions specific to Jewish experience and expressed in folk-song or religious ceremony. Wagner's anti-Semitism was, of course, not concerned with Jewish music in that sense (or, most likely, in *any* sense at all).

It is vain to imagine that in a dozen pages – of, for that matter, in a dozen books – these questions might be answered. It is hardly less vain to imagine that the close and, I believe, highly relevant parallels between the place of opera in Germany and Italy can be developed beyond the reminders of affinity which are scattered through these pages. At best I hope to suggest what might be productive ways of thinking about the problem, and to use our study of the traditionally separate worlds of Wagner and the novel as pointer to these wider issues. Just as the earlier chapters tried to listen to Wagner's music rather than read his theories, in a similar fashion this chapter is more interested in Wagner's experiences than in his opinions, which are quoted only when they underline general truths about his age.

Socio-economic arguments for the well-being of the novel

From the earliest days, as they tried to account for Germany's failure to produce a novel both of international stature and of emblematic national quality – such as that achieved by Scott, or Dickens –, critics looked at issues of German society. They argued that the weakness of the German novel was attributable to deficits in German society, and in particular to the underdevelopment of various social institutions. In a celebrated review of the novels of Fenimore Cooper, the critic Ludwig Börne wrote in 1825:

> We have no history, no climate, no national community, no market-place of life, no patriotic hearth, no major trade, we do not go to sea, and we have – no freedom to say what further things we lack. Where are novels going to come from? The English write them, and we simply *read* them. (1825:396-97)

[We briefly add that the failure to produce a novel is a defining feature of Italian literature in the nineteenth century. Between Alessandro Manzoni's *I promessi sposi* (a romantic historical novel of 1827) and the rural naturalism of Giovanni Verga (1840-1922), whose *Vita dei campi* (1880) is known best for having been adapted into the libretto of Mascagni's *Cavalleria rusticana* (1890), there is a considerable void. In particular, the Risorgimento produced hardly any novels, their function – as Volker Kapp's history of Italian literature explicitly states – being taken over by the opera. The history of Italian literature in these years is the history of the opera – from it alone the intellectual history ('mentality history') of the country can be drawn (Kapp 1991:302).]

Börne's argument is a double one. In common with other contemporaries, he laments the absence of certain institutionalized experiences, symbolized in

Germany's lack of one central metropolis. It was not just political exile which sent so many German writers and artists to the great cities of London ('not a city, but the world', sighed Verdi) and Paris, but a thirst for experience. The lack of comparable German cities was a product of the proliferation of small German states (this was the so-called *Kleinstaaterei*) and its effect was that German writers felt, as Börne explained, that they had no contact with a wider experience of life, or with the major historical impulses active at the time. In a similar fashion – although after Unification – the Italian intellectuals known as the *scarpigliatura* (whose number included the librettist of Verdi's later years, Arrigo Boito) complained of their 'age-old lagging behind other literatures' (Kapp 1992:286). By this they clearly meant the failure to produce *national* works of art, and their desire was to follow the route Börne had identified, namely to modernize literature by modernizing society. This was certainly how Italian intellectuals were understood in Germany. In an encyclopedic work on European cultures, Theodor Mundt (once a radical Young German) identified the principal effort of Italian intellectuals 'once again to participate in the highest level of European cultural life' (1853:751). In an interesting letter to a friend in Bologna, at the time of a performance of *Tannhäuser* in the city – after the achievement of Italian unity –, Wagner revealed that he understood the situation in Italy to have been identical to what he diagnosed in Germany, namely one in which political change would enable national art to flourish. In the new Italy, he writes, 'I saw again – leaving behind us the strange century of Italian decadence, with its castrato singing and its pirouettes – the incomparably productive popular spirit [of Italy], to which the post-Renaissance world owes all its art' (ix,289).

Leipzig and Dresden, where Wagner's early years were spent, had certainly lacked neither culture nor rich tradition – no child christened, like Wagner, in St. Thomas Church in Leipzig could feel himself in a provincial backwater, for the spirit of Bach was still alive in his church; but Wagner's artistic ambition clearly depended on city experiences which these places could not offer. He felt the need for that pulse of life and history which flowed only in Paris and London. It is not enough to say that he sought fame in the only markets large enough to meet his ambitions – it was a tempo of life, an interconnectedness of experience and an openness to the new which were his real goals. We need remind ourselves only that when Balzac began to write the *Comédie Humaine* Paris's population made it nearly a modern metropolis; in contrast, when Goethe finished his Wilhelm Meister novels, Weimar was a town of hardly more than six thousand inhabitants. Travel was the only way out, whether in exile or for experience. Brecht's famous phrase that he changed country more often than he changed his shoes would equally apply to Wagner's life, and it draws attention to a national, rather than merely personal feature of both periods of history. It was therefore no mere rhetorical trope when Mazzini compared his country, Italy, to the hardly more restless Wandering Jew (cit. Wilson 2007:144). The fact that none of the specific experiences of the city found any direct reflection in Wagner's work in no way contradicts his need for the city. Like the nation, only the city could provide the environment in which great art could be produced. It was the touchstone of what was important.

Historians follow Börne in extending his argument from the social institutions, to the importance of political factors in the emergence of the novel. Börne's comments are deliberately foreshortened, in that he refers only to censorship, the lack of freedom to discuss other deficits, and as a result has nothing to say of specific political forms. Historians argue – in part on the basis of the explicitly middle-class standpoint of the Realist novel – that more serious deficits existed in the political structures of Germany. In successive political systems following the defeat of Napoleon in 1815, the German middle-classes were barred from meaningful participation in the political life of their nation, and thus – so the argument runs – the experiential basis on which Realist novels were produced and read was eroded. The frustration of the democratic aspirations of the German intellectuals was marked at two highly significant moments, both of which possessed massive importance in Wagner's biography: the defeat of the revolution in 1848 (a defeat shared by Italian patriots) and the establishment of the Empire in 1871. The revolution failed to implement proper parliamentary structures: still worse, it witnessed the surrender of many intellectuals to the forces of reaction. From 1849 on middle-class intellectuals lacked any sense that it was worth seeking to be involved in public life, except in the de-politicized worlds of the professions and commerce – or, in the case of artists, public entertainment. This situation was sealed by the fact that the unification of 1871 took place without that democratic involvement so central to the English or French revolutions. When Bismarck claimed to have united Germany by 'blood and iron', he was pointing – without regret – to the absence of formal democratic or informal cultural support for his project. The once liberal middle-classes compromised with the old feudal system, and thereby prolonged it. Intellectuals – in the cases where they had gone neither to America nor to prison – made their peace too, and retreated into a world of private culture unconcerned with their political environment, Thomas Mann's description of Wagner's 'inwardness protected by the might of the state' (ix,419) is characteristic of Wagner's whole generation after

1871. It is hard to see how the Realist novel could thrive in such an environment.

None of this should be confused with cultural backwardness. It cannot be said that German novelists lacked a modern and commercial publishing industry to distribute their works. Perhaps the only difference between German circumstances and those which we quoted from Balzac's *Illusions Perdues* was that Germany did not know the contrast with the capital city on which Balzac's passage was constructed. Germany was all province. It's important to emphasize this point, since it is possible – when discussing the emergence of opera in Germany – to argue from the comparative excellence of the infrastructure necessary to that art-form. Notoriously, as a result of the plethora of small states and separate courts in mid-century, Germany (and Italy) had a relatively large number of opera houses – certainly more than other European states. However much both the musical directors and the repertoire of these operas may have been foreign – it was not just in Germany that the literary caricature of the Italian music director arose –, there was an outlet for new opera and a reasonable chance of new operas being performed. These favorable circumstances did not guarantee international success to a young composer – the absence of a metropolis meant that Wagner needed Paris and London to become known. Indeed he explicitly blamed *Kleinstaaterei* for the lack of proper German opera. 'Where was the public I was to appear in front of?', he asked in 1840 (i,151). If he went an hour down the road (i.e. into the neighboring German state), even the next opera house would not have heard of him. There was no national public. The continuation of patronage was perhaps more marked in Germany than in France or England, certainly in terms of literary activity. The survival of patronage in music was more general and was broken only by the creation of large public subscription orchestras at the end of the nineteenth century. It was the experience of patronage which forced Wagner into a series of humiliating subserviences to the rich and powerful. His humiliations were equaled only by the way in which Paris theaters treated him, where – as Goldsmith had remarked a hundred years previously – there was no other patron than the public, mediated by the theater owners. It was in Paris that Wagner experienced what was to become the more familiar phenomenon of rampant commercialism, to which – picking a current metaphor of the day – Wagner gave the label 'the art industry' (3,69). But if it is impossible to say that it was poor infrastructure which disadvantaged the novel, it is no more true that a good infrastructure advantaged the opera. Significant works of art feed off other factors – there are no simple recipes and no obvious material explanations.

Deep down, the critics of the nineteenth century, such as Börne himself, knew that, and the greatest mystery – why great artists arrive at particular times in particular societies – stayed decently unanswered. But it remained a popular theme among critics contemporary with Wagner to identify socio-economic reasons for the failure of particular cultural forms to develop. They ran the risk – not unknown in other areas of sociology – of appearing to deal in formulae, suggesting that there was a causal relationship between certain social concomitants and the appearance of the great novel or opera. A glance at the backward state of Russia at this time – backward in all those respects which made the Germans feel ashamed of themselves – suggests that the genius of Tolstoy and Turgenev was not that fussy about the society in which it would flourish: indeed that sense of the connectedness which democracy and a modern metropolis were supposed to bring to characters' experience of life is noticeably absent in many of their works, without impairing the Realism or universality of the work.

There is one example, however, which most strongly underlines both the nature of a longing for the novel and the arbitrariness of the conditions diagnosed for its emergence: namely the United States of America. We listen – after Börne's remarks with some surprise – to Nathaniel Hawthorne writing in the Preface to his novel *The Marble Faun* (1860):

> No author, without a trial, can conceive of the difficulty of writing a Romance about a country where there is no shadow, no antiquity, no mystery, no picturesque and gloomy wrong, nor anything but a common prosperity, in broad and simple daylight, as is happily the case with my dear native land. It will be very long, I trust, before romance-writers may find congenial and easily handled themes either in the annals of our stalwart Republic, or in any characteristic and probable event of our individual lives. Romance and poetry, like ivy, lichens, and wall-flowers, need Ruin to make them grow.

It is worth considering this long quotation for three of its features. First, Hawthorne's uncertainty about terminology – it seems remarkable that in 1860 he is short of a word for a genre which has literary ambitions and which we would unhesitatingly diagnose as the novel. Wagner was not alone in the shortage of his vocabulary. Secondly, in however perverse a manner, Hawthorne clearly sees a direct connection between the state of his country and its ability to produce novels. This connection is so significant that the final point – the amusing claim that all those features of Europe in which Börne had diagnosed the *impossibility* of writing novels were in fact *essential* to the novel – seems less incongruous.[16] Hawthorne, like Henry James some twenty years later, did however see literary development as the outcome of some kind of social recipe – perhaps in our age we are more sanguine about such forms of cooking and regard them at best as aspirational, rather than diagnostic, certainly never as prescriptive.

Behind these discussions of the novel, present, absent, and aspired to, lies the issue which is our central concern in this chapter: the readiness of the nation to identify its 'imagined' greatness[17] in works of art and the consensus of population and cultural elite in this process. Clearly we must formulate our question differently, moving our focus away from mere socio-economic background. We should ask less in response to which conditions the Germans and Italians carried out this national identification through opera, rather than the novel, and rather focus on what were and are the implications of their having done so.

We knew the answer anyway

It will have been clear for some time that the easiest way to focus on the issue of German and Italian predilection for the national opera is to see the question in terms of the hare and the tortoise. For if we look at the finishing line – or at least the only one we have access to, namely the present – it is absolutely evident not only who won the race, the opera or the novel, but that the result was inevitable. Despite moments when the tortoise appears to make up ground, the hare has sprinted to the line and long since crossed it. While new operas are still being written today, the dominance of the novel seems unchallenged. Other combinations of music and story overshadow the opera – in that sense film and musical are the reality and opera itself the phantom – while opera seems to have receded into the pre-nineteenth century role of court entertainment. Our question as to the shifting generic dominances of the nineteenth century is by now firmly historical.

For many observers in the nineteenth and early twentieth century such an outcome had been entirely predictable. While Wagner shared with many of his generation a confidence in the renewal of genres, even for him the sense of working against the stream grew ever stronger. He spoke often of the

---

[16] It is the more ironic since the point of Börne's review had been enviously to praise the Americans for having so quickly achieved the national novel. Börne writes: 'the Americans have got there before us, a young nation, hardly forty years old, it makes you blush, it takes away all your self-confidence'. He would not have enjoyed Hawthorne's Preface.

[17] I refer to the seminal work of Benedict Anderson: *Imagined Communities* (1983).

secret accord between the work of art and the historical period, still more strongly the dynamic historical *movement*, but at every turn he failed to recognize that the market was moving in a different direction. The market which he, and all worthwhile artists, speculated on increasingly vanished over the horizon, and for the real market (itself a product of history) he had nothing but contempt. That's why his confidence in renewal is so striking, for by the time of his death the weight of opinion in cultural circles was that all traditional culture was doomed and that materialism, populism and Americanism would sweep all before them.[18] Wagner had observed that tendency in the novel (perhaps one reason why he did not go into the genre himself – its descent into 'journalism' and 'politics'), he saw that the mass appeal of the *Opéra Comique* had what he regarded as a catastrophic effect on artistic quality, and yet he still briefly believed that opera – and with it German art – could be renewed.

So our question is easily answered. Opera was on a downward path long before *Rienzi*. For all the moments of artistry, for all the magical achievements of Mozart, Meyerbeer, Auber and Wagner, they were traveling on the same doomed ship. And it was in the very nature of their chosen genre that their defeat would be major. One might argue (many poets have argued) that lyric poetry was traveling on the same route, yet poetry is so much cheaper to produce that it may well survive everything, even if in an extenuated condition. How much easier Wagner's life would have been, how free of boot-licking and fawning, if he had not had to find the finance to produce his operas. Just as the life of his chosen art-form was more strenuous, so its defeat was more bloody.

A more positive understanding of this outcome would be to recognize in the film and film music the continuation of Wagner's work. It is clearly a thoroughly worthwhile and significant approach, for it involves not just the biographies of those composers who came through the school of Wagner (who had not done that?) and ended in Hollywood, or Babelsberg, or Moscow. It raises the central issues of Wagner's aesthetics (simultaneity of word, music, gesture and the invisible orchestra) and offers an opportunity to recast much of Wagner's theory in a cinematographic mode. When Adorno rather contemptuously spoke of 'the birth of film from the spirit of music'[19]

---

[18]   This view was held no less firmly (and pessimistically) by many intellectuals in the USA (cf. on the American 'politics of cultural despair' HR 2007:58f).

[19]   (1964:114). The phrase is an inversion of Nietzsche's famous title: *The Birth of Tragedy from the Spirit of Music* – a process which Adorno clearly felt to be more important than the birth of Hollywood. In particular Adorno disliked what he called 'the hiding of production

he had, fortunately, not spoken the last word on the subject. Where none of this discussion helps is in the exploring the field of aesthetic development *before* the finishing-line. After all, we have simply agreed that the demise of opera is part of 'modernization', and therefore that Germany and Italy held on to the opera because they were so slow to participate in that modernization – they were 'backward' – and this says nothing of aesthetics. Yet it is precisely the outcome of our study of Wagner and the novel to show how clearly he participated from the start in the tendencies of the Enlightenment – tendencies which (as Adorno and Horkheimer's study predicted) would turn into the more negative form of modernization. We have seen that Wagner participated not just in Enlightenment, but in that modernization of musical and theatrical practice with whose consequences we still live today. How was it that modernization in Germany and Italy took a form which stayed within an archaic form (opera) rather than tamely settling for the 'modern' genre of the novel? So our last question concerns the ebb and flow of artistic movements: 'when one particular art starts, whether it is extinguished, and when, whether it is transformed into another, why one or other art-form is missing or is dominant at a particular time' (Spengler 1923:289). In short, we need to take a final look at the theory and the practice of the novel and opera.

Grand Theory and Grand Opera

Two types of theory offer themselves to anyone thinking about problems of the evolution of art-forms and literary style. Not surprisingly both were products of the very period we are discussing, when literary and cultural history seemed undermined by massive change. On one hand there is the cultural morphology which set out – on the broadest of all canvases – to see cycles rather than meaningless change and chaos, coherent patterns of evolution and – in consequence of that – some kind of sequence in cultures and their art-forms.[20] The other is Russian Formalism – a movement which set out to identify the constituting features of art, and of literature in particular. By focusing on those features alone which made art art – what in

---

behind the appearance of the product'; this basic dishonesty he held to be both 'the formal law of Wagner's work' (xiii,82) and the ethos of the commercial cinema.

[20]   This cultural morphology is an activity distinct from the scientific field which shares the same title. The subtitle of Oswald Spengler's major work was 'the morphology of world history' and it is from there that the name derives. Elements of it had evolved in nineteenth century anthropology and in progressive classical studies. Much of Nietzsche's writing is influenced by such currents of thought and strongly encourages them.

literature they called *literaturnost* – and eliminating everything which was socially determined or mimetic in art, the Formalists set out to explain how genres and art-forms evolve and to offer a corresponding understanding of literary history. It's very late in my book to introduce two mega-theories, and I expect neither to explain them fully nor to commend them to further attention. Nevertheless, both offer interesting perspectives on our question.

Spengler's main work is dauntingly long and intimidatingly broad in the knowledge it presupposes. From ancient Egyptian architecture to Renaissance painting, forms of military and political organization, Dutch interiors, Indian and Islamic culture and religion – no area of world history is closed to him. Spengler organizes these vast panoramas into historically and stylistically shaped groups and periods of evolution. He breathes (limited) life into these dry categories by two organic metaphors: the seasons of the year and the stages of human life. So world history moves from culture's spring (its infancy, producing creations of 'an awakening soul still heavy with dreams') through the high summer of maturing consciousness, the autumn of enlightenment and metropolitan science and intellectuality to the winter of our globalized urban civilization, in which 'men have lost the spiritual power to shape their world' (1,70f). Already in this brief outline one major drawback of Spengler's methods becomes clear – his prophecy of doom for western civilization, from which the book took its ominous and politically fateful title: *The Decline of the West*.[21] Yet this panoramic view can fascinate, showing up affinities between cultural and artistic phenomena which we would normally think of separately – for instance, in one section of his periodic charts: Impressionism, Wagner and American architecture. Three impulses which bear on our problem can be taken from Spengler's general argument:

1. Spengler is a great opponent of seeing cultural history as a kind of cafeteria in which each age must produce for consumption the same range of dishes as its predecessors. To 'explain' gaps in the menu (e.g. the

---

[21] First published in 1919. The title was such a success that a perfume under that name – *Der Untergang des Abendlandes* – became popular in mid-1920s Berlin. Decline might as well smell nice. Some forty years ago, a prominent member of the Nazi movement – Hanns Johst, who was to become President of the Chamber of Culture in the Third Reich – told me of first meeting Hitler ca. 1925 in the house of the piano-manufacturer Bechstein and listening entranced to Hitler telling his fashionable fellow-guests: 'The West will not decline. I can guarantee that.' Spengler's own attitude to the Third Reich is best described as ambiguous. His influence on English-speaking intellectuals was considerable: among professional historians it was Arnold Toynbee whose work is most often compared to Spengler's, and D.H.Lawrence was influenced briefly by Spengler's thinking.

absence of a novel in the Risorgimento) merely 'by postulating an accidental lack of creative personalities or the lack of corresponding circumstances' is, he argues, to misunderstand the whole nature of art (1,11). Our question is his type of question.

2. It follows that Spengler is contemptuous of critics' failure to understand the uniqueness of individual works of art. He may generalize a period – as when autumn turns to winter – but he never underestimates the uniqueness of the achievement of the individual artist, which is by pure artistic creation to encapsulate, often to *create* the period. His examples are Rembrandt's 'The Night Watch' and the *Meistersinger* (1,289). A great art-work participates in and makes visible the deepest complexities of history: 'If an art has limitations, these are historical, not technical or physiological' (1,288).

3. In consequence, it is part of Spengler's broad vision not to make absolute distinctions between genres, or indeed between the separate arts. Although, for instance, the novel belongs in a distinctive epoch of world-history it shares with other contemporary forms more than it shares with earlier prose writing. The clearest indication of this is seen in Spengler's attitude to Wagner. He obviously feels huge admiration for Wagner but he makes no bones about ascribing Wagner's work to the same period of 'winter' culture as the novel. In particular, the inclusion of words into music illustrates for Spengler an absolute and irreversible shift from earlier art. Wagner is as much part of the decline as his contemporaries in other forms, his dream of emulating the Greeks is illusory. There is no way back, no revival is possible, Spengler sums up this argument as follows: 'For this [i.e. Wagner's] music, seeing and hearing were a bridge into the soul, nothing else. For the Greeks such a visionary type of art reception was completely alien. The Greeks stroked marble with their eyes; the earthy sound of the *aulos* was tangible and corporeal to them.' (1,288)

So, if for different reasons, Spengler agreed with Nietzsche in arguing that Wagner's music came last in the sequence of the arts; that it was at the leading edge of the decline. Despite the fact that his own first publication had insisted that the supreme works of Greek tragedy had been products of the historically much earlier 'spirit of music', when Nietzsche looked at his own age music seemed to him (in a characteristic organic metaphor) 'the last of all plants in the last autumn blossoming of every culture it belongs to' (vi,3:421)

208 Wagner and the Novel

the most orientated towards the masses.[22] For that reason opera was a symptom of decline, the last in the line of the arts. A sequence of art-forms had also been a central element in Hegel's *Aesthetics*: that was in part the reason for Hegel's low estimation of the novel, which represented the decline in 'modern' art vis à vis classicism. We would have to stress only that decline, especially in the case of the novel, did not mean extinction. Hegel was not so committed to theory that he turned his own tastes into predictions.

I have not introduced Spengler in order that he tamely justifies the genre-hopping of this book, and I cannot claim to have lived up to the massive challenge hidden in the second point above. What Spengler does show is that to understand works of art we need not concern ourselves overly with the ideology which they contain or the fashions which they follow. The real level on which art-works make sense is the process of creation, and the closer we can come to that, the more we can discard extraneous elements and focus on the making of the work of art, the greater the affinities we shall find across genres. Comparing the opera with the contemporary novel is, by Spengler's standards, hardly bizarre, and if it is unorthodox then perhaps we need a new orthodoxy.

As we turn to the offerings of the Russian Formalists, we refer to the important elements of their theory which we have previously found relevant to our discussion of Wagner. The first was their sense of the relationship between artistic innovation and the renewal of the technical devices of the genre. Our comparison of *Tristan* and *Tristram Shandy* in Chapter Five suggested that in this respect the two works belong together, both being written on the very edge of the collapse of the formal means of the genre. They respond radically to the crisis of the material of their genre. The Formalists' awareness of the clock ticking in the genre illuminates these works as symptoms of the need for change. Opera and the novel were not cozy art forms happily engaged in predictable routine, but – where we are dealing with serious art – areas of struggle. What Wagner wrote at the start of his career - 'German opera suddenly no longer functioned'[23] – is an indication of a continuous rather an once-off crisis in the art. It was this

---

22 Repeatedly in Nietzsche's works we find echoes of what was manifestly the daily table-talk of Wagner. These echoes are heard in Nietzsche's criticism of music that wishes only for effect (that had been Wagner's criticism of i.a. Meyerbeer in *Opera and Drama* – iii,301) – Nietzsche applies almost the same words to Wagner's chasing of effects – and the echo is unmistakable here too: obviously Nietzsche had taken in much of Wagner's diatribes against the *Opéra Comique* and he was merely passing them on as his own. For himself he knew little of the music world.

23 '[M]it der deutschen Oper ging es auf einmal auch gar nicht mehr' (ix,47).

which made artists especially frightened of parody – they knew on what thin ice their works were always condemned to skate.

One of the other important shifts of mind-set which the Formalists wished critics to practice was to move from thinking of literary history merely as duration (i.e. as periods) and to think of it also as a cross-section through literary culture at one given moment. The shift is close to the revolution that Saussure introduced into linguistics, moving attention from *langue* (the language as it exists and develops across time) to *parole* – the language of the everyday moment, a concrete selection from the possibilities contained within *langue*. (A frequently used metaphor was the contrast between a rope – thought of as length and duration – and a cross-section of the rope, in which the interrelation between the individual strands of the rope can be seen.)

Most of this book's discussion has been concerned with literary history as length, although our brief departure into discourse theory in Chapter Five examined the understanding of Realism at particular historical moments and its interrelations with other discourses – that is, in historical cross-section. In fact everywhere we discuss the individual work of art we are concerned with *parole – parole* is what the artist uses from the totality of possibilities open to them to fashion the individual work at discreet historical moments. While the work passes back into *langue*, in as much as it has changed the global possibilities of the genre – after *Tristan* one must write differently, just as Scott, Balzac, or Tolstoy altered the general landscape of the novel – the work itself is a revelation of the momentary cross-section. And within each work there is a multitude of voices and forms of expression. *Parole* is a totality, a world in itself, a system held together by balance and difference. Each work of art is a system to itself, and therefore, the Formalists Tynianov and Eichenbaum argued, literary history is not just the rope as a length, but it is the juxtaposition of an infinite series of cross-sections, which behave to each other in the same way as the elements within the individual art-work – that is, in difference and balance. And while we can see change by comparing the position of the two ends of the rope – Romanticism and Naturalism, for example – the Formalists propose that we should see change in the relationship between cross-sections, those micro-systems illuminated and illustrated by individual works of art. And it is this thought which, I would like to suggest, can help with our question.

To illustrate the argument in brief is not easy,[24] but since we have been talking of the novel let us take three well-known scenes from novels with

---

[24] For reasons that will become clear, the best – but by no means the shortest – approach is to see the progression within a series of poetic expressions of a fixed topos. An obvious

which we have become familiar, and which range in time across the nineteenth century. We pick one theme, the death, ultimately the suicide, of a significant character and briefly sketch the nature of the contrasts.

At once her lungs began to heave rapidly, the whole of her tongue protruded from her mouth, her rolling eyes turned pale like the globes of two guttering lamps: she might have been dead already, but for the frightful oscillation of her ribs [...] As the death-rattle grew louder, the priest hastened his orisons; they mingled with Bovary's stifled sobs, and sometimes everything seemed to be drowned in the dull murmur of the Latin syllables, that sounded like the tolling of a knell. Suddenly there was a clumping of sabots on the pavement outside, the scraping of a stick and a voice came up, a hoarse voice singing: *When the sun shines warm above, / It turns a maiden's thoughts to love.* [...] A convulsion flung her down upon the mattress. They moved nearer. She was no more. (1857:336,337)

So Emma Bovary goes to her death in 1857. The language is naturalist in its physical detail – we might remember the care Flaubert took to discover the sensations and symptoms of arsenic poisoning –, in the contrast which it establishes between the romantic illusions which Emma has lived and died by and the realities of her final hours. Its effectiveness consists in the contrast and balance between the explicit and shocking realities and the conventional tropes – with familiar metaphors and 'poetic' figures, appearing in a form that was once called 'poetic justice'. The scene is also emblematic of the social ensemble; all agencies are represented, and even at this extreme moment Flaubert's skepticism about the Church and his scorn for provincial mediocrity and stupidity find continuous expression.

She wanted to fall under the first carriage, the midpoint of which had drawn even with her. But the red bag, which she started taking off her arm, delayed her, and it was too late: the midpoint went by. She had to wait for the next carriage. A feeling seized her, similar to what she experienced when preparing to go into the water for a swim, and she crossed herself. [...] Yet she did not take her eyes from the wheels of the approaching second carriage. And just at the moment when the midpoint between the two wheels came even with her, she threw the red bag aside and, drawing her head down between her shoulders, fell on her hands under the carriage, and with a light movement, as if preparing to get up again at once, sank to her knees. [...] And the candle by the light of which she had been reading that book filled with anxieties, deceptions, grief and evil, flared up brighter than ever, lit up for her all that had once been in darkness, sputtered, grew dim, and went out for ever. (1877:768)

---

candidate would be the Ophelia topos, as it is worked on across the centuries from Shakespeare to Baudelaire, Rimbaud, Heym, Benn and beyond. With a stable mass of content and an established intellectual-emotional range (reflections on death and nature, sexuality, pity and indifference, beauty and cruelty etc) the wide variety of devices and their interdependencies become evident in the different balances through which the 'same' content gets expressed. (cf. Blume 1954).

In this, no less famous scene (from 1877), it is Anna Karenina who dies, and in perhaps a still more contemporary fashion. The modern world is as present therefore at Anna's death as it was round Emma's bed, and Anna dies under the wheels of the symbol of modernity – the railway. Yet we see no details. Her red bag represents to readers the physical suffering Anna's body is about to undergo – it is one of the most famous pieces of metonymy in literature. The traditional metaphor of the candle, which Flaubert needed to evoke naturalistically in the flickering of Emma's rolling eyes, is used in full poetic expression, something which Flaubert avoided, perhaps because it would have destroyed the balance of his scene; while the physical identification with the dying woman – to achieve which Flaubert himself took arsenic – becomes possible in an extraordinary evocation of what it feels like before lowering oneself into cold water, a comparison which lies outside the traditional reference of this scene yet serves to make death more prosaic and everyday. It may be unconventional, but it is so strong that it binds in the metonymic features and allows the full horror of the scene to be captured.

> Cases of typhoid fever take the following course. The patient feels depressed and moody – a condition which grows rapidly worse until it amounts to acute despondency. [...] Cases of typhoid take the following course: When the fever is at its height, life calls to the patient: calls out to him as he wanders in his distant dream, and summons him in no uncertain voice. [...] he may recognize a bond existing still between him and that stirring, colorful, callous existence which he thought he had left so far behind him. Then, however far he may have wandered on his distant path, he will turn back and live. But if he shudders when he hears life's voice, if the memory of that vanished scene and the sound of that lusty summons make him shake his head, make him put out his hand to ward off as he flies forward in the way of escape that has opened to him – then it is clear that the patient will die. (1901:585,587)

The reader does not learn whose death this is until the beginning of the next chapter, when it is clear that Hanno Buddenbrook, the last of the family, has died. For the reader the death is tragic and heart-rending – no less than the deaths of Emma and Anna –, although for each of these characters death is a release. As the quotation makes clear, 'the patient' determines the outcome of the illness by his will to live, and Hanno is too disgusted by life to want to turn back. So the scene provokes profound reflections on the nature of death (like the Latin prayers of the priest and the 'book' of her life that flashes in front of Anna). Its objectivity has been so enhanced that the readers meet death, so to speak, as a separate character in the novel. The essence of all three scenes is to objectify death and yet keep the individual in sight. The documentary element of the scene could not be stronger, moving from physical effects of poison and the steam-train we are simply presented with a few pages from a medical encyclopedia and the individual character is objectivized into 'the patient'. Yet the reader is as shaken as by the death of Mimi or Little Nell.

In each of these situations, therefore, reflecting cross-sections of literary history situated more or less within the length of rope we call Realism, something very similar is being evoked. And it is happening within more or less the same ideological frame and with a similarly defined emotional spectrum. No flights of angels take off and land, there is no 'beautiful' death and the reader's emotions are handled in a similar way. Of course the reader cares and is saddened by what happens – how could these be three of the world's greatest novels if readers did not care or were not deeply moved? The conventionalities are established, the objectivity of Flaubert's description means that Tolstoy does not need to say as much and Mann needs to say next to nothing. Within that objective context very conventional motifs can be built in – the prayers as a death knoll (Shakespearean, I think, though the translation furthers this interpretation with the word 'orisons'), life as a candle (certainly *Macbeth*) and an almost medieval discussion between the patient and death: will you join the dance? The objective framework permits these ancient tropes to become expressive once more, not to be sentimental and archaic. In just this way the lyrical moments of *Elektra* are the more powerful for being embedded in disharmony, and the occasional traditional tonality produced by Schönberg's twelve-tone music is electrifying to hear, rather than conventional. The range of devices remains as constant as the emotions to be expressed: what the Formalists help us to observe as the process of literary history is the re-occupation, re-functioning[25] of the devices, the balanced, systematic character of change within literary works.

So we can see how Tynianov compared literary history itself with a work of art, and how the idea of the literary system embraces both the equipping of words and tropes with interrelated significance[26] and the evolution of macro-systems over the generations. This recognition brings me to my final point, which – again I stress – is an attempt to see things differently, rather than a fixed conclusion. Formalist theory invites us to think of systems of culture – the *langues* embedded in whichever macro-unit one chooses: nation, continent, whatever – as oceans of potentiality. From these oceans of

---

[25]   Brooks would describe this as the re-cathexizing of tropes – i.e. altering the choice of tropes into which the psychic energy of author (and reader) flows (cf. above, p.105).

[26]   A Formalist reading of music history would be very rewarding, since everything we said about music in Chapter Two was predicated on the idea of music's systematicity: things mean something in music only in relation to other things. Otherwise music is simply a noise. That is the starting-point for Levi-Strauss' explorations of Wagner.

possibility works of art pick out the *parole* appropriate to their situation and
to the situation of their genre. All cultures have the same things to say – like
poetry they question values, they celebrate positive feeling, they practice
melancholy and grief, and they reflect on experience – and in each
generation, at each cross-section of the long thread which is their life,
cultures will pick on different combinations of the available forms of
expression. Spengler's view that art-forms can simply vanish for ever, that
there is no repetition and no revival, does not have to be true: it is easier to
think of forms retreating into a lower water table from which the efforts of
subsequent generations can rescue, if not them, then their component parts. In
this subterranean stream Wagner found not only his themes, he found too the
novelist's devices which he re-fashioned into the structure and balance of his
operas; in the same way his own achievements and innovations went into the
stream from which novelists subsequently fashioned the devices of new
novels. We do not enter into the same river twice, Heraclitus famously
remarked. But equally there is only one stream and, as we saw in the
collaboration of artists from different genres in the common, synthesizing
activity of making an opera (and in the dual operation of Wagner's own
mind, as librettist and composer), it is from that one stream that artists drink.
Our view of the making of opera, the games we play to see the distinctive
features of each genre, both sharpen our eyes for genre and blur the certainty
with which we place genres as defining blocks for art and for the
communities in which art is produced.

Wagner draws on those same energies which others refashion as novels,
the devices – objectivity and personification, symbol and detail, cleverness
and feeling, loud and quiet, large and small – are mixed afresh in each genre,
at each cross-section of the continuity of an age. The choice of genre is
driven by identifiable factors – the drive for success, a desire to match one's
vision with the precise state of play in the various genres (the one thing we
have never contemplated is that Wagner would have wished to write *old-
fashioned* novels), perhaps too, as Börne suggested, the restrictions placed on
the various genres – and even the artist's personality is in complex ways a
product of the historical moment. What emerges at one moment as opera
becomes novel: whether today's novels will ever re-emerge as operas may
seem unlikely, but we are not at the finishing-line.

Bibliography

Abbate, Carolyn & Parker, Roger, *Analyzing Opera. Verdi and Wagner* (Berkeley/London: University of California Press, 1989)

Ackermann, Peter, *Richard Wagners 'Der Ring des Nibelungen' und die Dialektik der Aufklärung* (Tutzing: Schneider, 1981) (Frankfurter Beiträge zur Musikwissenschaft, 9)

Adorno, Theodor W., *Gesammelte Schriften* (Frankfurt: Suhrkamp,1971)

Adorno, Theodor W. & Horkheimer, Max, *Dialectic of Enlightenment* (1944), translated by John Cumming (New York: Seabury Press, 1972)

Anderson, Benedict R. O'G., *Imagined Communities: Reflections on the Origin and Spread of Nationalism* (London: Verso, 1983)

Aspden, Suzanne, Arne's Paradox. National Opera in eighteenth-century Britain, in: Lodato, Aspden & Bernhart (2002), 195-215

Balzac, Honoré de, *Lost Illusions*, translated Herbert J. Hunt (Harmondsworth: Penguin, 1971)

Baudelaire, Charles, *Richard Wagner et 'Tannhaüser'* [sic] *à Paris* (6 April 1861), in: *Oeuvres complètes: L'Art Romantique* (Paris: Conard, 1923), 199-252

Becker, George Joseph, *Documents of Modern Literary Realism* (Princeton, New Jersey: Princeton University Press, 1963)

Becker, Heinz, Die historische Bedeutung der Grand Opéra, in: Salmen (1965), 151-160

Beller-McKenna, Daniel, *Brahms and the German Spirit* (Cambridge Ma./London: Harvard University Press, 2004)

Bendix, Regina, *In Search of Authenticity. The Formation of Folklore Studies* (Madison: University of Wisconsin Press, 1997)

Blackbourne, David, *The Conquest of Nature. Water, Landscape and the Making of Modern Germany* (N.Y./London: Norton, 2006)

Bloch, Ernst, Rettung Wagners durch Karl May, in: *Anbruch: Monatsschrift für moderne Musik*, 11/1 (1929), 4-10

————., *Gesammelte Werke* (Frankfurt: Suhrkamp, 1965)

Bloom, Harold, *The Anxiety of Influence* (Oxford: Oxford University Press, 1973)

Blume, Bernhard, Das ertrunkene Mädchen. Rimbauds ‚Ophélie' in der deutschen Literatur, in: *Germanisch-romanische Monatsschriften* NF 4/35 (1954), 108-19

Börne, Ludwig, Coopers Romane (1825), in: *Sämtliche Schriften*, vol. 2 (Düsseldorf: Melzer, 1964), 395-403

Borchmeyer, Dieter, *Das Theater Richard Wagners. Idee – Dichtung –
Wirkung* (Stuttgart: Reclam, 1982), esp. 125-151
———., Thomas Mann und Richard Wagners Anti-Poetik des Romans, in:
Poetik und Geschichte: Viktor Žmegač zum 60. Geburtstag, ed. Dieter
Borchmeyer (Tübingen: Niemeyer, 1989), 390-411
Brecht, Bertolt, *Werke* (Suhrkamp: Frankfurt/Berlin, 1988)
Bronfen, Elisabeth, Das Lachen Kundrys, in: Bronfen, Santer & Žižek
(1999), 47-66
Bronfen, Elisabeth, Santer, Eric, & Žižek, Slavoj, *'Enden sah ich die Welt'.
Wagner und die Philosophie in der Oper* (Vienna: Turia u. Kant, 1999)
Brooks, Peter, *Reading for the Plot. Design and Intention in Narrative*
(Oxford: Clarendon, 1984)
Brown, Matthew, Isolde's narrative: From Hauptmotiv to Tonal Model, in:
Abbate & Parker (1989), 180-201
Buchan, John, *The Three Hostages* (1924) (Harmondsworth: Penguin, 1981)
Capra, Marco, 'Effekt, nichts als Effekt'. Aspekte der Rezeption der Opern
Verdis im Italien des 19. Jahrhunderts, in: Engelhardt (2001), 117-142
Carnegy, Patrick, *Wagner and the Art of the Theater* (New Haven,
Conn./London: Yale University Press, 2006)
Cicora, Mary A., *From History to Myth. Wagner's 'Tannhäuser' and its
Literary Sources* (Bern/New York: Peter Lang, 1992)
———., *Wagner's 'Ring' and German Drama. Comparative Studies in
Mythology and History in Drama* (Westport, Conn./London: Greenwood
Press, 1999)
Dahlhaus, Carl, Wagners Begriff der ‚dichterisch-musikalischen Periode', in:
Salmen (1965), 179-194
———., Das ‚Verstehen' von Musik und die Sprache der musikalischen
Analyse, in: Faltin & Reinecker (1973), 37-47
———., *Musikalischer Realismus. Zur Musikgeschichte des 19. Jahrhunderts*
(Munich: Piper, 1982). *Realism in Nineteenth-Century Music*, translated
Mary Whitall (Cambridge: Cambridge University Press, 1985)
———., *Richard Wagners Musikdramen* (Stuttgart: Reclam, 1996²)
Darcy, Warren, *Wagner's 'Das Rheingold'* (Oxford: Clarendon, 1993)
Deathridge, John, *Wagner's 'Rienzi'. A Reappraisal Based on a Study of the
Sketches and Drafts* (Oxford: Clarendon, 1977)
Dellamora, Richard & Fischlin, Daniel (ed.s), *The Work of Opera: Genre,
Nationhood and Sexual Difference* (New York: Columbia University
Press, 1997)
Del Mar, Norman, *Richard Strauss. A Critical Commentary on his Life and
Works* (1962) (London: Barrie & Jenkins, 1978)

Demet, Michel-François, Cosima Wagner, in: *Richard Wagner. Wie antisemitisch darf ein Künstler sein? Musik-Konzepte*, 5 (Munich: text + kritik 1985), 50-53

Dettmering, Peter, *Dichtung und Psychoanalyse: Bd. 1: Thomas Mann, Rainer Maria Rilke, Richard Wagner* (Frankfurt a.m.: Fachbuchhandlung für Psychologie, 1976)

Dierks, Manfred, Traumzeit und Verdichtung: Der Einfluss der Psychoanalyse auf Thomas Manns Erzählweise, in: E.Hefterich and H. Koopmann (ed.s), *Thomas Mann und seine Quellen: Festschrift für Hans Wysling* (Frankfurt a.m.: Klostermann, 1991)

Döge, Klaus, Jost, Christa, & Jost, Peter (ed.), *,Schlagen Sie die Kraft der Reflexion nicht zu gering an'. Beiträge zu Richard Wagners Denken, Werk und Wirken* (Mainz: Schott, 2002)

Döhring, Sieghart, Puccinis ,Italianità', in: Motte-Haber (1991), 122-31

Edler, Arnfried, Zur Musikanschauung von Adolf Bernhard Marx, in: Salmen (1965), 103-112

Engelhardt, Markus (ed.), *Giuseppe Verdi und seine Zeit* (Laaber: Laaber Verlag 2001)

Faltin, Peter, & Reinecker, Hans-Peter (ed.), *Musik und Verstehen. Aufsätze zur semiotischen Theorie, Ästhetik und Soziologie der musikalischen Rezeption* (Cologne: Arno Volk Verlag, 1973)

Flaubert, Gustave, *Madame Bovary* (1857), transl. by Alan Russell (Harmondsworth: Penguin, 1967)

Fontane, Theodor, Unsere epische und lyrische Poesie seit 1848 (1853), in: *Sämtliche Werke* (Munich: Nymphenburger, 1963), xxi, 7-33

———., *Effi Briest*, translated Helen Chambers & Hugh Rorison (Harmondsworth: Penguin, 2001)

Frank, Manfred, *Die unendliche Fahrt: Ein Motiv und sein Text* (Frankfurt a.M.: Suhrkamp, 1979)

Freud, Sigmund, *Werke* (Frankfurt: Fischer, 1966)

Freytag, Gustav, *Die Technik des Dramas* (Leipzig: Hirzel, 1863)

Gabriel, Francis, *Richard Wagner: le chant de l'inconscient* (Paris: Anthropos, 1998)

Gay, Peter, *Education of the Senses* (New York: Oxford University Press, 1984) (*The Bourgeois Experience*, vol. 1)

Geck, Martin, *Zwischen Romantik und Restauration. Musik im Realismus-Diskurs der Jahre 1848 bis 1871* (Stuttgart: Metzler/Bärenreiter, 2001)

———., Richard Wagner und der musikalische Realismus, in: Döge, Jost, & Jost (2002), 182-192

Goffman, Erving, *Behavior in Public Places. Notes on the Social Organization* of *Gatherings* (N.Y.: Free Press, 1963)

Graf, Max, *Richard Wagner im ,Fliegenden Holländer'. Ein Beitrag zur Psychologie künstlerischen Schaffens* (Schriften zur angewandten Seelenkunde, hrsg. von Prof. Dr. Siegm. Freud, 9. Heft, 1911) (Kraus Reprint: 1970)

Gregor-Dellin, Martin, *Richard Wagner. Sein Leben, sein Werk, sein Jahrhundert* (Munich: Goldmann/Schotts 1983)

Grey, Thomas, Metaphorical modes in nineteenth century music criticism: image, narrative and idea, in: Scher (1992), 93-117

Grimm, Reinhold & Hermand, Jost (ed.s), *Re-Reading Wagner* (Madison: University of Wisconsin Press, 1993) (Wisconsin Workshop 21: *Monatshefte*, occasional volume 13)

Gutman, Robert W., *Richard Wagner: the Man, his Mind and his Music* (London: Secker and Warburg, 1968)

Hanslick, Eduard (anonymous review of *Vom Musikalisch-Schönen*), in: *Die Grenzboten*, 1/1 (1855), 475

——., *Was denken Sie von Wagner? Mit Eduard Hanslick in der Wiener Hofoper. Kritiker und Schilderungen*, ed. Michael Jahn (Vienna: Verlag Der Apfel, 2007) (Schriften zur Wiener Operngeschichte, Bd. 4)

Hebbel, Friedrich, *Werke* (Munich: Hanser, 1963)

Heftrich, Eckehard, *Zauberbergmusik. Über Thomas Mann*, vol. 1 (Frankfurt: Klostermann, 1975)

Helmstetter, Rudolf, *Die Geburt des Realismus aus dem Dunst des Familienblatts. Fontane und die öffentlichkeitsgschichtlichen Rahmenbedingungen des Poetischen Realismus* (Munich: Fink, 1998)

Hemmings, F.W.J. (ed.), *The Age of Realism* (Harmondsworth: Penguin, 1974) (Pelican Guides to European Literature)

Hermand, Jost, *Glanz und Elend der deutschen Oper* (Cologne, Weimar: Böhlau, 2008)

——., Wagner's Last Supper. The vegetarian gospel of his *Parsifal*, in: Grimm & Hermand (1993), 103-118

HLWC, *Brünhilde* [sic]: *A Psychological Study* (London: Theosophical Publishing Society, 1909)

Hömberg, Walter, *Zeitgeist und Ideenschmuggel: Die Kommunikationsstrategie des jungen Deutschland* (Stuttgart: Metzler, 1975)

Hohendahl, Peter Uwe, Reworking history. Wagner's German myth of Nuremberg, in: Grimm & Hermand (1993), 39-60

Ingenhoff, Anette, Wagners Romankritik, in: Anette Ingenhoff, *Drama oder Epos. Richard Wagners Gattungstheorie des musikalischen Dramas* (Tübingen: Niemeyer, 1987), 80-100

Irwin, Michael, *Words and Music* (Canterbury: University of Kent, 1991)

Janowski, Franca, Ottocento, in: Kapp (1992), 249-302

Jauss, Hans-Robert, *Literaturgeschichte als Provokation der Literaturwissenschaft* (1967) (Frankfurt a.m.: Suhrkamp, 1970). *Towards an Aesthetic of Reception* (Hassocks: Harvester, 1968)

Jung, C.G., Psychology and Literature (1930), in: *Collected Works of C.G.Jung*, vol. 15 (London: Routledge & Kegan Paul, 1966), 84-105

Kamuf, Peggy, The Replay's the Thing, in: Levin (1994), 79-105

Kapp, Volker (ed.), *Italienische Literaturgeschichte* (Stuttgart/Weimar: Metzler, 1992)

Kelly, Barbara L., (ed.), *French Music, Culture and National Identity, 1870-1939* (Rochester: University of Rochester Press, 2008)

Kimbell, David, *Italian Opera* (Cambridge: Cambridge University Press, 1991)

Kittler, Friedrich A., *Aufschreibesysteme 1800-1900* (Munich: Fink, 1985)

Kramer, Lawrence, *Music and Poetry: the Nineteenth Century and After* (Berkeley/ London: University of California Press, 1984)

——., *Music as Cultural Practice 1800-1900* (Berkeley/London: University of California Press, 1990)

Kurth, Ernst, *Romantische Harmonik und ihre Krise in Wagners ‚Tristan'* (1923) (Hildesheim: Olms, 1968)

Laing, Alan, *Tonality in Wagner's 'Der Ring des Nibelungen'* (Ph.D. Thesis: Edinburgh, 1973

Lauster, Martina, *Sketches of the nineteenth Century. European Journalism and its Physiologies 1830-50* (Houndmills: Palgrave Macmillan, 2007)

Levin, David J., *Opera Through Other Eyes* (Stanford, Ca.: Stanford University Press, 1994)

Lewin, David, Musical Analysis as stage direction, in: Scher 1992, 163-176

Lissa, Zofia, Ebenen des musikalischen Verstehens, in: Faltin & Reinecker (1973), 217-246

Lodato, Suzanne M., Aspden, Suzanne, & Bernhart, Walter (ed.s), *Word and Music Studies and on Cultural Identity and the Musical Stage. Essays in Honor of Steven Paul Scher* (Amsterdam/New York: Rodopi, 2002)

Lukács, Georg, *Die Theorie des Romans* (1918) (Neuwied: Luchterhand, 1963)

Lytton, Edward Bulwer, *Rienzi; The Last of the Roman Tribunes* (1835) (London, Paris etc: Cassels, n.d.)

McClatchie, Stephen, *Analyzing Wagner's Operas. Alfred Lorenz and German Nationalist Ideology* (Rochester, New York: University of Rochester Press, 1998)

Maffei, Giuseppe, *Storia della letteratura italiana, dall' origine della lingua sino á nostri giorni* (1834) (Italia,1884[3])

Mann, Thomas, *Buddenbrooks* (1901), translated by Helen Lowe-Porter (Harmondsworth: Penguin 2000)

———., Ibsen und Wagner, in: *Gesammelte Werke in zwölf Bänden* (Frankfurt a.m.: Fischer, 1974) vol. 10, 227-29

———., Versuch über das Theater, in: *Gesammelte Werke in zwölf Bänden* (Frankfurt a.m.: Fischer, 1974) vol. 10, 23-62

———., Blood of the Walsungs, & Tristan, in: *Stories of Three Decades,* translated Helen Lowe-Porter (London: Secker and Warburg 1946), pp. 297-319, 133-166

———., Sufferings and Greatness of Richard Wagner (1933), in: *Essays of Three Decades*, translated Helen Lowe-Porter (London: Secker and Warburg 1947), 307-52

Marquard, Odo, Zur Bedeutung der Theorie des Unbewußten für eine Theorie der nicht mehr schönen Künste, in: Hans-Robert Jauss (ed.), *Die nicht mehr schönen Künste. Grenzphänomene des Ästhetischen* (Munich: Fink, 1968), 375-392

Martens, Wolfgang, *Lyrik kommerziell. Das Kartell lyrischer Autoren 1902-1922* (Munich: Fink, 1975[2])

Matejka, Ladislav, & Pomorska, Krystina (ed.s), *Readings in Russian Poetics. Formalist and Structuralist Views* (Cambridge Ma./London: MIT Press, 1971)

Matt, Peter von, *Verkommene Söhne, missratene Töchter. Familiendesaster in der Literatur* (Munich/Vienna: Hanser, 1995)

Meisel, Perry, *The literary Freud* (New York/London: Routledge, 2007)

Melville, Herman, *Writings of Herman Melville* (Evanston and Chicago: Northwestern, 1968).

Mila, Massimo, Melodramma Romantico, in: Caretti, Lanfranco, & Luti, Giorgio, *La letteratura italiana per saggi storicamente disposti: L'Ottocento* (Milan: Mursia, 1973), 848-853

Mitford, Mary Russell, *Rienzi. A Tragedy in Five Acts*, in: *The Dramatic Works of Mary Russell Mitford*, vol.1 (London: Hurst and Blackett, 1854), 1-79

Morris, Christopher, *Reading Opera between the Lines. Orchestral Interludes and Cultural Meaning from Wagner to Berg* (Cambridge: Cambridge University Press, 2002)

Motte-Habe, Helga de la (ed.), *Nationaler Stil und europäische Dimension in der Musik der Jahrhundertwende* (Darmstadt: Wissenschaftliche Buchgesellschaft, 1991)

Mueller, Norbert, *Die Nibelungendichter Hebbel und Wagner. Der Tragiker und seine ,Nibelungen' im Widerstreit mit dem Musikdramatiker und dessen ,Ring'* (Essen: Frohn Verlag, 1991)

Mundt, Theodor, *Geschichte der Literatur der Gegenwart. Vorlesungen [..]. Von dem Jahre 1789 bis zur neuesten Zeit* (Leipzig: Simon, 1853)

Musil, Robert, *Tagebücher*, ed. Adolf Frisé (Reinbek: Rowohlt, 1976)

Nicolodi, Fiamma, Nationalistische Aspekte im Mythos von der 'alten Musik' in Italien und Frankreich, in: Motte-Habe (1991), 102-121

O'Grady, Deirdre, *Piave, Boito, Pirandello – from Romantic Realism to Modernism* (Lewiston, New York: Edward Mellor, 2000)

Phillips-Matz, Mary Jane, *Verdi – A Biography* (Oxford: Oxford University Press, 1993)

Prawer, Siegbert, *Karl Marx and World Literature* (Oxford: Oxford University Press, 1978)

Rabinowitz, Peter D., Chord and discourse: listening through the written word, in: Scher (1992), 38-56

Rank, Otto, *Das Inzest-Motiv in Dichtung und Sage. Grundzüge einer Psychologie des dichterischen Schaffens* (1912) (reprint: Darmstadt: Wissenschaftliche Buchgesellschaft, 1974). *The Incest Theme in Literature and Legend.* Translated by Gregory C. Richter (Baltimore: John Hopkins University Press, 1991)

Ridley, Hugh, Myth as Illusion or Cognition, in: *German Life and Letters*, 34/1 (October 1980), 74-80

——., *'Relations Stop Nowhere'. The Common Literary Foundations of German and American Literature 1830-1917* (Amsterdam: Rodopi, 2007)

Roden, Eva, *Einflüsse auf Richard Wagner vor Schopenhauer* (Vienna/Münster: Literatur Verlag, 2006)

Rosen, Charles: Happy Birthday, Frédéric Chopin!, in: *NYRB* June 24 2010, pp.4-6

Rüland, Dorothea, *Künstler und Gesellschaft. Die Libretti und Schriften des jungen Richard Wagner aus germanistischer Sicht* (Frankfurt a.M./Bern: Peter Lang, 1986)

Salmen, Walter (ed.), *Beiträge zur Geschichte der Musikanschauung im 19. Jahrhundert* (Regensburg: Bosse, 1965)

Scher, Steven Peter (ed.), *Music and Text: Critical Enquiries* (Cambridge: Cambridge University Press, 1992)

Schmid, Manfred Hermann, *Musik als Abbild. Studien zum Werk von Weber, Schumann und Wagner* (Tutzing: Schneider, 1981)

Schmid, Marion, À bas Wagner, in: Kelly (2008), 77-91

Schnebel, Dieter, *Denkbare Musik. Schriften 1952-1972* (Schauberg: DuMont, 1972)

Schopenhauer, Arthur, Zur Metaphysik der Musik (1819), in: *Die Welt als Wille und Vorstellung*, in: *Sämtliche Werke* (Stuttgart: Cotta/Insel 1987), vol.2 573-86

Schorske, Carl E., *Fin de siècle Vienna. Politics and Culture* (1961) (New York: Vintage Books, 1968)

Selinker, Larry, Interlanguage (1972), in: Jack C. Richards (ed.), *Error Analysis: Perspectives on Second Language Acquisition* (London: Longman, 1974), 31-54

Shaw, George Bernhard, *The Perfect Wagnerite: A commentary on the Niblung's Ring* (1923) (New York: Dover, 1967)

Spengler, Oswald, *Der Untergang des Abendlandes. Umrisse einer Morphologie der Weltgeschichte* (1919) (Munich: Beck, 1923)

Starobinski, Jean, *Psychoanalyse und Literatur* (Frankfurt a.M.: Suhrkamp, 1973)

———., Opera and Enchantresses, in: Levin (1994), 19-23

Stein, Jack M., *Richard Wagner and the Synthesis of the Arts* (Westport, Ct.: Greenwood Press, 1960)

Strauss, Richard & Hofmannsthal, Hugo von, *Briefwechsel*, hrsg. von Frank u. Alice Strauss (Zürich: Atlantis,1955²)

Stuckenschmidt, Hans Heinz, *Schoenberg. His life, world and work* (London: Calder, 1977)

Tolstoy, Leo, *Anna Karenina* (1877). Translated by Richard Pevear & Larissa Volokhonsky (Harmondsworth: Penguin, 2001)

Urban, Bernd, *Hofmannsthal, Freud und die Psychoanalyse. Quellenkundliche Untersuchungen* (Frankfurt a.M./Bern: Peter Lang, 1978)

Vogel, Martin, Nietzsches Wettkampf mit Wagner, in: Salmen (1965), 195-223

Voss, Egon, *Richard Wagner und die Instrumentalmusik. Wagners symphonischer Ehrgeiz* (Wilhelmshafen: Heinrichshofen, 1977) (Taschenbücher zur Musikwissenschaft 12)

Wagner, Richard, *Sämtliche Briefe*, ed. Gertrud Strobel & Werner Wolf, vol. 2 *1842-1849* (Leipzig: VEB Deutscher Verlag für Musik, 1970)

———., *Gesammelte Schriften und Dichtungen* (Faksimiledruck der einmaligen Vorzugsausgabe, Leipzig: Fritzsche 1887: Moers: Steiger

1976). Where a quotation does not come from this anything but complete edition (which is cited in the form: Roman numeral for volume, Arabic for page), its volume number will be in Arabic and it comes from: *Ausgewählte Schriften*, hrsg. von J. Kapp (Leipzig: Hesse & Becker, 1914)

Weinland, Helmut, Wagner und Meyerbeer, in: *Richard Wagner zwischen Beethoven und Schönberg, Musik-Konzepte* 59 (Munich: text + kritik, 1988), 31-70

White, Harry, *Music and the Irish Literary Imagination* (Oxford: Oxford University Press, 2008)

White, Hayden, Form, reference and ideology in musical discourse, in: Scher (1992), 288-319

Whyte, Lancelot, *The Unconscious before Freud* (London: Tavistock, 1962)

Williams, Ralph Vaughan, *National Music and other Essays* (Oxford: Oxford University Press, 1987²)

Wilson, Alexandra, *The Puccini Problem. Opera, Nationalism, and Modernity* (Cambridge, Cambridge University Press, 2007)

Wiora, Walter, Die Musik im Weltbild der deutschen Romantik, in: Salmen (1965), 11-42

Wiseman, Boris, *Lévi-Strauss: Anthropology and Aesthetics* (Cambridge: Cambridge University Press, 2007)

Worbs, Michael, *Nervenkunst. Literatur und Psychoanalyse im Wien der Jahrhundertwende* (Frankfurt a.M.: Athenäum, 1988)

Žižek, Slavoj, 'Es gibt kein sexuelles Verhältnis', in: Bronfen, Santer, & Žižek (1999), 7-46

——., Why is Wagner Worth Saving?, in: *Interrogating the Real* (London/New York: Continuum, 2005), 307-29

Index

Individual Operas

Wesendonck, Mathilde von
    32
Götterdämmerung: 47, 150n,
    176n
    and novel 46
    and potions 163

Parsifal: 106, 114, 194
    general interpretative
    problems 105, 170f, 176, 194
    Act 1 129-31
    Act 2 178f
    Act 3 186

Theoretical comments

DATE DUE

DEMCO 38-296

CPSIA information can be obtained at www.ICGtesting.com
Printed in the USA
BVOW011821111012

302703BV00001B/57/P

9 789042 035218